Lifeworlds and Learning

Essays in the Theory, Philosophy and Practice of Lifelong Learning

Lifeworlds and Learning

Essays in the Theory, Philosophy and Practice of Lifelong Learning

Bill Williamson

NIACE
THE NATIONAL ORGANISATION
FOR ADULT LEARNING

Published by the National Institute of Adult Continuing Education
(England and Wales)
21 De Montfort Street, Leicester, LE1 7GE
Company registration no. 2603322
Charity registration no. 1002775
The NIACE website on the Internet is http://www.niace.org.uk

First published 1998
Transferred to Digital Print on Demand, 2002
©NIACE

CATALOGUING IN PUBLICATION DATA
A CIP record for this title is available from the British Library
ISBN 1 86201 044 7

Typeset by The Midlands Book Typesetting Co., Loughborough
Cover design by Boldface, London EC1
Printed in Great Britain by Antony Rowe Ltd

'Tell me, Major, how can one make the best of one's life, in your opinion?'
An ambulance bell, shrilling like a danger signal, sped past them and receded.
Garcia was pondering.
'By converting as wide a range of experience as possible into conscious thought,
my friend.'

Andre Malraux, *Days of Hope*

Those who do not have power of the story that dominates their lives – power to
retell it, rethink it, deconstruct it, joke about it, and change it as times change –
truly are powerless because they cannot think new thoughts.

Salman Rushdie

What is the true value of knowledge?
That it makes our ignorance more precise.

Anne Michaels, *Fugitive Pieces*

Contents

Preface

This book of essays was completed during a period of research leave granted to me in 1996–7 by the Research Committee of the University of Durham. I would like formally to record my gratitude to the university for this period of uncluttered time which enabled me to write free of normal departmental responsibilities.

Many people have helped make this book possible. Colleagues in the Department of Continuing Education of the University of Durham, both past and present, will recognise the ways in which our conversations over the years have influenced my thinking. I am particularly grateful to Professor Ben Knights, now of the University of Teesside, for discussions on the meaning and purpose of adult education and for his suggestion which I have taken up, and probably abused, that archaeological metaphors are powerful in what they reveal of the structure and functioning of educational organisations. John Smith, now retired, triggered many ideas with his unique reflections on the history of adult education in Britain. Tim Bond, now of the School of Education in the University of Durham, talked me through many a tangled thought about morality and the psychology of personal change. Carol Newsom and Steve Cooke have read chapters for me and commented both critically and helpfully on them.

The secretarial staff of the department, usually thanked for their skills on the keyboard, helped me far more than they realise in developing my ideas. In many tea-break conversations, they gave me new ideas to think about, new angles of approach, a lot of encouragement and in their well-intentioned criticism and sound common sense, sharpened up much of my thinking. There was genuine dialogue in those friendly exchanges and my work is the better for it. Many thanks, then, to Jean Jobling, Bernie Athey, Susan Mather, Susan Temperley and Maureen Oliphant – adult educators all!

Students on the MA course in Adult Education have always been an encouraging influence and a critical audience. I would like to thank them for the stimulus for me of their commitment to lifelong learning.

Dennis Doran of the Department of Continuing Education helped me with word-processing problems and the final preparation of this manuscript. He, too, is a good teacher and I am grateful to him for his patience and help. My wife, Diane Williamson, another adult educator, read chapters and steadied my nerves to complete the project. However, all its faults are all too obvious.

Bill Williamson
Durham 1998

Introduction

The cistern contains; the fountain overflows
William Blake, *Proverbs of Hell*

I'll ha'e nae hauf-way hoose, but aye be whaur
Extremes meet – it's the only way I ken
To dodge the curst conceit o'bein' richt
That damns the vast majority o' men.
Hugh MacDiarmid, *A Drunk Man Looks at the Thistle*

At the end of the twentieth century, the idea of lifelong learning dominates all contemporary discussions about the continuing education of adults. It is an idea central to the search for economic prosperity and social justice, though the two goals are often contradictory. Lifelong learning is meant to close the gap, which exists both within and between all societies in the modern world, between the 'learning-rich' and the 'learning-poor'.

New technology, new modes of learning – such as distance education – new opportunities for learning at work and in the community, innovations in curricula, teaching materials, the assessment of learning, improved learner support, and profound changes in our understanding of how best to help people return to learning, all promise a widened educational franchise for adults, whoever they are and whatever their age.

The underlying idea both of lifelong learning and this book is that learning in adulthood is continuous and ubiquitous; it is not confined to and should certainly not be limited by what is offered to people through the institutions of formal education. Further, the full development of lifelong learning presupposes a dense network of effective provision from childhood to old age, which is imaginatively conceived to be qualitatively different to all the existing educational provision.

The opportunities for learning that are currently provided through universities and colleges as well as the market, through the mass media, work-based training, and the culture and leisure industries are, despite the vastness of their promise, still a mere shadow of what could be were people really given the chance to develop and to grow. Much of what is available is unchallenging and demands very little effort or attention. Richard Hoggart surely got it right when he noted that we now live in a society 'whose members are insufficiently educated for its complexities, educated only to the level at which they may be exploited' (1995, p. 226).

He is also right in noting that it need not be so; that there is another agenda, a democratic one in which people can be engaged with the political and cultural life of their societies and finely tuned into the public debates about what values should govern their lives. 'A well run democracy', argued Hoggart, 'will constantly quarrel with itself' (1995, p. 340). A culture of quarrel, however, needs learning and sustained learning needs appropriate support.

The dense and creative networks of 'civil society' provide clues about what lifelong learning could be. In the groupings people form to indulge their pleasures, fight their political battles, worship their Gods and meet the needs of the diverse communities – for better schools, hospitals, cleaner air, efficient transport – and wherever they come together to talk, grumble, be entertained or demonstrate, people learn much about themselves and their world. These ordinary practices which Gellner (1996) characterises as the genius of civil society, are the essential ingredients of liberty. They constitute the institutions that stand between the individual and the state. They are crucibles of hope and of imagination, settings for the best sort of personal growth and development: the freely chosen kind.

A buoyant civil society requires, however, an open society. In none of the modern societies that claim democratic credentials are the conditions of the open society fully met. The political and legal conditions may be in place: the rule of law, democratic elections, a free press. But the social and intellectual conditions needed are far from being realised: an informed and educated citizenry, a widespread acknowledgement of the importance of taking everyone into account when all important decisions are made; an acute understudying that all authority is necessarily fallible and that its effective exercise requires disciplined cross-examination and clear public accountability. It requires real respect for human rights, an unswerving commitment to the freedom and security of all citizens and to the open possibilities of their personal and intellectual development.

These conditions are not fully met anywhere. To secure them, all the institutions of society have a role to play. A particularly decisive task falls to those with responsibilities for education and learning. It is, in essence, to continue to explore how adults actually learn. It is to examine who is denied the opportunity to learn. It is to search for the explanations for the current structure and distribution of educational life chances. It is to evaluate alternatives to what is currently available. Each of these tasks requires direct engagement with public debates about the patterns of change and of development in society and about the values governing them; for it is these which shape the experience and aspirations of people.

Debate needs to be focused into decisions and actions. Those who exercise political authority live in a world of priorities, resource constraints and difficult choices. Though containing no blueprint for policies, no five-point plan, these essays contain a central message for the politician: there are no levers of power that can be pulled to produce predictable changes in educational opportunities or outcomes. We do not live in a social universe of causes and effects but of relationships, meanings and morals. Peter Jarvis (1997) has reminded us that learning is an essentially moral activity because it takes place within and builds upon a framework of social relationships. These either nurture moral sentiment or erode it.

Building on what we already know, much can be done to widen people's choices to promote learning at work, and to break down the barriers that exclude people from new learning. To do so involves a recognition that such changes both require, and will in their turn produce, more fundamental changes in the organisation of society itself and its structures of inequality and power. New opportunities for learning presuppose a new kind of society to sustain them and a political will to open them up. The challenge for political leaders is to have the courage to work for these ends knowing beforehand that they cannot predetermine what use people will make of their new-found knowledge and ideas.

Frameworks of debate

These debates now take place on an international scale. Information technology makes this possible but it is the globalisation of economic and political life which makes it necessary. The societies of the modern world are interdependent; the impersonal flows of trade and investment and the direct movements of people and ideas ensures it; military and political alliances compound its complexity and history shapes the patterns which it takes. The scientific and technical knowledge which drives the modern economy is itself international and the competition which the international system generates between the different states of the world is at once a source of innovation and change in economic life and a major threat to the stability of all the societies of the world.

In Europe, this competitive interdependence is at the centre of all public policy debates about education and training. In its 1995 White Paper, *Teaching and Learning, Towards the Learning Society*, the Commission of the European Communities (EC, 1995) spelled the problem out clearly. It noted that: 'The internationalisation of trade, the global context of technology and, above all, the arrival of the information society, have boosted the possibilities of access to information and knowledge for people, but at the same time have as a consequence changed work organisation and the skills learned. This trend has increased uncertainty for all and for some has led to intolerable situations of exclusion' (1995, p. 2).

In response to this the Commission is clear: the society of the future will be a learning society in which education and training 'will increasingly become the main vehicles for self awareness, belonging, advancement and self fulfilment' (1995, p. 2). The future of the European Union itself, the Commission argued, 'will depend largely on its ability to manage the progress towards this new society'.

For the Commission, the main task is to develop a sound system of basic education for everyone followed by further vocational training geared directly to increasing the employability of people. People need to be flexible, to know foreign languages. Companies need to work more closely with government and other 'social partners' to improve the stock of skills in society. Education, the Commission emphasises 'must be opened up to the world of work' (1995, p. 36). And the educational policies of member states should be directed also at combating social exclusion.

In its outline proposals in 1996 for the European Year of Lifelong Learning, the Commission was very explicit that 'Europe is faced with a situation in which its success in terms of economic growth is not matched by an equal capacity to create jobs' (EC, 1996, p. 5). Lifelong learning was outlined as the appropriate response to this problem. It is intended to foster a 'competitive economy anchored by solidarity'. Programmes such as Leonardo da Vinci, Socrates and Erasmus are designed to achieve these goals and each member state of the European Union (EU) is devising policies to meet the broader European objectives.

If one reads these documents with Beethoven's ninth symphony playing in the background the alchemy of it all is complete: 'Alle Menschen werden Brüder' is the European anthem and it dignifies the idea of Europe as a coming together of people and not merely as a more efficient organisation of a market. The problem, of course, is that the sentiments that inspired the symphony are not those that drive the bureaucrats in Brussels. The European reality behind the rhetoric, though we have to acknowledge some recognition of this by the Commission, is still that of a divided Continent.

The North–South, East–West axes of the map of Europe describe well its patterns of economic and social inequality and the political divisions which generate its conflicts. The Commission wants to overcome these divisions, but insists on a framework of economic life that could well exacerbate them. The Commission wishes to revitalise economic enterprises but there is little sign that it recognises the central contradiction of doing so: that firms will become more competitive by shedding labour thereby deepening the problem of social exclusion.

On a broader scale, the societies of Europe connect both with those of the wider world and with a new world order in politics, international affairs and economic life. As a new century dawns, no one can predict how the dynamics of this world order will develop. We cannot know, therefore, what kind of education will equip people to meet its challenges. It has to be lifelong; it has to help give people a purpose which is valued in the societies in which they live. It need not necessarily be democratic or secular. There are other political frameworks of economic life that can guarantee growth and prosperity. East Asia provides many examples of this where great economic success is not tied to any profound respect for the rights of individuals or commitments to help them develop their personalities to the full.

If lifelong learning, therefore, is to be given a strong democratic meaning, current models of what it is need to be rigorously debated. What the essays in this book seek to do is encourage that debate and to work towards a view of lifelong learning that is not restrictive or tied so directly to the arrangements of society as we currently know them. The aim is to make people involved in helping adults learn take a broad and critical view of their task, in whatever context they perform it.

I am not pleading here for lifelong learning to be brought into the fold of formal education or to be tied too closely to the needs of vocational training; quite the reverse. That would restrict ideas both of what it is and what it could be. It would define its starting points too narrowly, measure its achievements too restrictively and confine its purposes in too tight a frame. Formal education makes learning exclusive; vocational training is inevitably narrowly focused on current technologies. The real challenge is to break learning free and to help people engage with the important issues of their times in ways that reflect the dilemmas, contradictions, doubts and enthusiasms which are both at the centre of human lives and of human knowledge itself.

Hugh MacDiarmid has his drunk man say: 'For I've nae faith in ocht I can explain, And stert whaur the philosophers leave aff.' Precisely! All creative people do the same and this is the point where all new learning starts: with curiosity, with doubt about what has gone before and with hope that new questions will produce new answers; it is an open-ended, continuous challenge to conventional wisdom. It concerns everything, it cannot be confined; it goes on all the time and in modern societies there are more opportunities than at any other period of human history for more people than ever before to be part of it, to communicate what they know, question what is, and imagine alternatives.

This, anyway, is the spirit that animates the essays in this book. It is an article of faith for me that every human being has the capacity to grow, create and understand and to live their lives at the frontiers of creation in their culture. What prevents millions of them from doing so is not their human nature or the point they occupy on some statistical curve defining the distribution of some narrowly conceived human ability. It is the organisation of their societies and the ways in which life chances are distributed. The challenge is to transform the frameworks of opportunity and hope within which people live their lives. Those that currently exist limit the lives of too many people and by doing so deny everyone the possibility of living in a society which solves its problems by building on its best ideas and on the energy and creativity of all its members.

The social institutions of modern societies must be challenged. A new critical edge is required to the ways in which citizens judge what is done in their name. Prevailing ideas about what it means to learn and to know and to claim to have knowledge need to be profoundly reassessed; for too often they reflect the dominant discourses of the powerful within existing institutions. The terms of this debate have been too narrowly confined to the practical tasks of making what already exists more effective. The challenge, in fact, is to define radical alternatives to the status quo, for what currently exists is narrowly conceived, exclusive and deeply conformist. And in so far as debates about adult learning are confined to the contexts of either formal education or employment training, they fail to embrace all the other contexts in which adults learn or are prevented from so doing.

Much contemporary debate about the form and purpose of continuing education is tied to an agenda set by the needs of industry and commerce and focuses attention on skills and competencies relevant to only one version of how economic life should be organised. The dominant ideal is to make the capitalist economy more efficient. That economy is global in its reach and its centres of decision-making, connected to one another electronically, are no longer confined within the boundaries of nation states.

It is as if there is another level of human social reality which does not touch the more intimate settings in which people live their lives. People live in families, villages, towns and cities, each with their own unique characteristics, problems and identities. Yet the decisions which affect them are taken in the corridors of political power, in inter-governmental international bodies and in boardrooms of multinational companies and these in their turn are driven forward by the merciless logic of international trade, finance and investment. All is impersonal and the institutions involved are beyond the controlling reach even of elected governments.

Modernity is now global, though the gradients of wealth, power and inequality are steep. This is the central contradiction of it all: we have built an inter-dependent world. Our fates hang together in the same balance but the very mechanism which has achieved this, the global, profit-driven economy generates too the conditions which nurture conflict, insecurity, social fragmentation and a kind of institutionalised powerlessness to do anything about it.

Yet the twentieth-century project of modernity – the belief in progress through economic growth – is a god that has failed. Whether in its capitalist or communist forms, modern industrial society is unsustainable as a human social formation. Its modern, global forms have resulted in an inequality between nations which has set free the horseman of the Apocalypse, to ride with impunity through Africa, Asia, Latin America and the Middle East. It has catalysed a social and cultural fragmentation that almost defies sociological description in the complexity of its individualism, its consumerist values, its moral diversity and its ultimate loss of agreed human purpose.

The central meanings and values of the system are centred on production and consumption: on work and family life; on effort and pleasure. Those excluded from those roles – because of unemployment, age, poverty, family circumstances, chronic illness, disability, discrimination and oppression – have few chances to reap the rewards the system is claimed to deliver. Were they to think of themselves as others define them – as people who in some ways are either deserving of their fate or incapable of realising more in their lives – they would be truly wretched.

Many, of course, are; but need not be. There are and have to be alternative discourses which celebrate human potentiality, collective responsibility and the open society in which all can participate. It is why the idea of lifelong learning has to be much more widely conceived to embrace not only skills and competencies, but ideas, thoughts, feelings and self-awareness as much as knowledge acquisition. It is why lifelong learning has to lead to new ideas, ever-renewed ways of thinking and of doing things and why a worthwhile vision of what it could be has to be anchored in a lively image of the open society itself, the moral principles which should guide it and the social institutions which must protect it.

Without such a vision, not only will economies falter, so, too, will democracy itself, a rather poor outcome as a new century dawns, of a struggle for freedom which has lasted two hundred years and which is by any test a struggle not yet over. Learning opportunities for adults should not be judged by their utility but by how far they promote the imagination, and release the potential within all human beings to enrich the lives of others, seize their own destiny and contribute their distinctive knowledge and understanding to the solution of collective problems. Gellner (1996, p. 95) was surely right to insist that the economic and technological success of modern societies requires, as he put it, 'pluralism among cognitive explorers as well as among producers' and any imposed consensus would be disastrous for them. What they need, Gellner contends, is not shared faith but shared doubt, individual inquiry and scepticism.

What we have falls far short of what could be. The result is that literally millions of people are denied the chance to realise their full potential as human beings and the collective life of all is diminished as a result. The consequences are visible everywhere as blighted hopes and as the tangled webs of complex and unsolved problems in and between all the societies of the modern world. Lifelong learning is not the panacea solution to the problems of global society or to the personal dilemmas of individual people, but it has to be part of their solution. Matthias Finger (1995) put it aptly when he insisted that we have to learn our way out of the problems we face.

To do so requires skill, understanding, imagination and an ability to influence the ways in which decisions are made. People need continually to renew their knowledge if they are to understand the complexity of their world. But they need more than that; they need the power to act on the basis of what they know. The National Union of Mineworker's lodge banner of Murton Colliery, County Durham, is emblazoned with the words KNOWLEDGE IS POWER. This image holds for me that essence of the problem in all its ambiguity. Knowledge does bring power; but power undisciplined by morality is dangerous. And without the challenge to authority which only an open society can offer, knowledge itself is threatened.

When knowledge and power are combined to define truth, as the twentieth-century history of Fascism and Communism has shown, the first casualty is truth itself. And when the knowledge–power link is not challenged with an alternative vision of the possibilities of organising society, the alternative never becomes explicit. The tragedy of the labour movement in the twentieth century is that in the West it was too ready to sup with the Devil and strive mainly to get for its people more of the kind of things capitalism wanted to sell them. In the East it became trapped in an ideological frame which denied people the freedom upon which all radical creativity demands. The collapse of Communism at the end of the twentieth century is the symbol of the final demise of the hopes framed in the nineteenth-century modernist project. Postmodernism offers no coherent framework for the future either for the collapsed communist states of Eastern Europe or the capitalist countries of the global market place.

People without knowledge lack power. They cannot act to defend their interests or to change the circumstances of their lives. People do, of course, survive. Modern societies are not so complex that people with a modicum of education, native wit and the advice of others cannot flourish within them. People acquire the most complex of skills and develop a deep understanding of their world just by being part of society. But there are limits to what people can know before they need the help of experts and this is when they can become dependent on the skills of others.

With a highly specialised division of labour such dependency is inevitable. It defines a peculiarly modern state of ignorance. No one in a modern society can understand fully how their societies work or how the technologies on which they depend, function. People have become specialised in what they do and what they know. But most could understand much more than they do about the world beyond their immediate experience and thus feel less dependent on the expertise of others. The lives of most people could be significantly enlarged if there were real opportunities open to them, throughout their lives, to continue to learn and to develop and improve their skills and understanding.

But the problem of ignorance is not a problem only of those who lack formal education nor, indeed, necessarily a consequence of that. There is an ignorance, too, among the learned and the powerful which can show itself as indifference to the plight of other people in the world in which we live. The social organisation of modern industrial societies has often been described as rational, scientific, secular and bureaucratic. As Ulrich Beck (1992) has argued, however, there is a deep irrationality to the ways in which modern societies generate uncertainty and risk and build into themselves the possibility of destroying the very circumstances upon which their economies and political systems depend.

Ignorance, in fact, is pervasive and reveals itself most strongly among those who lay claim to the truth. Politicians with fixed ideas and ideologues of any kind are dangerous examples of it. They remain a threat because too many people are gullible or lack the means to evaluate critically what they are told. Ignorance is not therefore a condition. It is a facet of the social relationships, opportunities and circumstances of communication and understanding within modern societies themselves. The fundamental challenge for educators is to enable more people to be able to join in critically in the discussions and decisions which shape their lives.

The essays in this book have been written with this idea in mind. Behind them is a commitment to help build a better world and a belief that the way to do this, ultimately, is through education. Put thus, the claim may appear to have a naive, romantic ring to it. The Enlightenment Project, so the cynics say, is dead. Knowledge and wisdom may be what people search for; but darker forces shape our fates. It is easy to see the modern world driven on to its demise through conflict, the exercise of power and the pursuit of self interest.

It is easy to see why people could come to believe all this was true. And it is certainly no mystery why millions of people recall their schooldays as days not of hope but of humiliation. But there is another truth to contend with: people can act together to build a better world. They can imagine alternatives to the present mess. Democratic political institutions are built on the premise that people can make a difference to what happens in their lives. The whole of modern science and scholarship is built on the realistic hope that through greater understanding of nature and society, people can shape the world according to the values they believe in. And the most fundamental value of all education is that people can be enabled to choose their values rationally and be critical of all claims to truth.

To argue that something of the Enlightenment Project deserves to be rescued is not just naive optimism. If significant numbers of people do not acquire a critical understanding of their own view of the world, and of themselves – their ideas and values – what would the consequences be? People do learn quite successfully to become racist, nationalist, sexist, criminal and violent. The history of the twentieth century could be written around the world-destructive consequences of political movements based on wilful ignorance and gullibility. People easily absorb prevailing values which justify self-interestedness and materialism. The highest hopes of millions of people are to possess and consume the goods and experiences that the consumer markets offer them. People happily live their lives secure in the belief that what happens elsewhere in the world and what is reported daily in the news, is someone else's concern. People do learn to take the world as it is for granted. How they continue to achieve this (discussed in Chapter 1) is also a key concern for those interested in the lifeworlds of adults and the forms of learning from which they are constructed.

The tragedy, of course, is that the world does not change in ways that people either value or can control. The world for many has become an impersonal, threatening place and their previous understanding of both it and of their own roles within it, appears inadequate. Worse still, people too readily believe that the ways of thinking of their immediate social mileu are valid for everyone. Rigid, narrow-minded thinking is a dangerous form of ignorance. So, too, is that crippling feeling of powerlessness that so many people have. They are aware of the problems of the world but feel unable to do anything about them. The dawn of a new century underlines how vital it is that new forms of thinking are required if people are to grasp and celebrate the interdependence of their lives and control the consequences of that in the global contexts of postmodernity.

It is not in the gift, thankfully, of educators to provide people with those new forms of thinking. The new forms emerge from new actions. The people engaged actively to bring about change in society outside the conventional discourses of political life are the ones who confront the present with alternative views of the future. When Raymond Williams (1983) pondered these questions in the 1980s he found resources for hope in the Women's Movement, the Peace Movement and the Environmental Movement. These have continued in different ways through the 1990s and each responds to new threats in innovative ways. The recent battles in Britain about the export of live animals, road building and the demonstrations in France and Germany against extreme right-wing parties or in the South Pacific against French nuclear testing, are all high-profile examples of action to change the world by people who seek to break free from conventional ways of thinking and who struggle to learn their way out of the problems they face as citizens. The same probing, imaginative concern goes on in work organisations – in trades unions – and in community groups where people meet to defend their rights or overcome problems of urban squalor. It goes on in churches and voluntary associations of all kinds. Some are local; others, like Amnesty International, are global in their commitment. All represent contexts in which people express their commitment to their ideals in association with others and in so doing seek knowledge to bring about change in the world. The relevance of these movements to our understanding of learning in modern society is discussed in Chapter 1.

These essays represent an honest attempt to join in the debate about how people can be helped to a more critical understanding of their world and to a deeper understanding both of themselves and of what interests them in it. The prime value of modern developed societies and the one which legitimates democratic government the world over, is freedom. Such freedoms that we have, however, have been bought at a high price. It is an idea for which millions of people, quite literally, have died. What is still not clear is how that freedom should best be organised and how it can be maintained. The strength of its greatest enemy – oppression – which can take many forms, is founded ultimately on credulity and ignorance. These essays, written for educators throughout the world, are intended as a contribution to the discussion of how best to reduce both, in the interests of a just, decent and fair society with a sustainable future.

The essay form of this volume is deliberately chosen. It allows for the free exploration and development of ideas. It encourages reflection and tentative conclusion. It enables dialogue between reader and writer. Since dialogue and 'communicative competence' is the central educational idea of the volume – for it is only through dialogue that learning and real understanding develop – the essay form is particularly suited to the argument.

Dialogue is not confined to conversation with others; it embraces, too, the conversations we have with ourselves as we each of strive to find purpose and meaning in our lives. This particular theme is the focus of Chapters 9 and 10 but in one sense runs throughout all the chapters of this book. The search for purpose, for authenticity and meaning is ultimately rooted in a process of learning. People who return to learning in adulthood, as most adult educators know and as Linden West (1996) has eloquently explained, are pursuing more than career options, though this may be the language they are required to use to justify what they are doing. They are rediscovering themselves through learning and often recovering as adults the blighted hopes of their younger days. It is not an easy or painless process. It involves shifts in self understanding and awareness of a kind that can shake the foundations of people's lives and encourage them to reframe their life plans. At the heart of it are conversations or dialogues in which people explore with themselves the fundamental assumptions that govern their lives and through which they interpret their experience.

The themes developed in these essays and which derive from particular sociological traditions (discussed in Chapter 1) reflect, too, my own moral concerns as a citizen and what I have come to believe is flawed in the current organisation of society. Open debate with others, which the essay form allows and, indeed, encourages, is the way forward to a more decent society. It is the only alternative to imposed blueprints or the fatalism of much current social and political thinking which describes the world as it is as if it could not be otherwise. It is only through dialogue (discussed in Chapter 11), discussion, the refinement of ideas and the courage to translate ideas into action in full knowledge that they are necessarily flawed, that sustainable and life-enhancing change in modern society can be assured.

The character of the essays is theoretical. Nevertheless, there is an underlying concern for policy and practice in continuing education. Theory without practice is pointless; practice without theory is blind. My interest is to clarify the contexts and contradictions of policies for continuing education. The main focus of these essays is on the developed societies of contemporary Europe, the United States and the rest of the English-speaking world. Since those societies are global in their reach and are part of global networks of trade, aid, politics, knowledge generation, information flow and migration, their policies for continuing education cannot be evaluated in isolation from this broader context. The economic instrumentalism of education policies, the belief that education is justified for the contribution it makes to economic life is a very narrow discourse. The common sense practicality of its underlying logic is, however, hugely deceptive.

Seen from the periphery, from the underdeveloped parts of the globe, or from within the underdeveloped contexts of the developed societies themselves – Paulo Freire was quite right to point out the Third World is not a place, but an idea – what takes place in education in the developed societies takes on a meaning people living in those societies do not appreciate. Education is inextricably bound up with power and reflects in its assumptions and its forms the *Weltanschauung* of the dominant groups of society. The lifeworlds of people (discussed in Chapter 1) have been colonised by the dominant rationality of western societies and the ways of thinking encoded in it.

From this point of view, it stands out clearly that social and educational policies are never politically neutral; that policy discussions are never merely technical. Policies reflect values and priorities and in this way are always facets of the conflicts between the competing demands of different interest groups. Policies are entrenched in political discourse. Some, such as those of many modern European governments to limit the idea of continuing education to continued vocational education, are driven forward from firm ideological convictions. They are to privilege the interests of employers and the needs of what is always referred to abstractly as the 'economy' as if it was possible to separate this off from the wider society which constitutes it.

Other policies, like those of the European Commission, to promote greater opportunities for the long-term unemployed, are less tainted ideologically and reflect, in however ill-defined a way, some general and widely supported vision of a common purpose in which it is in everyone's interest to secure once more the conditions of full employment. Rarely questioned is whether the kinds of jobs likely to be created through community employment initiatives are of a kind likely to nurture in those who do them a commitment to continued learning and personal development or, indeed, whether such opportunities will be on offer.

An important role for social science, given this background, is to expose the ways in which interests are translated into policies and are cloaked with a legitimacy which is not perceived to be ideological. The development of the analytical tools which will enable people to understand better the role of ideological thinking in their societies, is one of the main goals of social science. These essays are conceived as a contribution to that essential tool kit. They are not essays in educational policy, but they are intended to be a contribution to the debates about policy which are currently taking place.

The book is organised into three main parts, each reflecting a particular level of analysis of the themes set out above. One of the essential elements of the sociological perspective running through these essays, is the effort to see the 'personal' in the 'political', to see the ways in which individual actions and identities are woven into the patterns of social structures and, indeed, constitute those patterns. In Part One, therefore, the essays explore facets of the social structure of modern societies. In this way, the broad, changing contexts of all adult learning are highlighted.

Part Two contains essays which explore various institutional contexts in which adult learning takes place. Their aim is to clarify the ways in which the institutional arrangements of education and learning either facilitate or inhibit the learning they are expected to nurture.

Part Three is focused much more on the experience of learning and on what it implies for the ways in which adults come to see themselves and their world. These essays probe the social psychology of adult learning at the point where it is happening – in the minds of adult students themselves. They seek to communicate something of the power of learning to transform awareness and to empower learners to greater levels of understanding. It becomes clear at that point that the analytical wheel turns once more, bringing back into view the changing social structures within which people lead their lives. For what do people do with their learning? What are they allowed to do with it? These questions about the structure of the distribution of power and opportunity in modern societies are explored in Part One.

The book arises from my own experiences as a sociologist and an educator. It has been written for other educators to read and I hope they will enjoy debating the claims I make. When one of my secretarial colleagues asked me what I was writing and 'What will be the gain to anyone from it?' I was stopped in my tracks. But the question is highly relevant and demands an answer. The gain, I hope, will be in the opportunity the book offers to help practitioners to have more confidence in promoting a broader idea of lifelong learning than the ones that currently dominate the educational agenda. It is to open outwards from the instrumentalism of current thinking to discuss questions about education and experience, education and democracy, education and values.

My hope is that the sociological frame around this discussion facilitates the debate. The core of it, for me, is the idea that social structures are not immutable; they are in constant change as the social values, rules and ways of thinking that support them are altered by the actions of real people exploring ways to change their world. It is in the inter-play of history, social structure and social action that hopes, experiences and identities of people change.

Of particular importance to me is the hope that the approach of these essays will encourage people to take their own experience of learning seriously. Personal biographical reflection is an important tool of self awareness and those who wish to help others to learn need to confront their own experience of learning directly to be able to understand their own learning styles and approaches to understanding. I aim to encourage learners to reflect on how they have become the people they are, to enable them to reflect critically on their own experience as an essential first step in transforming it.

Experience does matter. It is the experience of people which acts to govern whether they will develop themselves further through learning or limit themselves to live with what they already know. All learning involves a reframing of experience and a shift in self awareness and understanding. Those denied the tools to do this are condemned to live as others determine and to see themselves as others see them. Too many people labour under false images of themselves and of their abilities and their potential. Several chapters discuss the consequences of this, not just for the individuals involved, where the story is often of unrealised opportunities and low self images, but for society as a whole which also loses out.

In my own case, a sociological education and an historical cast of mind encourage me to see in the experience of individuals the unfolding moments of profound historical change. As the new Millennium approaches, though not because of that, it is clear that a new order of society is emerging. Eric Hobsbawm characterised the twentieth century as the age of extremes (1994). The twenty-first century threatens to be no less challenging. One of the key lessons learned from the age of extremes is that democracy is a fragile flower.

To protect and develop it, truth needs to be separated from power and all ideas, all claims to knowledge, all values need to be subjected to critical, open debate in an open society. We are nowhere near that yet. But there are firm grounds for hope but only on the basis of enabling more people to grow to have the confidence to join in and enjoy the debate about how their world should be organised and new possibilities for people opened up. An enriched idea of lifelong learning has to be a central element of the new thinking required by a new form of society.

Part One:

Theory

1 The sociology of lifelong learning

'Expect poison from the standing water'
'If others had not been foolish, we should be so'
William Blake, *Proverbs of Hell*

In his *Diagnosis of our time* (Mannheim, 1950), a book of essays written in wartime, Karl Mannheim outlined an argument that the task of a sociology of education was to identify the ways in which education could be changed to create the social conditions of 'militant democracy'. He was writing during World War II in full awareness of the horrors of Fascism, in a country which had received him as a refugee and whose government had committed itself to policies to slay the 'five giants' identified by Lord Beveridge: Want, Ignorance, Disease, Squalor and Idleness.

For Mannheim and others in his generation, there were clear connections among these issues. Fascism was for them a political ideology and movement born of social and economic breakdown, political gullibility and the weakness of democratic institutions. The postwar vision for a reconstructed Europe had to be based on stronger democratic values, social planning and international co-operation.

This was the context in Britain for policies to promote secondary education for all. In Germany and the rest of occupied Europe it was to plan for democratic schools. It was a time of hope, compromise and uncertainty. The future had to be better than the past. In 1945 Europe was, literally, a continent strewn with corpses. There was no going back to the conditions which spawned Fascism. It was a time of compromise because resources limited what could be achieved. The uncertainties which were to engulf the whole world after 1945 were the politics of Cold War, the nuclear nightmare, struggles for colonial freedom and competition among the world powers for economic dominance in the world economy.

Hope translated into expectations. In the field of education, these centred on free secondary education and educational opportunity open to ability and merit. Policy development sought a balance between the claims of social justice and economic efficiency. Throughout the developed industrial world the decades after World War II were decades of educational expansion. It was a time of expanding opportunities in which increasing numbers of people from ordinary backgrounds got the chance of secondary and higher education and the opportunity, denied to their parents' generation, of social mobility and full employment. The expansion of opportunity was both a demand-led phenomenon and an economic requirement.

These criteria set the terms of the debate among politicians about how educational expansion could be financed, what forms it should take, how it could be managed and its outcomes measured. They also defined the concerns of professional educators who tried to understand what functions expanded systems of education were performing for the societies in which they functioned. Theories developed about how education systems reproduce the social relations, values and ideals of their host societies. Debates about how to change education were either confined to a realistic politics of piecemeal social engineering or, later, in the 1960s and afterwards, particularly in the 1970s as the long, postwar economic boom came to its end, to ideologically driven demands – from the Right and the Left – for fundamental change in both education and society.

Basil Bernstein (1971a) noted that the sociology of education had grown up by 'taking' problems set by politicians rather than by 'making' their own. A quarter century on, it remains an area of academic enquiry framed tightly by the problems of school-based education and the political agendas of government. Radical educational thought of a transformative, democratic kind, is now at the margins of academic discourse. The dominant discourse about education has been set by the radical Right and focuses on issues of individual opportunity, parental choice and economic efficiency. Parents and children have come to value education in the same way that politicians do: it is something which leads to a job and it is by these standards that the performance of schools and colleges are judged.

The same point can be made about adult education. As an area of research, debate and reflection, adult education responds to problems taken from the political agendas of others rather than on those made or defined by adult educators themselves. The outcome is that the field has become much too narrow in its intellectual concerns and in its social and political vision. There are those who have tried to define a radical edge to work in this field. Throughout the 1980s radical adult educators, finding no radicalism in the organised labour movement, which once set the agenda for debate and research in this field, drew their inspiration from feminism, from Marxism and from the radical philosophical perspectives of writers from the Third World. Cultural studies and post-modernist theorising provide some kind of framework for asking new questions about lifelong learning but work of this kind is both marginal to educational studies as a whole and political practice in particular. Adult educators have lost control of their own agendas and the field itself has been largely ignored by social scientists.

Retrospect and prospect

Adult education services expanded after World War II, building on hopes for a better world. As a colleague of mine whose career in adult education started in 1956, put it to me, the 'retrospect' of adult education then was to the issues of the 1930s: to philosophy, international relations, democracy and the social, political and cultural emancipation of working class people. Its pioneers, inspired by the legacy of R H Tawney – educators like Richard Hoggart, Roy Shaw, E P Thompson and Raymond Williams – had cut their educational teeth in combat, in Army education, in the Labour Movement and the Workers' Educational Association. They were heirs to a tradition of liberal adult education stretching back into the nineteenth century and were inspired by what Fred Inglis has called 'radical earnestness'. After 1945 its supporters looked forward to a fair and civilised modern society in which all citizens could have unlimited access to the best in their culture and civilisation.

That tradition – the Great Tradition – has come to an end. Adult education now, rising like a phoenix as continuing education or lifelong education, has both wider and narrow foci of concern. They are wider in that they concern lifelong education and have broken free of the orientation of the liberal tradition towards both the political concerns of the labour movement and particular academic subjects such as history, politics and economics which were in the 1950s and early 1960s extremely popular. The political frames have widened. They embrace and reflect the needs, interests and struggles of a wider constituency of students: women, ethnic minorities, the socially excluded and, at the edges of its mainstream academic concerns, of the poor and dispossessed of the world as a whole.

As a field of academic reflection, it has broadened out, too, to consider the complex processes of adult learning and cognitive development. Those who work in this area have done much to explore how adult people are denied opportunities for further education, how academic institutions can be made more accessible and responsive to their needs and how learning can be promoted in the community, at work and through the mass media. The new information technologies open up prospects for lifelong learning that are truly global in their scope and promise an opening up of learning opportunities that will change the world. The direction of those changes will not, however, be determined by the technology available, but by the interests of those who control it. The bonds between knowledge and power (discussed in Chapter 2) remain tight.

In other ways the field of continuing education has narrowed. The focus of much contemporary research on the issue of adult access to learning opportunities is built on a political agenda which is full of contradictions. Increased access to education can be justified on grounds related to personal growth and the development of a decent, fair, cultured and democratic society. It can also be supported to promote the employability of people in labour markets whose structures and opportunities are designed to meet the needs of employers for employees equipped with the competencies and skills they require. This has been the context for policy debates about continuing vocational education, professional development and the measurement of academic and vocational competencies. The thrust has been to make modern capitalism work more effectively to steal a lead on competitors and keep shareholders – still the major 'stakeholders' of the modern economy – happy.

The retrospect of the Great Tradition of adult education was to a world of extremes, of class inequalities and political ideology. Its prospect, to recall a striking phrase of Raymond Williams, was in a vision of a common culture and a just society. The newer, contemporary models of adult education have a retrospect in a world of affluence, high expectations and fear of global economic competition. The prospect is completely unclear.

There is no agreement about the idea of culture or about how society itself should be organised. Postmodern politics, no longer containable within the framework of the nation state, are as fragmented and incoherent as the world itself. There are no inspired visions of a glorious future in our grasp. Neither the older 'free world' models of the future which looked to a period of affluence and the 'end of ideology', or the communist versions of the planned society, have any credibility. The Berlin Wall is down. And it is only on a very narrow geographical version of capitalism that it could be said that the free market succeeds in delivering growth with any success and happiness. Outside its metropolitan centres where it is regulated strictly, though not too tightly, by relatively open, democratic politics, capitalist enterprise is still, in many parts of the under-developed world, raw-toothed and brutal – exploitative, violent, indifferent to the environment and unstable.

In the under-developed world which is so much part of our own, though this may not be widely acknowledged or its implications realised, the giants of Want, Ignorance, Squalor, Disease and Idleness, rule with ever greater savagery. To poverty has to be added something Lord Beveridge had no need to consider: injustice, corruption, the systematic denial of basic human rights, environmental degradation and hopelessness, all bound up, though people in the developed societies are not fully aware of it, with the politics of international aid and trade, diplomacy, military alliance, the development strategies of major world institutions like the International Monetary Fund or the World Bank and, of course, as a necessary corollary of it all, debt.

What, then, should a diagnosis of our time look like? What is the prospect for lifelong learning? What frameworks of ideas enable us to consider what lifelong learning should be? What conclusions about policy and practice in lifelong learning should be drawn from our understanding of how our world is changing? And what values should govern our attempts to give that change some direction and purpose? For Mannheim and other writers of his generation, the underlying task was to give an account of how society itself was constituted and how it was changing. For them there was no prospect for social reconstruction without a sound understanding of society itself and the theories needed to explain its development. They were possessed of a strong sense that a new society was being created and that it needed firm, democratic foundations.

Fifty years on it is clear the project failed. It began to falter as the Cold War divided the world into competing ideological blocs. The educational preconditions of a healthy democracy have nowhere been met; too many people are still denied access to educational opportunities on account of their class, their gender or their ethnicity. The gradients of social inequality in the developed industrial societies have widened, driving millions of people to the margins of their societies. Democratic citizenship is a stunted little flower growing on the meagre ground of mass politics, animated by self interest and conducted through debates based on carefully honed sound bites. The North–South fault line running through the global economy is a source of world political instability and as the Millennium approaches, no one can seriously imagine that what Hobsbawm (1994) has called 'the age of extremes' is over.

Social theory and lifelong learning

A new world requires new theories to help us describe it. Social scientists are heirs to several traditions of social theory with their roots in nineteenth-century attempts to understand and explain the development of, and changes within, industrial capitalism. In the radical tributaries of these traditions – in Marxism in particular – as well as in its conservative channels – in functionalism – and, finally its essentially liberal forms, in the work of writers like Max Weber, much was written about the ways in which human life and thought, and human social action, were shaped by social circumstances. Patterns of thought and action have been tied to religion and culture, to class position – and, in Marxism, to the ideologies related to different class positions – as well as to the subtle cultural frameworks of particular milieux or sub-cultures.

What has been missing in all of these perspectives – though they contain clues to the problem – is any serious interest in how human beings actually come to learn what they claim to know and believe and, more importantly, how their knowledge changes as the circumstances of their lives alter. *Homo sociologicus*, the individual human being trapped in an iron cage of roles, customs or ideologies, is a pale shadow of real human beings who do think, dream, imagine alternatives to their present lives and, above all, learn continuously throughout their lives. It is only on the basis of knowing more about how they do that, that we can imagine the ways in which their learning can be facilitated And it is only through new learning that people in modern societies will solve some of the complex problems they face.

The essence of the argument of this chapter is this: the social structures of modern societies are rooted in particular patterns of learning of which formal education, both at school and afterwards, is only one. Learning is continuous; it builds on lived experience. It is part of the structure of the lifeworld itself. It has a history – both in the content of what people think they know and in the ways in which they acquired their knowledge. It anticipates the future, for all learning has a purpose. The structures of learning – which are both formal and informal – like the structures of the lifeworld which constitute them, are part of the structure of modern societies themselves. Learning takes place in the struggles of individuals and different groups of people to justify and achieve their ends.

In complex societies, learning takes many different forms among different groups of people. Some forms of learning, as well as ways of knowing, are valued more than others and all forms of learning are governed by rules which determine who has access to them. The distribution of learning opportunities and, therefore, of the kinds of personal identities open to people from different social backgrounds, always reflects, therefore, the distribution of power in society. It follows that changes in the subtle structures of learning are always facets of changes in the distribution of power.

To point this out is to do much more than state what, to many, would be sociologically obvious. It is to encourage reflection about what is taking place in particular contexts of learning and to invite questions about how those contexts might themselves be changed. For the postwar generation, the hope for change rested on some idea of social planning. Modern societies are far less manageable. The challenge for those who wish to promote lifelong learning is to understand its constraints in the context of a new kind of society and to map out the alternatives for its development.

Two ideas, both of which must be grasped historically, provide the clues as to how this can be done. Learning by individuals – including learning about themselves – must first be related to the structure of the lifeworlds of different groups of adults. From this angle, learning, as will be seen, cannot be viewed as a purely psychological process or something detached from the social and historical contexts of its occurrence. Second, changes in the structure of lifeworlds must be carefully mapped out in acknowledgement of the fact that the forces which shape them are now global in their reach and cannot be contained either within the institutions of nation states or the cultural forms of particular societies.

That process of mapping is not one to be left to experts, though it requires expertise. To understand a society as complex as ours requires (and these issues are discussed in greater depth in Chapters 3 and 11) new forms of communication and dialogue among all the different groups within it. This is the great paradox of complexity: as societies become more dependent on specialised knowledge and expertise, they must widen the basis of all decision-making lest experts become totally incapable of understanding the implications of what they do.

A new theory of knowledge is needed. The best experts realise the fallibility of their claims to knowledge. The worst do not. The open society demands that all claims to knowledge and authority are tested. Under the social conditions of high specialisation and differentiation, everyone has some expertise relevant to a problem. The challenge is to develop institutions through which all can be heard – at work, in the community, and in politics – and which enable people, especially the powerful, if necessary, to change their views and learn. The role of lifelong learning in this is to enable people to acquire all the skills and competencies they require, to reflect on what they know and to communicate it effectively so as to test out the ideas of those who seek to govern them or manage them and who take decisions in their name.

Lifeworlds: structures and change

The notion of the lifeworld carries with it two ideas that more conventional, static accounts of the placing of people in society lack: the first is that people live their lives in and through others, so that their understanding of themselves and others is inter-subjective; people share interpretations of their world. They communicate with one another. What they understand of it, what they can communicate about it, is rooted in tacit agreements with others about how that world is constituted and how it functions. Second, it carries the idea that people strive to live lives which are meaningful, which have purpose and legitimacy and in which they can define a place for themselves which confers significance on them and on what they are seeking to do.

Several ingredients can be identified which enable us to begin to map the structure of the lifeworlds of different groups of human beings. They can be pictured as in Figure 1.1

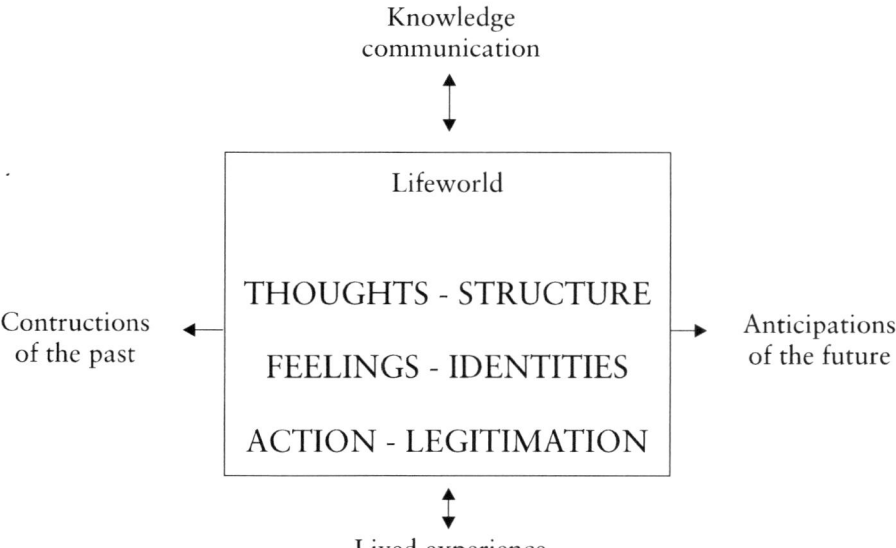

Figure 1.1   *Structure of the lifeworld*

The lifeworld is constituted of the thoughts, ideas, feelings, identities and beliefs of individual people. A full description of it would clarify how people make sense of their past, how they see themselves in time. It would extend further to clarify how they see the future, how they co-ordinate their present-day preoccupations with their hopes for the future. Both descriptions, adequately carried out, would reveal the ways in which people interpret their experience in the light of the knowledge and frameworks of understanding available to them in their society. The narrative structure of such understanding has often been commented on (Bruner, 1986; Josselson and Lieblich, 1993). In the stories people tell about themselves they make sense of their world.

Stories are never private nor ever entirely authentic. Linden West (1996) has shown, for example, that adult returnees to education will often justify their decisions by reference to their need to earn a living or build up qualifications for a job. Closer observation and deeper probing of their motives reveals that their decisions are much more complex than that, and are bound up with their attempts to find personal authenticity and fulfilment. It is through the terms of the dominant qualifications-seeking discourse that mature students often account for their return to study. It provides them with a clear, recognisable and legitimate narrative (or story) to tell. In fact, West claims (1996, p. 10), closer probing shows that people use higher education 'to compose a new life, a different story and a more cohesive self'.

Some of the stories concern the past and provide people with a way of making sense of their own lived experience. For some, these stories will be positive so that they can look back on their lives with some satisfaction and sense of achievement. For others, the past is an abyss of regret, a story of failure or unfulfilled ambition. It is never, however, a static image. Adults (and this theme is more fully explored in Chapter 10) can reach new understandings of their biographical selves. Therapy and counselling provide one means to do so. But so, too, does political action. Thousands of women who have been active in the women's movement have been able to see 'beyond the fragments' of their daily lives to reach a new understanding of their roles and experiences.

As with the past, so with the future. All of us live in the future; we make decisions all the time to try and shape the future we desire. Some can approach it with a sense of hope and optimism. For others (as some of those people discussed in Chapter 4 make clear) it is a brooding threat. The stories they can tell themselves about the future have a social shape to them. It worked for some to believe that if they worked hard, saved, looked after their families then 'things would be OK'. The underlying metaphysic to such views is a belief in steady progress as something inevitable in a modern society. For those thrown out of work or threatened with redundancy or who, for whatever reasons, find they can no longer pay their rent or mortgage, the future looks much more uncertain. Because of that, people then have to redefine their hopes and understand their past in a new light.

In some societies these dislocations of the lifeworld are profound. There are millions of people in East and Central Europe who were forced through the break-up of the Communist order of things, to re-evaluate everything they once believed in. The further back in time we go in the history of Europe, the more occasions we see in which people were forced by historical circumstance to redraw the boundaries of their world, their sense of belonging, their personal identities and their views of history and the future. People caught up in the throes of political revolution – the Nazi seizure of power in 1933, the setting up of the People's Democracies in the late 1940s – and, of course, all those caught up in war – as soldiers, migrants, citizens of occupied territories – have all been presented with the task of rewriting their personal scripts in a profoundly changing world. For some people – I am thinking here primarily of those who survived the Holocaust – the task of doing so is ultimately impossible – for their experience is actually beyond the limits of normal narrative representation (Friedlander, 1992). Others would require sustained therapeutic help to arrive at a comprehensible account of what has happened to them.

Eurocentric versions of the boundaries of the lifeworld will not do. If the experience of people in Africa, Asia and South America is brought into the frame of the account, it becomes clear in an instant that the lives of millions of people have been profoundly transformed by the impact of economically powerful Western societies on the structure and functioning of their societies. The gains made by people – especially the well-off among them – in underdeveloped societies, from their trade, alliances and cultural exchanges with the West, have to be offset against the miseries of urbanisation, rural depopulation, hunger, obscene social inequalities, political repression, war – in some cases genocide – and, everywhere, environmental degradation and poverty.

The narratives available to people in these contexts to explain their past and anticipate their futures are very different to those that can be heard in the metropolitan comfort of modernity and development. Yet there is only one world and all our fates are connected. People do learn, however, to draw tight boundaries around themselves and their lifeworlds, to be able to insulate themselves from the full implications of their global interdependence.

Jeremy Seabrook (1997), who has travelled much in what we call the Third World, commented recently on his twenty-year association with Mumbai (formerly Bombay) in India. He writes powerfully of the oneness of the modern world and draws challenging conclusions. Of Mumbai (1997, p. 1) he writes:

> I have been returning there again and again over the past 20 years. I have seen global integration leading to even greater convergence between the experience of workers of North and South. We now have our increasing pockets of dereliction among those who have been evicted and marginalised by the industrial system, just as the cities of the South have their enclaves of staggering wealth, guarded by barbed wire, armed guard and high walls. Working conditions in the sweatshops of Sydney and Toronto increasingly resemble those slums of Dhaka and Jakarta. The homeless on the streets of New York evoke the pavement dwellers of Mumbai.

His main point is this: the cities of the South provide powerful images of our future 'unless we rapidly learn or relearn the lessons of solidarity, collective resistance and internationalism'. The very same global economic forces which shape the experience and set the constraints within which slum dwellers in Third World cities must live their lives, are at work in the developed societies of the world. We must find ways to bring them under control and avoid the worst of their damaging effects.

The resources at hand to do so, however, reflect our social placement as members of a society. How we do it reflects our class, our gender, our ethnicity and the problems of our own generation. Each of these dimensions of social placement offers different resources of understanding and of experience. Each provides different kinds of opportunities to learn and to act on the basis of what we know. It is a vital task of those who wish to understand lifelong learning, to find out how different groups of people in society actually construct their understanding and interpretations of their world.

People live their lives in particular places. People who live in towns lead lives very different to those who live in the countryside. Those in affluent suburbs experience the world in different ways to those in and on the edges of poverty in the inner city. Each setting provides different interpretive frameworks through which people can make sense of their world, in which they can acquire a sense of what is valuable and what is not. It has been well-noted, for example, that people trapped in poverty have a low self image and fatalistic outlook (Barke and Turnbull, 1992). Their lives are a daily struggle against adversity in environments where crime is a real threat to their security. Long-term planning is a luxury they cannot afford. In contrast, the socially successful can contemplate with pleasure and hopefulness an open-ended future of interesting possibilities.

Lifeworlds are socially structured. The meaning they confer on what people do and what lends legitimacy to their thoughts, feelings and actions, are both shared and change through time. Finally, the ways of thinking – the modes of knowing – and the beliefs and values and perceptions which are at the centre of the lifeworld, all have to be learned as people become part of the social groups in which they live their lives.

It is a major task for research in this area to explore how that learning takes place. The study of lifelong learning has for too long been confined to the contexts of education or professional development in employment. We need to know, too, how people become prostitutes as well as priests, poets as well as professors, card-sharps as well as computer experts, nurses as well as nationalists. We need to know how people learn to become parents; how they learn to cope with the stresses of urban life and, most importantly (as is discussed in Chapter 10), how and what they come to know and believe to be true about themselves.

Changes in lifeworlds

The underlying problem in exploring the contours and boundaries of the lifeworld is to know how people have come to learn the ways in which they frame their experience and perception of the world they inhabit. Just as difficult is the task of describing how that world itself is changing. One of the key propositions in Habermas's notion of the lifeworld is that, in modern societies, the lifeworld – which he sees mainly as the arena of the personal in which people live with and communicate with others – has been 'colonised' (see Bernstein, 1995; Crossley, 1996). Comparing the process to the ways in which colonial masters colonised tribal societies, Habermas sees the world of every-day consciousness as having been invaded by the impersonal logic of the market place, by the power of political and economic institutions.

These institutions are part of the 'system' of society and their manner of operation is not always clear to people. Ordinary people come to be dependent on the experts who manage the system and who possess specialised bodies of knowledge. What people come to value and prioritise in their lives, is no longer something they come to know about in conversation with one another; it something imposed on them through the impersonal media of the market place and the operation of political and bureaucratic power. The roles that come to be valued are those of client or customer. As Nick Crossley (1996) explains, the role people can play as citizens is much reduced. Solutions to the problems they face in their ordinary lives, both as individuals and members of a community, are not found in discussion, dialogue and debate, but are imposed on them by outsiders who legitimate what they do through reference to their specialised knowledge.

It is not entirely a bleak view of the world. The imposition is not mechanical; it is achieved through the lifeworld itself by influencing how people think about themselves and relate to one another. For this reason, the influence of these abstract 'systems' and, therefore, the ways of thinking, feeling and valuing associated with them, can be redefined. In the politics of radical social movements, Habermas finds the sources of new ideas and new meanings which will resist the colonisation of lifeworlds.

Whether this faith of his that a democratic form of life can be maintained is credible or not, depends on how we view the changes taking place in modern societies and on how we assess the changing balance of lifeworld and system. The problem can be differently stated: if the balance is to shift, if the colonisation of the lifeworld is to be resisted, what must people come to know and understand? How can they be helped to a critical understanding of their world? How vital in any case is such an understanding?

Ernest Gellner (1996, p. 137) noted that the Soviet regime rested ultimately on a fusion of truth, power and society. The regime carried authority because of its claim to have grasped the truth of history and to be the caretaker of 'absolute righteousness'. Any opposition to the state had to be a kind of moral offence. Those who criticised the state had to be shown to be wrong, to have ideas that were fundamentally misconceived. Gellner believed that oppositional thinking, especially of a rational critical kind, requires the support of civil society to flourish. Civil society breaks the 'circle between faith, power and society' (1996, p. 141). Loyalty, Gellner insisted, no longer entails credulity.

How far does modern, liberal capitalism depend upon credulity? Gellner's view is that civil society allows for a wide range of views about the world and that the modern economy is not necessarily threatened by the existence of wide differences of political opinion among people. Indeed, he goes further than that and suggests that a successful social order does not need strong commitments of faith on the part of citizens to the state itself. Faith, he believed, was in any case not very deep. When the Soviet world collapsed it was astonishing, he claims, to realise that its citizens had simply gone through the motions of believing in it all without either active doubt or affirmation. It had kept them reasonably happy for a time; but its inability to deliver the living standards of the West, and the perceived freedoms of people who lived there, undermined it.

The legitimacy of it all did leach away; people were no longer prepared to live inauthentic lives or to be denied access to the goods and experiences they saw were available to people like them in the West. There is an underlying moral here for western societies themselves. The morally superior *schadenfreude* of people in the West about what happened to Communism is a premature response to the changes they have observed. For western societies themselves could lose their legitimacy as they, too, fail to deal with the unintended, damaging consequences of their own success. For economic success has been paid for at a high price and the effects of that can be traced out in the contours of the lifeworld and how they have changed.

Some of the most important changes (with all their associated social and psychological costs) include the following: the growth of home-centred privatism; of social and economic complexity; of uncertainty; of dependency on experts of all kinds to meet basic needs; of the steady erosion of social capital and of the public realm itself as an important framework within which people can plan their lives; of the disembedding of personal identities and lifestyles from local contexts and the growth of essentially 'open' – and necessarily precarious – identities. These themes are discussed in greater depth in Chapters 6 and 9 of this book.

There is in modern society a prevailing sense of a loss of tradition and of moral certainty and a loss of faith in the validity of all the old 'grand narratives' of progress and orderly change in society. Many experience their lives as being ultimately without meaning. Many more search for meaning among the chaos in religion, political movements, or in forms of personal activity – travel, drugs, music, friendship – in a world where none of these frameworks of meaning are stable. Nor are they free from the influences of commercial colonisation. The travel and tourism industries, for example, bind private dreams to their commercial products offering carefully packaged experiences which sustain temporary opportunities for escape and for trying out new identities.

Modern societies disempower people; millions feel they can have little real say in what happens to them. The feeling of powerlessness is widespread; people feel their fate is in the hands of others, unknown to them. As explained in Chapters 5 and 6 of this book, where connections are made between the historical contexts of personal experience, hopes for the future and political action, the ways in which different groups of people respond to the changes they experience in their lives, reflects their opportunities to re-frame that experience and articulate new goals for themselves. The social and political movements of the twentieth century which carried forward democratic ideals and the hopes of ordinary people for a better life, have run their course. New models of democratic practice are required to understand and manage the conflicts and uncertainties of an increasingly global society.

The dangers are clear. The threat to democratic institutions comes from the still unresolved problems of modernity as these exemplified themselves in the history of the twentieth century. There are inequalities and social exclusions which nurture resentment and fear. The political Right in Europe is still an untamed beast capable of racial violence and intolerant nationalism. The formal politics of the developed industrial societies in the period after the end of the Cold War rest on a pragmatic discourse of economic liberalism and social democracy which depends for its legitimacy on its continuing ability to deliver steady economic growth and progress. It is a discourse under threat not only from economic competition from societies who do not carry the high social costs of a democratic polity, but also from social and religious movements – in the Middle East, North Africa, Central Asia and the Far East – which regard the Godless, materialist civilisation of the West, including its liberal democratic values, as a serious threat to be overcome.

The social institutions to support 'militant democracy' are essentially the same as those required to sustain lifelong learning of a critical and reflective kind. Just as Mannheim's plea in 1944 (Mannheim, 1950) was for democratic education in schools, the case has to be made now for a democratic programme of lifelong learning. The sociological understanding of education which developed in the years after World War II, rested on the observation that education systems functioned more effectively to reproduce social orders than to challenge them. Lifelong learning is a radical idea but is equally in danger of doing the same.

Lifelong learning is not to be equated with the current forms and levels of provision of adult education. It embraces much more: people learn at work, in the community and through their ordinary participation as citizens in the political and cultural life of their society. They learn through their experience of being human beings who suffer, who grow old, who are bereaved but also who enjoy their pleasures and find all sorts of life-enhancing fun. Formal adult education touches such a small fraction of the population that it has to be judged in some major ways to be a failure. In Britain, at least, its wings have been clipped as well: much of what passes as adult education is focused on the development of either leisure interests or work-related skills. Its older, radical agendas have been superseded and the critical, creative impulses which defined them, find their expression now in social and political contexts not connected with formal education or, for that matter, mainstream politics.

Just as it is not inevitable that schools should reproduce the social orders of the society in which they function, there is no necessity for the concept of lifelong learning to be confined to its present meaning. Schools possess a degree of autonomy to define their mission and the best of them can overcome the constraints faced by their pupils to enable them to reach high levels of academic attainment. Lifelong learning is an activity which can be promoted and demanded in many different contexts. Just as any school education worthy of the name nurtures in pupils self confidence, good study skills, an ability to question ideas and statements; lifelong learning which is worth the support of communities, employers and the state, but which at the same time is capable of transcending the demands each of these make of it, is equally possible. Its practitioners are not only those who work in education. They exist, too, in factories, communities, political groups, hospitals, social service departments, the professions and the media. Wherever and whenever adults are faced with problems for the solution of which they require new ideas, new information, knowledge, help and advice, those they turn to are performing an educational function. For their task is to help people learn something new.

A depressingly negative conclusion to be drawn from this is that too many people live out their lives at a low level of critical awareness of the world around them and that the socio-economic conditions of modernity are such, that millions of people can live quite successfully and happily not knowing very much. Millions can read their newspapers, watch TV, have access to vast sources of information about almost anything imaginable, but process it all with indifference and in ways which do not challenge them in any way at all.

The positive conclusion is that we now have available the material resources to enable all adults to learn continually to whatever level takes their fancy. The state can be pushed to facilitate this. Policies can be designed to promote higher rates of participation of the young in education. They can be developed to promote more effective work-based learning. Public policies to facilitate community education initiatives are not difficult to define. The climate has never been better to build into all forms of professional education the requirement for further education and training and to help all professional groups be better facilitators of the learning of their clients.

What prevents the full articulation of the positive agenda for lifelong learning is not people themselves, for they are learning all the time, but the quality of the vision of what it could be, among politicians, educationists and employers. Politicians need help to see different possibilities for the ways in which learning is supported; educators need a deeper understanding of how their own practices and institutions can limit learning opportunities (this theme is taken up directly in Chapter 7) and employers need encouragement and incentives to invest more in training and education. All need a clearer vision of the challenges before them, a critical reading of the situation we all face in building up more coherent strategies to secure sustainable, democratic futures for modern societies.

Vision is inseparable, however, from values and from our understanding of what gives shape to them in the conditions of postmodernity. Reflection on this question (discussed in more detail in Chapter 9) leads to this: values are inseparable from social circumstances and how people themselves are valued in the settings in which they live. Too much of what is done in the field of the education of adults has been done in the interests of a very narrow version of economic efficiency – where education is equated with training – or on grounds of political expediency, where inadequate funding has been justified on the grounds that public funds cannot support the activity. Both sets of arguments have had damaging consequences for the opportunities in, and quality of, people's lives. The terms of these discourses have limited severely the prevailing sense of what people could be and what they could do. The loss to individuals is also a collective one, for the quality of public life itself is diminished as the capacity of people to engage creatively and critically with the decisions which shape their lives, is eroded. Too much is left in the hands of the few and the powerful, and democracy itself is devalued.

Karl Mannheim wrote in 1943 (see Mannheim, 1950, p. 74) that: 'The educational aims of a society cannot be adequately understood as long as they are severed from the situations that each age is called upon to face and from the social order for which they are framed'. His recipe to avoid after the war the kinds of catastrophes which caused it, was 'militant democracy', planning and social justice and education for everyone of a kind which acknowledged that 'social awareness becomes a moral obligation' (1950, p. 113). A democracy in which people were merely expected to fulfil their social roles and which failed to arouse a deep interest in its own achievements, would not be safe.

The world he described was one of nation states in which democratic politics had collapsed. The thrust of his analysis, though, remains relevant to us now. Democracy is not a final achievement, a kind of political end state. It is a framework of values and institutions which evolve, adapt and enable people collectively to seek creative solutions to the problems they continue to encounter. They do that through analysis and reflection, debate and discussion. In the course of this they arrive at an understanding of their past; they evolve the narratives which make sense of their experience and which help them to understand their relationships with others.

These efforts to achieve structure and meaning in the lifeworld are never complete. They are a process of dialogue and learning which people engage in – with different degrees of success and very diverse outcomes – throughout their lives. People who acquire a critical, reflective understanding of their world are much more likely to be the agents of social change than its victims. For the state, of course, there is a paradox to be resolved. As Peter Jarvis (1992) has noted, reflective learning is a democratic undertaking, but it is also potentially a subversive activity. It is a process which requires public support for without it, there will be no public to support. Lifelong learning is from this angle a necessary requirement of sustainable development and democracy. Whether it happens, of course, is another matter, a question of life chances and social organisation, of awareness and understanding, of lifeworlds and learning, of how society itself is governed and the values by which its citizens choose – or are sometimes forced – to live.

2 Knowledge, power and ignorance

> Strange to know nothing, never to be sure
> Of what is true or right or real
> Be forced to qualify, or so I feel,
> Or Well, it does seem so:
> Someone must know.
> Philip Larkin, *The Whitsun Weddings*

> If the lion was advised by the fox, he would be cunning.
> William Blake, *Proverbs of Hell*

Science and the cast of mind it nurtures, is at the heart of the culture and civilisation of the modern world. The achievements of scientists and engineers have been engines of profound economic change and growth. The development of what has been called the 'knowledge system' in the developed industrial societies has had major implications, too, for cultural life and politics and for the patterns of thought, feeling and action which are woven into the textures of the daily life of millions of ordinary people throughout the whole world. Western developed societies have both imposed their technology, their media of communication and the patterns of thinking and education associated with them, on the whole world and found ways to exploit the graduates and the indigenous knowledge of Third World societies for their own ends (Altbach, 1987; Apffel-Marglin and Marglin, 1996).

The dominant patterns of modern consciousness are, as a major consequence of the growth of science, overwhelmingly secular, rational, pragmatic, logical and practical; embedded in an essentially scientific world view. Modern life styles are essentially private and the strong undertows of individualism and self preoccupation, which are part of what Charles Taylor (1992) has called, 'the modern identity', are connected in subtle ways with the development of the social sciences and the resources they offer people to describe both themselves and their world in new ways. To put it graphically: after Karl Marx, no one could underestimate the role of economic interests as the driving forces of history and after Sigmund Freud, no one could believe that human beings were entirely rational. Both men have altered not only our view of ourselves; their ideas have changed the world we live in. We are no longer economic or psychological innocents.

What I want to suggest in this chapter is that the cultural contours of modernity which I have hinted at, are intimately bound up with the way in which knowledge is produced and disseminated and that the contradictions and conflicts of modern industrial societies are bound in the logic and contradictions of a new kind of society – the expert society. It is not a new idea. Some nineteenth-century social theorists saw science and technology as the driving force of history. Throughout the twentieth-century, social scientists have highlighted the increasing importance of knowledge in shaping the fabric of society. Given the revolution in information technology and global communications, contemporary writers are struggling to express the idea that a new kind of society is being born. Manuel Castells (1996) has described it as the 'network society'. Nico Stehr (1994) has used the term 'knowledge society', to describe the ways in which modern societies are changing. In each of these accounts, there is a new emphasis on the importance of knowledge, information and expertise as its driving forces, the source of its conflicts and instabilities and the source and guarantor of its freedoms.

To understand this society, it is essential to grasp that the experts who drive it – in the state, industry, commerce and the professions, but also, as Castells (1996) reminds us, in the criminal underworld, in money-laundering financial networks (as well as the street gangs who run the drugs trade) and in other groups like the international news media – cannot be adequately described using the older terminology of specialists, elites or of intellectuals. Unlike the technical specialists and intellectual leaders of previous generations, the experts of modern society are drawn from a wide spectrum of social groups. They are formed in the public institutions of higher learning, or in the sub-cultures which generate 'illegitimate knowledge'; they work anonymously in large organisations and are deeply embedded in international networks of communication.

Nor can they be described as the agents, conscious or otherwise, of different social classes. They are neither the agents of capital or labour, for the structures of class inequality no longer follow the logic of such differentiations. In so far as they represent and promote demands for efficiency, growth and innovation in the modern economy and the modern state, they represent the desires of millions of employed workers who see their own futures in precisely these terms. For the values of modern society centre on a search for affluence and, as Galbraith has described it, 'contentment' (1992). Experts – legal or illegal – provide the means to achieve it. But in doing their work, in laying down the criteria for admission to their occupation, they set up new structures of social exclusion which define new patterns of social inequality and, ultimately, of dependency.

To understand, therefore, both the patterns of differentiation and sources of change in modern societies, it is vital to consider changes in the role of knowledge in the metabolism of their social institutions. From another angle, it is important to assess the role of ignorance in such societies for as social differentiation based on the possession or non-possession of knowledge increases, so does the role of ignorance. It is a paradox of the expert society that as more people acquire specialised knowledge, their ignorance about other fields of activity increases. Ignorance, therefore, is not just 'knowing nothing', being stupid or uneducated; there is an ignorance among the experts and the powerful who are dependent on other experts. Ignorance is a feature of the social organisation of the expert society and its dimensions are global.

Ignorance of the uninformed, uncritical kind is, however, a problem. Writers who fear the growth of 'mass societies' have correctly drawn attention to the growing credulity and gullibility of people in the developed societies. Richard Hoggart (1991, p. 21) has argued in relation to mass schooling that:

> The literacy given to most people is insufficient for the needs of increasingly complex societies, and, more important, inadequate in ways essential to a democracy. Most leave school critically, culturally and imaginatively sub-literate.

Paul Fussell (1991), in a savage counterblast against what he takes to be the dominant trends in American culture, which he regards as BAD, has made a very similar point. Things that are just ordinarily bad on this analysis are legion; but to be really BAD, something must exhibit 'elements of the pretentious, the overwrought or the fraudulent' (1991, p. 32). He sees BAD things in the mass media, advertising, the publishing industry and in education. 'About a century ago,' he writes:

> Americans set out to experience the higher learning, but after a brief trial they found they did not like it. It was too hard and serious. An acquaintance with the principles of logic and evidence was found an actual impediment to enthusiasm and good fellowship and skeptical studies seemed undemocratic (1991, p. 32).

The result, he has argued, is that Americans are credulous, uncritical and pliable; he sees them as being devoid of curiosity about anything other than money, sports or entertainment and living a life untroubled by thought. Conversation, he feels, 'dwells all but exclusively on personal desires and images' and amounts to no more than an 'unvoiced cry for help which, although touching does not make it any less boring'. With hopes and ambitions shaped primarily by advertising, Americans, he claims follow a way of life which has 'elevated banality and deception to cultural principles . . . in which mendacity and mediocrity must govern.'

This is too savage. It underestimates the resilience, scepticism and creativity of people and of the ways they cope with the changing complexities of their lives. (This theme is taken up in more detail in Chapters 6 and 7.) It ignores how much learning is going on in their lives as they participate in their community groups, trades unions, professions, political parties, pressure groups, churches, leisure interests, hobbies, street gangs, crime syndicates, militias and in the ordinary routines of their workplaces. It fails to capture the healthy cynicism and unwillingness to be duped, to have the wool pulled over their eyes, that is so much part of the culture of everyday life. Nevertheless, the pressures on people to conform and consume, to keep themselves to themselves and to embrace a very narrow view of what their citizenship means, is enormous.

The experts driving forward this style of life are the anonymous employees of the media corporations, the marketing executives of industry and commerce. In Eastern Europe, before the collapse of Communism, it was the *apparatchiks* and *nomenclatura* of the state and party bureaucracies. The state sought to control information and ideas and to keep the aspirations of people limited to what the state itself felt they needed. Even with such control, a subversive 'culture of quarrel' emerged which finally eroded the legitimacy of the communist social order. For this is the paradox: the expert, knowledge-based society is not containable within the boundaries of a nation state. Watching western TV and reading the western press was something the state could not control. Nico Stehr (1994) is quite right to point out that although knowledge does bring power, the diffusion of knowledge in modern societies is on a global scale and generates instabilities which the powerful cannot control. Knowledge societies, he insists, have 'fragile' social orders: for knowledge empowers people to take control of their own fates.

The conditions for the production, dissemination, understanding and application of knowledge are not stable. They alter rapidly. If European governments are not careful, their economies will become dependent on the superior Research and Development achievements of the Pacific Rim economies. Increasingly, the global gradients of dependency and underdevelopment will reflect global differences in the R&D capacity of modern economies. And within modern societies themselves, the groups of experts who drive the knowledge system and legitimate its achievements, will bring to their work and express their interests in, a framework of thinking which is essentially international, communicating with one another through the modern media and the ether of cyberspace. RH Tawney's comment in 1931, that 'life is a swallow, theory is a snail', has never been more apt. A new kind of society is emerging. Global in its reach, driven by powerful interests in business and the international institutions of modern states, it is an unequal, unstable, culturally varied order in which knowledge confers but can never guarantee power, but where ignorance is a certain element of powerlessness.

Scientific rationality

Václav Havel, echoing the Czech philosopher, Belohradsky, noted in his essay, 'Politics and Conscience', that 'the rationalistic spirit of modern science, founded on abstract reason and on the presumption of impersonal objectivity, has, beside its father in the natural sciences, Galileo, also a father in politics – Machiavelli' (1987, p. 143). It was Machiavelli's contribution to formulate a theory of politics as a 'rational technology of power'. Both contributions – the rationality of science and of the technology of power of the modern state are central elements of the civilisation of modern capitalism.

They are what made possible the phenomenon Albert Salomon once called 'the tyranny of progress'. He was referring to the development of totalitarianism. Whether it was the Fascist or Communist version, a belief that the Party possessed the monopoly of truth, particularly about the direction of history, was at the core of it. Such ideologies brook no dissent or opposition. When the leaders march with destiny they expect nothing less than to be followed obediently.

Progress still has its tyrannical aspects. There is still a widespread belief that the future of industrial society is set in the moulds of its past; that technological change of a kind which results in the deskilling of work and the break-up of communities is relentless and inevitable. Faced with such a metaphysic, people can feel powerless, unable to act in ways that will alter their fate. And too many are likely to feel that the sheer complexity of modern society renders it beyond control or redefinition by ordinary folk. Such Promethean tasks are for experts.

That same tradition which nurtured the growth of science and technology and the belief that both hold the keys to a secure future, has produced also a much greater awareness of their limitations, particularly those of science. Peter Medawar expressed it eloquently when he wrote that he believed it to be 'science's greatest glory that there is no limit upon the power of science to answer questions of the kind science can answer' (1986, p. 87). The point, of course, is that there are many other worlds of discourse for which throw up questions unanswerable by science.

A firm and widespread belief in the necessity for and emancipatory powers of knowledge, particularly scientific knowledge, was a fundamental element of nineteenth-century social theory. Positivism was for some the basis of a new religion and within Marxism, a particular version of scientific knowledge became the basis for a revolutionary philosophy of history which, in the twentieth century, transformed the world. Whether it was 'philosophy' or 'myth' will always be debated. In the Soviet Union and in Eastern Europe it became, of course, the underlying creed for all scientific work and enquiry.

The history of twentieth-century science in Europe is one of startling achievement and horror. As an instrument available to politicians, science, through its applications in technology, has benefited millions of people. But it has been used, too, to justify and make possible the worst crimes that human beings have ever committed. Zygmunt Bauman's (1989) study of the Holocaust brings out forcibly that the destruction of European Jewry was achieved by the ruthless application of rational scientific methods to politics and is therefore inseparable from what we must understand as modernity.

The strengthening of America's global position within the Atlantic Alliance and NATO together with the division of Europe after World War II and the development of the 'People's Democracies' of Eastern Europe in the context of the Cold War, fractured European science and research dividing the cosmos of knowledge into competing ideological camps. The consequences of that division will be elaborated on in more detail later. For the moment it needs only to be noted that the search for, dissemination and application of knowledge took place under very different conditions each side of the Iron Curtain. Two different attitudes to knowledge and its development emerged: in one, the Party claimed vanguard status in its understanding of history and of nature. In the other, it was affirmed strongly that the growth of knowledge presupposed freedom of inquiry and of information.

The implications of this division for the organisation of knowledge and the relative success of West and East European economies, as well as for the intellectual openness of the two social systems, has been profound. Both systems have distorted their R&D efforts in the service of military competition and short term economic ends. The focus, forms and functions of the search for knowledge are therefore inseparable from the wider frameworks of power and of ideology of the society as a whole.

The legacy of the twentieth century's contribution to science is therefore mixed. Its achievements, though, are of world significance and its core element has been the discovery of how to make discoveries. Science is, as Peter Medawar once put it, the 'art of the soluble' (1986, p. 21). The result is that scientific discovery and the systematic search for knowledge and its applications has become fully institutionalised in to the fabric of modern industrial societies.

But it also means that modern knowledge, in all areas, is provisional. Max Weber noted this in 1918: 'scientific work,' he wrote, 'is chained to the course of progress' and therefore always to be superseded by new discovery (1970, p. 137). The scientific career becomes under these circumstances a specialised, restless, uncertain one. Scientific rationality must bend to the needs and interests of those who fund research. The intermingling of these pressures, from both the market place and the state, has nevertheless produced in western societies a vital scientific culture and rapid technological change. It is on the achievements of the western states in these fields that the new democracies of the East will have to depend if their economies are to recover from the years of stagnation which were part of the intellectual sclerosis of totalitarianism.

In the short run, however, the East–West differences in the volume, quality and achievements of scientific research, is something to reinforce the imbalance in the power of different states and the role they can play in defining the future shape of European institutions. Western *schadenfreude* at the demise of communism in Europe is not, however, an appropriate response, for it rests on the complacent premise that all is well with the western research system.

It is not; and there is much truth in the comments of Václav Havel, that what westerners see in the wreckage of the East – the pollution, the rape of nature, the distortion of science and scholarship to the needs of the state – is merely an awful intensification of trends and potentialities which exist too in western society (Havel, 1987). The totalitarian system, he claimed, was ultimately 'a convex mirror of all modern civilisation and a harsh, perhaps final call for a global recasting of that civilisation's self understanding' (1987, p.

145). If the global perspective is shifted from Europe to Africa, to Asia or Latin America, the other dimension of modern science and technology comes into view: its neo-colonial domination of the intellectual life of poor nations where the demand for its products and the legitimation a western scientific education gives, is crucial to the ways in which new elites define a place for themselves within the power networks of their own societies. Altbach (1982) went so far as to suggest that the dependency of Third World countries on the knowledge and education systems of the developed societies constituted a kind of servitude – a 'servitude of the mind' – which consolidated their economic and political dependency.

Science and the modern mentality

Disciplined, rational enquiry within a critical, questioning cast of mind, has become a feature of the way social structures are organised and of how those people at the centre of modern institutions actually think. Rationality and modernity are indissolubly linked. The consequences of such a mentality are legion: it results in the belief that all problems can be solved. Raymond Aron once referred to this as the 'ultimate inspiration of the modern age' and called it the 'Promethean ambition' (Aron, 1968, p. 216). It reinforces the belief that nature can be brought to order to serve the needs of men and that technology will overcome all the problems of society.

It nurtures an open-ended view of the future and, therefore, for the social and personal identities of millions of people. The openness of modern identities has often been commented on (Berger *et al*, 1973; Giddens, 1990); what has not been quite so strongly emphasised is that such openness is something dependent on the ability of people to acquire new knowledge and new frames of reference for thinking about themselves and their world. It means that, since the future can be to some degree engineered on the basis of the knowledge we possess, or will inevitably acquire, the past is no longer the guide to what the future will be. Our fate is finally in our own hands.

Such a belief, however, is ambiguous. If the fate of our times, as Max Weber once put it, is characterised by intellectualisation and rationalisation and if it is also true, as he claimed that the world is, on account of this, 'disenchanted', then our futures will remain uncertain (1970). Whatever is achieved by way of scientific understanding must necessarily be superseded. The certainty that what we presently know will be overtaken and revealed to be an inadequate guide to decisions and conduct, is something which drives on those who work in commercial enterprise to ever greater efforts and achievements.

To avoid economic failure and remain competitive, firms must remain abreast of modern technologies and the research and training associated with them. The requirement is relentless and governments must necessarily play a strong role in bringing this about, for they have high expectations to meet.

The metaphysic of progress encourages everyone to hope for and expect steady improvements in living standards and reduced effort at work. This particular feature of modernity has been described by Habermas (1976) as a key element of the 'legitimation crisis' of modern capitalism and by Daniel Bell as its major 'cultural contradiction' (1976). Where all theorists are agreed is that, given fierce competition, economic growth is the only route out of it so that the rising expectations of modern populations can be met.

These conditions nurture high hopes and real anxieties that they may not be realised. Such uncertainty breeds doubt. For those who possess redundant skills, the sense of being cast aside in the relentless march of progress can spawn resentment and nostalgia for better times past which both combine into a fear of the future. The emergence in modern Europe of anti-democratic, racist, right-wing political movements, is related to this particular 'structure of feeling'. 'Foreigners', especially if they are from a different cultural tradition, can still so easily become a target for aggression because of a belief that they are the cause of the economic problems faced in the host societies.

The growth of religious fundamentalism in many parts of the Middle East and central Asia is a response to underdevelopment in those regions. The search for a new kind of community – the Islamic Umma – is, as Gellner (1996) has argued, a response within Islam to find a future which is not western or secular or, for that matter, nationalist. It is certainly not a democratic future on any current western sense of the term. The emergence of such ideas and movements in countries like Algeria, Tunisia, Turkey, Iran and Pakistan has had direct consequences for Europe and for the political stability of the Mediterranean. The migration of workers from Africa into France or from Turkey into Germany – the *Gastarbeiter* – means that consequences of global economic forces have to be managed in particular towns and cities where different world cultures come into contact with one another.

These are the consequences of a global economy. They are among some of the most important factors breeding insecurity about the future. When it is further realised that the framework of western, liberal democracy is not of itself any guarantor of sustained economic success and, indeed, that this may well be a poor model for it, the uncertainty is compounded. The Pacific Rim economies did not develop on the basis of a liberal political framework which guaranteed the rights of individuals. Indeed, as Gellner (1996) has noted, individualism could well become redundant; cultures which are hierarchical, conservative and traditional can just as well engineer economic success with the tools of modern technology and science.

Long-term political stability in the advanced industrial societies of the world – particularly those in the West – presupposes Sisyphian labours from scientists, engineers, managers and planners. It requires institutionalised innovation of a self sustaining kind and constant re-education and training of all those who work. Only thus can the doors of the future be kept open and high hopes kept alive. The shadow over it all is that not everyone will be able to participate in the growth achieved. Nor will the information economy require everyone to have high-level skills in the new technologies. Much of the job growth in information technology application has been in the low-skilled, low-pay areas of service industries (Kumar, 1995).

Science, policy and politics

The belief in science and technology-led economic growth has inspired the prevailing modern vision of the role of European institutions. Indeed, modern Europe, particularly Western Europe, is organised through a range of international institutions and initiatives to develop the continent's base of research and development.

The European Commission is acutely conscious that in the global economy, success comes to those organisations in which knowledge can be translated into new products, new processes and the development of new markets. High growth rates are expected in the new information technologies, telecommunications and biotechnology. Growth here will transform all sectors of economic life. For the foreseeable future, it is commonly, though perhaps erroneously believed, the growth in the demand for labour will be in those areas where workers require high level skills.

From the early 1980s, the role of the European Commission has been to develop a co-ordinated framework of initiatives to promote European science and technology. The Single European Act in 1987 took this a step further to encourage cross-border co-operation in all aspects of research. At the core of the vision of the new Europe is a large market and an information society where strong links are cultivated between research and all its applications to economic life.

A whole new range of acronyms drawn from the large number of Commission-funded programmes, have entered the vocabulary of modern researchers. There is an acknowledgement here that the topics of research – on the environment, agriculture, radiation control, information networks, bioengineering, electronics, fisheries and much else besides – must now be approached within an international frame of reference and with a backing in resources well beyond the capability of any one nation. The European accelerator – CERN – designed for fundamental research in particle physics in Geneva is a dramatic case in point. Only on this scale can the looming threat of a superior system of R&D in the Pacific Rim economies be challenged. Throughout this rich rhetoric, Promethean assumptions abound. Whether they will provide the inspiration for the fundamental rethink of the basic assumptions of modernity that the long-term future, not only of Europe, but of the planet as a whole requires, is, of course, another matter.

In the world's industrial economies, and particularly in the most successful among them – in Japan, Germany, the USA – the search for new knowledge is institutionalised. Government and industrial R&D, especially in the areas of military technology, catalyses technological change. Universities and research institutes, often publicly funded, strive to develop new ideas and their applications. The links between scientific research in universities and commercial companies is strong. Only those companies which maintain their place at the leading edge of innovation can hope for a long-term future. The development of such relationships can no longer be left to chance.

Knowledge and power in the expert society

None of this is entirely new. Indeed, within the literature of economic development, it is a standard argument. It is, however, more than that, for it is an idea with very profound political and cultural implications. The people and the organisations that are specialised to produce knowledge are the central elements of the structures of power and social inequality in modern industrial societies. Their position in this respect is not fully dependent on their place in a particular nation state. The expert society has broken loose of the traditional historical boundaries of the nation state. The scientific and research communities which matter, are international in their composition and frames of reference.

It does not mean, however, that in all circumstances they work co-operatively together. For knowledge is also a commodity of the market place, a resource to be used in the competitive search for wealth, status and political power. The claim to posses distinctive knowledge and expertise is one of the most powerful those with power and authority in the modern economy can make to justify what they have and what they do.

Armed with their expertise, scientists can lay claim to their research funds and assert their right to undertake the research they believe is important. Expert officials can shape how elected politicians reach decisions on public issues. Specialists of all kinds, but particularly those who have undergone long programmes of education and training, can use their claims to possess distinctive knowledge to justify high monetary rewards and privileges. Those who possess special knowledge become, inevitably, to use a term from Max Weber, a 'positively privileged' group. Their expert opinions carry weight in the organisations which employ them so that a whole range of decisions can be justified on ostensibly rational or scientific grounds.

In societies where the cultural gap between experts and non-experts is high, where the experts have secured the high ground in forming the opinions of those who make important political, military, economic and scientific decisions, the role of the inexpert is to accept the legitimacy of what the experts say and do. And the fate of those who remain inexpert is to be unemployed and marginalised to the periphery of the flow of modern life. The point is this: in modern industrial societies there is a close connection between expertise and power. Stressing this very point, a group of American writers have characterised modern capitalist society as 'mandarin capitalism' (Derber *et al*, 1990). In this respect, despite its claims to neutrality, science can never be neutral.

Scientific work of all kinds is inevitably shaped by the society in which it is undertaken and is responsive to the needs and interests of those who fund it or apply its results.

Access to specialised knowledge, either to be able to acquire it in the first instance or simply to use it or call upon it, is always regulated. Modern knowledge embraces highly complex and specialised modes of understanding which may take years to acquire and considerable investment to maintain. Access to such knowledge has to bought at a price for the costs of its development have to recovered. Within most bodies of expert knowledge, there are clear hierarchies of expertise. Entry into a particular domain, for example medicine or law, is governed by clearly specified rules and standards which themselves reflect, as is well known, the social divisions of the wider society. Only those thought to possess the appropriate intellectual and social qualities, or who have undergone a period of training and prior preparation, are allowed to enter the academy to study. It is this feature of modern society which Randall Collins (1979) tried to evoke in his image of the 'credential society', a society in which people strive for the qualifications which will give them access to high status employment.

Similarly, because knowledge is expensive to acquire and costly to maintain and develop, because it requires continuous new research and documentation, the costs of gaining access to it have to be at least as great as those of making it available to others. The lawyer needs his fee; the research foundation must recover the costs of its research investment. The pharmaceutical company must build its research and development costs into the price of its drugs in the market place.

The development of new knowledge is costly. The scale of research and development required by the knowledge-based industries requires massive long-term investment. It can only be funded by well-resourced organisations or by the state, either directly or indirectly in the way in which, some European countries, fund basic research through the universities. Such government funding is invariably undertaken through close co-operation with the professional organisations of experts themselves upon whom officials depend for advice on scientific matters.

The experts involved may not feel that their views are the decisive ones or, indeed, that their views are taken seriously enough. They may not, therefore, feel they are a power in the land. But they are, nevertheless, for they possess the vital commodity upon which those with political and economic power ultimately depend – knowledge. It is for this reason that in all modern societies, there are complex cultural markets in which individuals, organisations and governments compete for knowledge and seek to control it for their own ends.

The economy based upon the exploitation of knowledge has come to replace the economy organised to exploit the physical power of labour. The proportion of the labour force engaged in manual occupations is declining in all advanced industrial countries. The long-term trend is for employers to demand ever higher levels of education and training among those they recruit. In great demand are skills connected with the new information technologies and people who are capable of learning new skills and thinking creatively throughout their working careers.

These long-term trends are inexorable with profound implications for the structure of the international division of labour, the economic fortunes of nation states as well as for the distribution of power and life chances in modern societies themselves. Seen from this perspective, the life experience of people and the political divisions of modern societies will come to depend increasingly on how the social mechanisms which distribute access to knowledge function, and much less, as before, on the mechanisms distributing income and wealth. The status people achieve on the basis of expertise is becoming as significant as that ascribed to them at birth by their parents' social class.

The expert society is geared to growth and commercial success. It promises a decline in heavy manual work. Automation and information technology carry the great hope that human beings can be liberated from the drudgery of heavy manual work. The promise is there of an expanded realm of freedom in which people will develop their skills and potentialities to the full.

In such a society, often envisaged by technological utopians, the arts would flourish and the quality of life for all would steadily improve. Framed thus, modern science and technology is a potent ideological force, the hope for all of humankind. Organisations that produce knowledge – companies at the leading edge of technology, universities, research institutes and academies of science – and those who work in them are widely held to be among the most important groups of workers and institutions in society.

Whether such groups feel that their standing in society is as high as they believe it should be is, however, another matter. Members of the intelligentsia became, throughout Eastern Europe, very active in reform movements because they believed their scientific work and status were not adequately recognised and that they themselves were accorded neither the appropriate resources nor the freedom to pursue their interests. There is also something of a global braindrain from Third World countries to the developed societies where research opportunities and employment prospects are greater. Between 1960 and 1990 Canada and the USA accepted more than 1 million professional and technically trained migrants from developing countries (Delors et al, 1996). In 1985 one half of all assistant professors under the age of 35 years in American engineering institutions were foreign. In Ghana, 60 per cent of the doctors trained in the 1980s now work abroad, leaving critical shortages of medical staff in the country (Delors et al, 1996, p. 73).

Nevertheless, the public image of science and of professional expertise generally is, a positive one and the professional bodies promoting expert interests reinforce it. The claims of such groups are at the heart of modern ideas of progress, where the central belief is that the steady improvement in the lot of mankind is the direct result of the growth and application of knowledge to human affairs.

Expertise and the lifeworld

The cultural force of such claims cannot be underestimated. They enhance the status of scientific experts and so help frame people's view of the world around them, value its elements and interpret its development. The progress of science in the field of warfare, particularly in the development of terrible weapons of mass destruction, shapes the modern sensibility of Armageddon. The ideological potency of science and technology promotes ways of thinking which devalue other forms of knowing about the world and of interpreting experience.

Without doubt, we now live in a science-saturated culture. The results are inescapable: in the ways in which we eat, care for our health, consume our time, travel and pay our bills, we all depend on the work of experts and the systems they have developed. Agnes Heller formulated this idea in her notion of 'an encapsulated scientific world view' (1984, p. 102). Her point was this: scientific ideas percolate into everyday life and thinking. They have to if people are to work pragmatically with all the technology also present in their lives.

The belief is widespread that the solution to most of the complex problems modern societies face – with, for example, the environment, disease, internal security and achieving steady growth in the economy – depends fundamentally on progress in science and technology. This metaphysic of progress has come to replace religious faith as the basis of all hope, ultimate redemption and salvation.

In the face of organised expertise, however, people are placed in a position of dependency. The word of the expert, often bought at a very high price, has simply to be trusted and that trust is embedded in a perception that experts are themselves subject to the moral regulation of either their professional bodies or their employers. Trust under these conditions becomes, necessarily, impersonal. But not necessarily widespread; one of the features of the former communist regimes of Eastern Europe was that ordinary people had no confidence that the experts with whom they came into contact were acting neutrally. There was always the fear that they were working in some way for the state. The State and the Party sought the trust of the people, but never really achieved it.

The language or, at least, elements of it, of different groups of experts has become, as has already been noted, part of general knowledge and the currency of everyday conversations. The mass media publicise scientific success stories to the full and the ordinary domestic equipment of most homes is stuffed with microchips, the everyday components of high technology.

Another angle from which to approach these features of modern everyday life is to see them as the almost magical elements of a grand narrative which has seeped into the modern soul. It is a story so well told it is no longer regarded as a story for it seems so obvious: progress depends on knowledge and expertise, particularly that of scientists and technologists.

The cornerstone of this narrative, at least as it is understood by the inexpert, is that 'They' will find the solution to all the problems that beset 'Us'. They will do so because they possess superior knowledge or because their work is designed for such an outcome. It is reassuring to know that 'They' work so hard on 'Our' behalf, that they can be called upon to help us if we need them. And it is particularly gratifying to know that, since western society has found the way to combine economic growth and commercial success with freedom and democracy. Since in fact, the highest hopes of the European Enlightenment have been realised in the practical ways in which society has arranged its institutions, expert knowledge of all kinds must necessarily be the most potent force for good in our culture; that, in a quite basic way, it can be relied on. If history has indeed, on this basis, come to an end, then this has been achieved above all else through the disciplined search for and application of knowledge to human affairs.

In this way of thinking, science is neutral; human beings may be at fault in the way they apply its results, but science itself and those who disinterestedly pursue it 'for its own sake' are not responsible for its misuse. Science itself remains in this view, objective, rational and, in relation to the differences in values and interests for which human beings sometimes kill one another, indifferent. The narrative, then, conjures up scientific and technical expertise in a way which detaches them from the conflicts and the contradictions of the society in which they develop.

That science and technology and expert knowledge of all kinds is clothed in the interests of not only those who possess it, but also those who fund it and define the research priorities and the uses to which the results are put, is something by and large unquestioned by most of those who are not themselves experts. This is, however, a changing situation. In western Europe, there has been, over the past three decades, a growth in the questioning attitude. More and more people have access to more and more information on the basis of which they can question expert judgement. In the East, this possibility opened up dramatically after 1989 and the results have been revolutionary. The opinions of scientific experts, however, remain widely respected.

One important outcome of the wide acceptance of the dominant narrative, is that the cultural forms encoded in expert knowledge, for example the belief that all problems are capable of solution or that western science represents the pinnacle of human achievement, remain unquestioned by the majority of ordinary people. The same trust does not apply, of course, to the rational technology of power, where scepticism about and mistrust of politicians is pervasive.

The idea that science is inseparable from its social context has been the stock in trade for social scientists and philosophers of science for a long time. But they are not part of ordinary discourse, for they are not part of the ordinary education people receive. The everyday awareness of the world of expertise of ordinary people is patterned to different preoccupations. Their understanding of the expertise upon which their lives depend is neither critical or for that matter historical. The result is that the achievements of science and technology have to be accepted as they are and as if they stood outside the social frameworks of economic and political life. The judgements of experts are accepted as if they were based solely on a knowledge of the truth of a matter. This belief is the source of the power of all experts. Paradoxically, it erodes the capacity to doubt, to be sceptical, to demand the evidence, which is the central component of scientific awareness and thinking.

But it is not the only source of that power. In modern societies the capacity to control the flow of information is a major determinant of power. There are many reasons why access to information in modern societies is socially and politically regulated. National security requires secrecy about military and intelligence information. Noam Chomsky (1992) has for two decades exposed the way in which military planners have kept the American public in the dark for fear that their real intentions would provoke public outcry. And they have been helped by American intellectuals, he claims, who constitute a kind of secular priesthood, legitimating government decisions in ways which make them acceptable to the American public.

Commercial firms must guard the secrets of their products or their marketing plans from competitors. Professional bodies must protect the rights of their members and keep under strict control the ways in which professional knowledge is made available to others. Not to do so is to risk losing not only the market monopoly of expertise in particular areas but also the cloak of legitimacy within which their influence is wrapped. The critical capacity of people to enter into discussions of these matters is necessarily limited. Where there is a complex division of labour and highly specialised bodies of knowledge, it is difficult for non-experts to comment on the work of experts. Different generations of people, because of their educational experiences, have markedly different levels of understanding of the main domains of modern knowledge. Throughout western societies, for cultural and political reasons, men have had readier access to scientific and technological knowledge than women. Those who are reasonably well-educated are more likely to be able to question the expertise of experts or think critically about the statements of politicians than those who are not.

Those who live in societies where access to information and to the means to learn about particular issues are open, are more likely to be able to join in critical discussions about their world than those who have lived in societies which are intellectually closed in various ways. Modern European states, particularly those in East and Central Europe, are becoming open in ways scarcely imaginable just ten years ago. The transformations in how people are coming now to understand their past and to regard the experts who interpreted the world on their behalf – the *apparatchik*, the party-approved intelligentsia in the universities, the journalists, the scientists and the engineers – is only now coming into view.

Knowledge, power and social change

The point is this: the production and distribution of knowledge and the modes of understanding woven into the lifeworlds of individuals are inseparable from their social and historical contexts. Those contexts change through time. There is a constant requirement, therefore, for new research, new technology, new systems of training and new ways to control information and its uses and for new ways to make sense of it all by ordinary people.

All our lives are structured by change. There is an inescapable requirement to understand and to reconsider our knowledge and experience. The old assumptions, ideas and bodies of information upon which our lives were lived are poor guides to our ever-changing world. How well people are equipped to accommodate the new is, of course, something shaped by their abilities, their experience and their surroundings.

Because the long-term secular trend is for modern economies to require less labour in the most advanced sectors, this need to be well-informed and highly trained is not a general one. The lives of millions can be uncoupled from the productive base of the economy and structured only to consume its products.

In this respect, modern societies differ significantly from one another. Within Europe itself, those differences, reflecting the vast canvas of unique patterns of historical change, follow in addition both North–South and East–West gradients. Modern science, by its very nature, is international in its scope and organisation and completely rational in its methods and assumptions. As Manuel Castells (1990) has shown, one of the implications of this is that in particular areas of modern technology – he was writing about electronics – international companies can concentrate their activities at whatever global site seems to the most convenient. Nevertheless, people still imagine their lives to be influenced primarily by what takes place in the political institutions of their own society.

The social construction of the lifeworlds of ordinary people and the character of their thinking is deeply rooted, therefore, in their experience and in the logic of the particular social and cultural settings in which they live their lives. It is telling, for instance, though cruelly ironic, that the internationalist outlook prized by official propaganda among the former communist states of Europe, never really penetrated the way different ethnic groups, nations and peoples perceived one another. *Mitteleuropa* is a cauldron of nationalism and seething resentments.

People differ enormously in the kind of resources available to them to help them map out their world and in the type of skills and understanding they possess. The bridges between the knowledge system and the rationalities it encodes, and the public understanding of its work are therefore not the same from one society to another. It is this variation, which remains substantially uncharted, that will be of decisive importance in shaping the political destinies of European states. The fracture lines of political interests and the propensity of different groups to act in pursuit of their interests, reflect how different groups perceive their world. The well-organised, knowledge-based interest groups of the international organisations, the public bureaucracies, the professions and scientific experts are well placed to achieve their goals.

This is not the case with millions of ordinary people who lack such knowledge and who are therefore dependent on the experts. We have to hope that ways can be found to help them become much more active and effective agents of their own fate. The danger is that too many could become the mere agents of the designs of others, trapped in narratives which are not of their own making and left merely to consume the products of a knowledge system from which they themselves are profoundly alienated.

The paradox is that modern society contains within itself the means to disseminate knowledge widely and empower its citizens to forms of thinking and understanding denied them both by capitalism and socialism in the earlier parts of the twentieth century. The politics of the twenty-first century must transcend the constraints of both if the promise of science is fully to be realised.

The practical conclusions of this analysis can be simply put. Knowledge does confer power. Even the knowledgeable, however, are in many domains of experience and understanding, ignorant and therefore powerless. If more people had more access to knowledge and to new ideas, modern societies could become much more open and much more creative in the ways they solve their problems.

Access to knowledge and information is not, however, enough. Conditions have to be created in which the views of people matter, in which the unique understanding each can bring to any problem is taken into account. Science itself develops through open dialogue and debate among scientists. The greatest technological achievements of the twentieth century – flight, medicine, space travel, telecommunications, the list is endless – have depended fundamentally on co-operation among experts and workers of all kinds finding ways to solve problems together.

The solution to the social and political challenges facing modern societies – which the Delors report (Delors *et al,* 1996) to UNESCO on lifelong learning, described as the need to find harmonious forms of human development which 'reduce poverty, exclusion, ignorance and war' (1996, p. 13), will require new forms of co-operation and communication which are just as effective as those in the world of science and technology. The more people understand the collective nature of all knowledge and expertise, the more they can recognise the fallibility of all claims to knowledge and the more they acquire the skills they need continually to deepen their own understanding of the world, the more effective their communication, debate, analysis and problem-solving will be. The more open the society, the greater the likelihood that the power of experts can be tamed.

3 Knowing, understanding and feeling

> The Eagle never lost so much time,
> as when he submitted to learn of the crow.
>
> William Blake, *The Proverbs of Hell*

Through education, though not by any means exclusively, people come to a greater understanding of their world. What I wish to consider in this chapter is the question, 'What is meant by the term understanding?' The answer to it which educators arrive at will shape directly how they approach the process of helping others to learn. If teachers are unclear about what the term means, then their teaching will be inadequate; they will not know precisely what it is they are seeking to achieve for their students. The experience of the learner under these conditions will be a frustrating one, fraught with uncertainty, possible failure and corrosive self doubt.

If, on the other hand, both teachers and learners – in whatever context they work – can have a clear view of what it means to understand a subject or a theme, then they can work effectively with one another. When that happens, their relationship alters, their understanding deepens and so, too, does their sense of the possibilities in their lives.

The thesis explored here is twofold: first, understanding is best conceived as a social process nurtured in the most effective way, at any level, through dialogue, which is itself a special form of human communication requiring a distinctive competence. (See Chapter 11 for further discussion of the idea of dialogue.) It is a process in which learners come to acquire, through discussion and practice of various kinds, a confident and critical grasp of the grounds upon which arguments, propositions and truth claims are made. Second, when adults are helped to approach the business of understanding something from within these assumptions, they learn quickly and effectively, with profound consequences for the ways in which they see themselves and for the contribution they can make to the life of society as a whole.

The corollary is that, when people are denied the means to develop their critical understanding of their world, they become the victims of the way other, more powerful groups interpret it and are in effect denied the effective means to pursue the development of their own thoughts and feelings. Vast areas of human experience and understanding then become inaccessible to them and their lives are thereby diminished. There is great loss to everyone in this; the quality of and possibilities in all our lives, even for those who regard themselves as educated and cultured, but particularly for those who do not see themselves in this way, are, as a consequence, reduced.

The cultural context of understanding

Understanding is a process of making sense of the world around us. It is our way of reducing uncertainty, developing our curiosity and bringing our world under greater control. When we understand something we can explain it, describe it, analyse it in relation to other, similar phenomena and act on and in the world in new ways. Kant pointed to the ways in which the realities of the world we live in, are organised and experienced conceptually. The cognitive templates we employ to order experience – the fundamental categories of thought – are the constructs that enable us to confer our experiences with meaning and significance. It is a great achievement of modern science to have shown that there are disciplined methods available that enable us to refine, challenge and test out what we believe to be true in the open domain of public debate and thereby learn from the work of others.

If it was Kant who transformed our view of reason, it was only because Hume had demonstrated that reason itself was the slave to our passions. There is no experience without thought, and no thought without experience. Our key existential task is to bring the two together and to bring both into some alignment with what we feel, for there are, too, no feelings, no emotions, without words and thoughts to describe them. This insight of constructivist psychology and philosophy has profound implications both for what we mean by the term understanding and for teaching and learning. Cognitive development can never be separated off from feeling and emotion. What we feel shapes how and what we learn and what we know colours and conditions what we can feel (Harre, 1986).

All mental operations involve abstraction, generalisation, inference, deduction, classification and prediction. Science constitutes our most powerful model of this, with lots of parallels in ordinary, everyday thinking, both in modern technological societies and in traditional cultures (Horton, 1971). But abstract, conceptual thought, such as mathematics, is not the only mode in terms of which we understand the world. Aesthetic experience, insight, imagination and intuition are also part of our repertoire of ways of comprehending our world and conferring meaning on it.

The constituent elements of these processes – the language, narratives, symbols – are essentially cultural and are, therefore, both public and shared (Bruner, 1990). At the core of this perspective – what Bruner calls 'cultural psychology' – is a theory of the human mind itself which is construed in cultural terms. Our efforts to make sense of our lives and to interpret our experiences succeed only to the extent that we can draw upon the experiences of others and the resources of the culture around us. It is, therefore, only through other people that we come to know ourselves and our world.

This way of looking at learning is profoundly at odds with approaches that lay stress on individual cognitive processes and capacities and which treat learning as a hard, lonely journey, undertaken by people who are each equipped differently to complete it. The view that some people are equipped for education and some only for training to perform particular kinds of tasks, is from the cultural–constructivist perspective, deeply flawed. It is nevertheless the case, that much of the organisation and delivery of formal education in modern industrial societies, whether it takes place in school and colleges or in work organisations, is rooted in an individualistic psychology of learning and a deeply hierarchical and linear view of the process of knowledge acquisition. And it leads necessarily to the view that some people are better capable of understanding the world than others and this presumption slides easily over into another: that some people deserve more rewards, responsibilities and power than others.

There is a particular twist to this line of argument in formal education settings that concerns the curriculum and the organisation of human knowledge into subjects. In parallel to the conventional, linear, essentialist view of learning and understanding, there has prevailed in modern western societies a strong sense of the division of knowledge into subjects such as the arts, sciences and humanities and a belief that human understanding is organised into different forms of knowing, some of which are abstract and theoretical and some technical or practical.

These divisions (discussed in Chapter 7) tell us as much about the political divisions of academic communities as they do about the logic of particular disciplines or methods of enquiry. They certainly cannot be justified in terms of any credible theory of human learning. The institutionalised insulation of the arts and sciences, of the theoretical and practical disciplines, of reason and imagination, is something which not only runs counter to how people actually learn and understand the world, it reinforces inequalities in society and is immeasurably expensive in the way it leads to a terrible loss of human, creative achievement. When people are classified as failures because they are not good at certain 'subjects', the failure is less in the individual than in the way a society constructs human achievement and possibility.

Relationships between teachers and learners in modern societies are constructed in terms of hierarchies of authority and power and do not easily allow – though many attempt to achieve this – for the free flow of ideas, information, doubts and questions which are the necessary preconditions of all successful learning. Because teacher–learner relationships are imbalanced, and set up to ensure that learning will be measured and tested so that those who are successful can be distinguished from those who are not, they have an in-built potentiality to breed defensiveness, doubt and anxiety. Such conditions inhibit learning and stifle open dialogue. They prevent questioning and the development of a shared interpretation of the truly emancipatory kind that would nurture new perceptions and insights for both teachers and learners alike.

Open learning, open society

The cultural–psychological model of learning which Bruner (1986) has described – and which has many other echoes in different traditions of social, psychological and cultural theory – is profoundly opposed to the models of learning institutionalised in much formal educational practice and certainly to much that passes for training in work organisations. It is contrary, too, to the ways in which most modern societies construct their policies for education. By privileging the young and concentrating most of the resources for education in the early years of life and focusing them on formal education and training of various kinds, adults in modern societies are too often denied the help they need to continue the development of their understanding. Learning is, necessarily, a lifelong experience and human beings retain a far greater capacity for new learning than most are ever given credit for or opportunity to realise.

Many recent trends in education and in work-related training are, from the perspective being developed here, also of questionable value when set against the epistemological requirements of enabling people to understand their world in a confident and critical way. Throughout the advanced, industrially developed societies of the world, formal education systems have expanded enormously since the period after the end of World War II. Mass enrolments in further and higher education have spawned highly innovative curricular changes. Courses have been modularised. Access to further and higher education has been widened. Systems of credit accumulation and transfer have been developed. Educational institutions themselves have grown in scale and complexity and older subject boundaries have been and are eroding. Stronger links have been forged between the worlds of work and education and the interests and needs of students are taken much more seriously than they once were.

This opening up of educational opportunities to more people than ever before is something to applaud; it is surely a mark of progress, a contribution to the development of more open societies and to democratic institutions within them. There remains, none the less, a wide divide between what has been and what might yet be achieved. The forms and levels of understanding and of thinking achieved by different groups of people, remain both finely tuned to the operational requirements – particularly the economic ones – of contemporary societies, and they limit severely the potentialities of most people to think in different ways. The result is that many people experience their lives, often fatalistically, as a series of traps; they feel caught in a downward spiral of pressures confining them to the jobs they do and limiting the options open to them.

Carrying within themselves a shrunken view of their own competence and devaluing their own achievements, too many people – especially those thought of, conventionally, as failures at school and those who see no possibility of changing the work they do – underestimate what they are capable of and remain victims of, rather than agents of, their own fate. These are not the conditions which nurture the competence to learn new forms of communicative action of an emancipatory kind. These conditions do not allow people to challenge confidently the terms of the dominant discourses which confer such limited meaning on their lives or imagine alternatives to them.

The imagination schooled to believe that significant learning takes place only in college or in organised training programmes handled by experts, is not one geared to the full realisation of its own potential. A truly open society would not limit people to the narrow confines of learning currently open to them. Nor would it impose tight restrictions on how it would value the learning which takes place experientially as people cope with the growing complexity of their ordinary lives. It could not be restricted to forms of understanding that were primarily technical or theoretical, but would embrace others, including those that nurture sensitivity, insight, spirituality and an expansive and lively imagination.

Rational thought is only one of the ways – though, perhaps, in modern technological civilisation the most important – through which people interpret their world. In their efforts to understand their worlds, people in all cultures have imagined other ones. The past they have envisioned in their creation myths; the future through their religious eschatology. Through their art they have explored the boundaries of their imagination and stretched their comprehension to its limits, extending not only what they have had the power to 'see', but also what they could 'feel'.

Human creative thought (discussed in more detail in Chapter 8) is driven and excited by the imagination, by the ability, which can be cultivated, to think in fresh ways, to dream and to contemplate actively alternative worlds and of ways of doing things. The world of the imagination – expressed in all the visual arts, in science, in fiction, poetry and dance, as well as in the profound realms of religious experience – sharpens and shapes our understanding of the everyday, secular world of ordinary life and extends our emotional responses towards it.

When we understand something, it is no longer strange; we have a way of explaining it and reporting to others what we have come to know. In doing so, however, our world has altered; our boundaries of comprehension have been extended with subtle, but inevitable changes to our deepest sense of self. This has to be the case, for the self is deeply anchored in what we know and our knowledge defines the boundaries of our world. Extend that knowledge and, as I show in Chapter 10, the self itself alters.

Each act of understanding is simultaneously, however, one which opens up new questions which demand answers. When students achieve a deep understanding of their subject and of its epistemological assumptions, their prime experience is of how easily its boundaries and certainties dissolve into new unknowns (Bernstein, 1971a). A further dimension of this phenomenon is scepticism. Giddens has noted that 'high modernity' institutionalises what he calls 'radical doubt' (1991, p. 3). Traditional nostrums and taken-for-granted assumptions about anything – politics, medical knowledge, morality – are subject to constant questioning. Nothing any longer is certain. The key principal of rational science is 'the methodological principle of doubt' and this is something which intrudes into ordinary life (1991, p. 21). Something which serious students realise comes to be appreciated by people in general: they no longer feel their lives or their understanding can be governed by certainties of any kind.

Given this, it is clear that the processes of learning and understanding in modern society are limited, not by some natural distribution of ability, but by the social frameworks built on a too restricted view of knowledge and the clearly specified indicators of achievement and competency which accompany it. These processes, which determine, ultimately, the quality of all our lives, ought not be left to educators or to trainers alone to define. They cannot be confined to the early years of life or be constrained by the labour requirements of giant corporations or strained to fit the curricula of universities. The open society presupposes an open-ended commitment to the lifelong learning needs of people and be rooted in a strong sense of the creative possibilities of all our lives.

Levels of understanding

The counterpoint to the argument so far developed, is that not everyone can understand to the same degree, that people have different abilities and, more importantly, interests and inclinations. The point is not, however, that people are the same and not at all that they should be. Rather it is that there are no limits to what people can be helped to understand, should they wish to and be given the right kind of opportunity to learn.

There are, clearly, many different levels of understanding in any field of human enquiry. And there are some questions which are perhaps beyond human understanding. God remains a mystery to human consciousness and understanding. So, too, as Karl Popper has pointed out, referring to the beliefs of the physicist, Niels Bohr, is the problem of reconciling quantum mechanics with classical physics (1992, p. 93). Anyone who can join in and make a sensible contribution to debates about God or small particle physics, will have a much deeper understanding of the issues involved than the beginner in Physics or Theology.

To become such an expert takes time. All complex skills – like being able to speak a foreign language competently or play a Beethoven piano sonata so that others might wish to listen, take time to acquire. One psychologist, John Sloboda (Sloboda *et al*, 1994) of the University of Keele, claims the time required, whatever supposition of native ability, is 5,000 hours. The key difference between musicians thought to be gifted and those considered merely good, lay primarily in the quality of their practice. Whether or not complex skills and expertise are acquired depend upon the opportunities available to people and on the kind of help they get to benefit from them.

All of the higher levels of understanding involve epistemological insight – an appreciation of the methods through which knowledge is gained, a critical understanding of truth claims, and an ability to evaluate arguments and evidence. The skills which are part of this are those of logical thinking, hypothetical–deductive reasoning, an ability to infer reasons and explain data and, of equal importance, an ability to communicate confidently and coherently.

These are skills. But they are not skills in the sense of being competent to perform a task. The ability to perform a task is not synonymous with knowledge of or an understanding of the task being performed. It is possible to mend a motor car without fully understanding the engineering principles in the design of internal combustion engines. It is not, however, possible to judge the merits of competing theories in science without a deep understanding of the subject and grasp of the analytical skills in making such judgements.

These skills develop and improve with practice; they decline and ossify if they are not used. From this angle, it is clear that the practice of such skills is not something occasioned by self interest or inclination alone. Whether we use such skills depends on the circumstances of our lives and the demands made upon us. The relentless pressure within modern societies to mechanise work, to rationalise and simplify production processes, to simplify and commoditise leisure, is simultaneously a process of deskilling many people and of reducing their scope for independent thought.

Those who undertake the research and development to enable this to happen are not somehow free from these pressures. They are being limited, to our great collective cost, in other ways. Their work is to contain, to render the work of others predictable; it is only with difficulty that they can reframe what is expected of them by their own bosses and the anonymous shareholders who own the company and who can move their investment if they choose to wherever else it might be more profitable. This is not a problem unique to the private sector. It pervades all complex work organisations whether in the private or the public sector. It is a problem in universities as much as in business enterprises.

Nearly 40 years ago, at the height of the Cold War, C. Wright Mills (1959, p. 129) castigated intellectuals for being in default of their duty to mankind. 'By intellectuals,' he wrote, 'I mean scientists and artists, ministers and scholars; I mean those who represent the human intellect; those who are part of the great discourse of reason and enquiry, of sensibility and imagination that in the West began in Jerusalem and Athens and Rome, and that has been going on intermittently ever since.'

What puzzled Mills was that some of them could remain within the legacy of science and be, simultaneously, hired technicians of the war machine. Or that many accepted without scrutiny official definitions of reality. They did not, he claimed, 'examine the USA as an over-developed society full of ugly waste and the deadening of human sensibility, honouring ignorance and the cheerful robot, pronouncing the barren doctrine and submitting gladly, even with eagerness, to the uneasy fun of a leisureless and emptying existence' (1959, p. 132).

Mills' virulence was born of his context: the Cold War and, as many saw it, the imminent prospect of World War Three. Our context is different. The

Cold War has metamorphosed into an uncontrollable pattern of regional conflicts which threaten to destabilise a very divided, polluted world and in the developed and rapidly developing industrial economies, particularly in the West, there is widespread doubt that the forms of society being built will survive the next fifty years.

The critical default among the educated remains, however, an issue. Do those computer scientists building the world's information highway care very much whether the world's millions will consume culture or pornography? Do they sense a connection between their highly developed and practised skills and the discourse of reason to which they are heirs? Would it make a difference to what they do, even if they did? Do they feel themselves sufficiently independent of their paymasters to commit themselves to a different vision of how the future might be organised? Do those who develop the new drugs for the world's pharmaceutical industry care whether people lead healthy life styles which might reduce their demand for medicine?

Hard-won, detailed expertise acquired over many years may amount to a great understanding of a subject. But it could also amount to a naive, uncritical blindness to other perspectives and possibilities. Freed from open, critical discussion and lacking the kind of controls only democratic societies with heightened moral sensibilities can supply, expertise can become blind and dangerous. The German scientists and engineers who designed the concentration camps to exterminate Jews were, as Zygmunt Bauman (1989) has poignantly explained, part of the culture of modernity. But their critical, expert understanding of one domain of knowledge, was fatally flawed by their inability to understand the moral and political context of their work with anything like the same degree of critical integrity.

Those in contemporary society in the knowledge-generating roles, who have the responsibility to innovate and change, exercise high-level skills continually. Their opportunity to do so is a great personal bonus, for the skills they acquire carry over into other areas of their lives offering chances of personal growth and enrichment denied to those who are trapped in dull, unchallenging routines. Whether those roles nurture critical thinking is, however, another matter.

There is a confidence needed to think critically and unconventionally and to have the courage to doubt what is usually taken for granted or is widely believed. Those who have it are prepared to be seen as pariahs among their peers. Those who lack it are too often prepared to believe what is conventionally taken to be true or to be swept along in their thinking by what is popular and fashionable. The differences between the two groups are embedded in wider differences of attitude, value and education that themselves are woven into the institutions of society as a whole.

The aim of education is to enable people to understand their world better so that they can appreciate more of it and act much more confidently within it. Whatever the subject – art or astrophysics – the goal is to help people acquire the analytical and empirical skills to deepen their understanding further. It is not a question of filling their heads with received information; it is to help them locate information in a wider frame of reference; to help them see its relevance against a wider background of theory, practice and uncertainty. It is to help learners acquire the skills and the confidence to enter into dialogue with experts and to appreciate the significance of their learning. And it is to help experts realise the fallibility of their expertise and to live comfortably with doubt and uncertainty and be open to the influences of others.

This kind of understanding is not subject-based. It flows from a moral sensibility of human interdependence. It can only develop when there is a genuine confidence and openness to others. The most highly qualified scientist can, by this test, have a very limited understanding of themselves and their role and of the place of their work in the wider discourse of reason which supports the fragile structures of modern culture, society and citizenship.

The process and politics of understanding

Understanding is a process; a continuous, fragile, doubtful, provisional attempt to confer meaning and order on to experience and to open up new possibilities for action. The action can be technical or political, scientific or cultural. Though anchored in the minds of individuals, it is essentially a social process. The languages that make it possible and communicable are social. The epistemological criteria involved in deciding the validity of a knowledge claim are legitimated publicly; they are part of the ways of knowing within a culture.

Modern forms of understanding are saturated with science; premodern forms lack the explicitly secular, causal, reductionist characteristics of modern consciousness, but represent none the less, successful attempts to see order in chaos and meaning in what would otherwise be meaningless. This point is not, however, widely acknowledged. Western philosophers have typically only attached significance to propositional knowledge; the knowledge of how to do something – know-how – has been devalued.

One result is that a distinction has emerged between the practical and the theoretical, between education and training, between culture and craft, which is both socially divisive and epistemologically unsound. It drives a wedge, too, between thought and feeling, counterposing them in ways which value only those understandings rooted in conscious thought and playing down those rooted in intuition or in a well-developed aesthetic sensibility. The danger in doing this is that the role of intuition and feeling in the creation of ideas which later become tested and part of the wider public domain of scientific discourse, is devalued.

From the individual's viewpoint, the process of coming to understand something has to be seen as a phased one. At whatever level, understanding involves bringing new information, insights, ideas or experiences into a previous framework of concepts and beliefs, thus rendering them no longer strange and, simultaneously, altering what was known before. At the highest level, people have a capacity to generate new understanding, to induce what Kuhn (1970) called 'paradigm shifts' which alter how the world is understood.

Understanding is inseparable from the communication processes that sustain it. Those of organised scholarship are among the most powerful human societies have ever produced. But if the results of scholarship and research are not widely available or understood, then they remain the property of elites. Without the intellectual resources to order new information about the world, people can be trapped in narrow lines of thought, limited in what they can think and communicate and criticise. The communication revolution of the past 25 years has opened up literally unbounded possibilities for international, intercultural communication. The world information highways network the world's most advanced databases as well as, of course, the worst TV into every home with a satellite disc. Totalitarian attempts to control this have failed. Eastern Bloc countries could not stop their citizens watching western TV. Some of the closed cultures of the Middle East cannot shield satellite TV transmissions. The irony is that as the information available to people has exploded, the capacity of people to sift it and evaluate it and be critical of it, or to generate and communicate their own views, is much less than that of the corporate planners who straddle the globe.

Learning to effect

All understanding is shared; it is part of what a group takes for granted about itself. How groups of people account for their world has become one of the central questions of modern anthropology and several lines of contemporary social theory. From these angles, understanding is an active, social process of accounting for events and experiences and is inseparable from the kinds of rules which apply within a group or society. In some contexts, the accounting procedures are legitimated by someone in authority – scientists, priests, opinion formers of several kinds. In modern, expert-dominated societies, this is a common feature: experts possess understanding and make it available to others, who are dependent on them. Another model is possible: one in which people themselves can become their own experts, should they choose so. It is only in this way that people will acquire the confidence and skill through which to think critically about the discourses within which decisions are taken which shape their lives.

Set against what we know is involved in understanding something – the conceptual development, the hard work, the practice of a skill or technique and the solving of problems – it is easier to see how much of what people experience as education and of training at work, inhibits it. The new model requires a new system of learning, which is continuous, open, lifelong and critical. The institutional forms which would support it are very different to those which currently exist and to the assumptions of social policy which lie behind them. The entitlement to and need for continuous learning cannot be institutionally confined to education but must be acknowledged and met in the work place and in the community.

It must be based, too, on principles different to those of didactic teaching and the kinds of understanding aimed at should not be restricted to the narrow confines of particular subjects, competencies or employer's interests. Those who begin a journey of understanding can never really know beforehand where their destination will be. To believe that learning outcomes can be specified in advance is to fail to appreciate the intrinsic open-endedness of all learning.

All teaching must start from what the student knows. It must begin from the acknowledgement that adult students have a great deal of experience of the world. They may not have reflected fully on it, or even understand it. But they have it. They have come to know much about themselves and their world and their experience may in many ways be broader and varied than that of their teachers. Whatever the case, it must be taken seriously; it must be valued and understood, for it is through the interpretive frames of their own experience that people make sense of their world and arrive at an understanding of it.

Successful teaching and learning must extend that understanding in manageable stages and at the student's pace. Time must be allowed for people to try out, practise and use what they come to know, otherwise understanding slips and falters. The organisation of work in modern societies often prevents people from deepening their grasp of something so that people remain trapped within narrowly defined work roles or in the use of old technologies and methods. Those organisations which seek to prevent this and which see themselves as 'learning organisations' seek to overcome this and build positively on the recurrent learning of their employees.

Change, innovation and personal development are then institutionalised. But it does take a management culture that values people and is tolerant of risk and failure to nurture enthusiastic learning among employees. Such a culture could be profoundly threatening to some managers or officials who might perceive their authority threatened by bright subordinates.

Psychological research into the phenomenon of understanding failure, or comprehension failure, provides a further perspective on how to facilitate the development of sound understanding in students, whether they are in college or in a job. Comprehension failures are inevitable and with unique features in each individual. Students have to be helped to recognise their own failures and the reasons for them. They must be encouraged to a meta-cognitive awareness of how they deal with comprehension failures so as to know how to correct them. It is failure here which explains why so many people experience their education as something confirming their lack of ability and perceive the ability of others as a gift and not, as they should, as something based on a successful strategies for learning and understanding.

Understanding failures are not confined to 'subjects'; they are existential. Death, war, revolution, loss, illness and injury, accident – in general, the unexpected, the unknown, the random – test us out and find us wanting. As individuals grow and develop, therefore, their previous understanding of the world has to alter. Were it not to do so, then all of us would be trapped in completely unadaptive patterns of behaviour.

But it is not just a question of individuals needing to change. Organised, modern societies generate constantly new bodies of knowledge which, translated into technology alter the way in which society itself functions. Modern societies institutionalise change. They require of all of their citizens a constant updating of knowledge and understanding. Those who cannot achieve this find themselves increasingly driven to the margins of modern life incapable of comprehending it or altering the course of its development. Some groups are placed strategically to constantly update their knowledge and understanding of the world around them. The scientific community is one such group. All of those workers involved in specialised research and development function at the frontiers of human knowledge. Experts of all kinds play roles which require them to keep abreast of developments in knowledge and, indeed, to define new knowledge. Well-educated people with a capacity to interpret new information and with links into complex information systems, are well placed to change their view of the world and their own place within it.

On the other hand, those who are less well equipped or who lack the communicative competence to interpret the data with which they are daily bombarded, will find themselves living in increasingly narrow and circumscribed worlds. When the bonds between knowledge and power tighten, those who lack knowledge find themselves alongside the powerless denied opportunities to shape the development and future direction of their societies and communities. A major challenge confronting all adult education in all modern societies, is therefore, how to enable more people to build on their previous knowledge and acquire a new understanding of their world. It is to find the means to enable literally millions of people to gain access to the resources they currently lack, to help them articulate what they have come to know and to reformulate it in ways which enable them to explore it further.

Democratic modern societies require a stronger educational foundation. Ignorance and gullibility and a readiness to believe what so-called experts say, are the necessary, though not sufficient, conditions for the development of forms of totalitarian government. The social and political conditions of the modern economy and of modern society, which are deeply affected by the development of new knowledge, especially in the areas of science and technology, presuppose a much more effectively and widely educated society than most of the developed countries of the world have so far achieved.

But it is not only the political and economic dimensions of understanding which matter. The economic metabolism of modern society is an immensely productive one. The technical and economic means are widely available to sustain very high standards of living for most people who live in modern societies. What is less clear, however, is whether the quality of life can be sustained at the same level.

The danger is as more aspects of our lifeworlds become commoditised and commercialised, the range, quality and depth of our understanding both of ourselves and our world, will all diminish. The consequence is that many people will not live their lives to their full potential, that people will experience their world in wholly inauthentic ways and that the wider social benefits of enabling more people to participate in society to a far greater extent than they currently do, will be lost. What Paulo Freire once described as 'the culture of silence' is not a phenomenon only of the Third World. The poor and disadvantaged of modern industrial societies also lack the ability to articulate their experience so that others can understand it. The consequence is, not only that inequalities persist, but that the prevailing picture that we have of how our society is constituted and how it changes, is a distorted one.

The loss in this is a general one, for the vital, creative, developing society, which carries the promise of higher and better living standards for all, is one which nurtures learning and understanding throughout all social groups. Writing of the great engineering achievements of the late nineteenth century in the North East of England, Sid Chaplin, the region's most important modern literary voice, noted: 'The real wealth of a city or a region consists of the sum total of the skill and mother-wit of its people, sharpened and not spoiled by education and honed to a proper cutting edge by an open society' (1969a). Wit, which we all possess, and opportunity, which too many are denied, are the necessary conditions for successful understanding. What Chaplin knew intuitively, has now been proved, though as yet, not fully or with real conviction, acted upon: the developing understanding of individuals needs renewed opportunities for further development and these can only come from within a social framework – in education, at work, in society – which is itself open and developing.

4   Lifeworlds and learning

The cistern contains: the fountain overflows.
                            William Blake, *Proverbs of Hell*

For all adults, organised learning is a challenge with great risks attached, for it invites people to reconsider what they know. It requires them to re-evaluate their life experiences and their understanding, both of themselves and their world. Those unprepared to take such risks, or those who feel well enough equipped already to achieve their goals on the basis of the knowledge or skills they already possess, are unlikely to seek out opportunities for new learning. It does not necessarily follow, however, that those who are aware of a need within themselves to improve their knowledge or skills will actually take steps to do so.

Whether they do so or not depends, first, on how people perceive the constraints they must overcome to gain access to new learning opportunities, and second, on how they normally seek answers to questions, satisfy their curiosity and pursue their interests and enthusiasms. Both are facets of how they live their lives and reflect the tacit assumptions, attitudes, expectations and future hopes woven into the patterns of their everyday understanding and awareness. Moreover, as I hope to show, the precise patterns which make up the lifeworld (*Lebenswelt*) of different groups of people are themselves shaped considerably by the ways in which people anticipate, experience and interpret the changes taking place in their lives.

It follows from these observations that those who seek to provide greater educational opportunities for adults must seek to do so in ways which build upon an understanding, not only of the personal interests of different people, but of how they make sense of change, in their own lives and in the society in which they live. It is not sufficient to follow the market research model and ask individuals what kinds of things they might like to study, though this is an approach strongly recommended by marketing experts in their advice to educators. It is much too shallow as a way of probing learning needs and intentions, too individualised and too confined to the present tense. To achieve the understanding required is a complex sociological task. It can only be done on the basis of dialogue between those providing learning opportunities and those for whom they seek to do so. The outcome to be hoped for is an exchange of ideas and perceptions, so that each can learn from the other and on that basis, establish arrangements which will enable learning to take place, because they would then meet the special needs and circumstances of the learners themselves.

This chapter reports the results of two sessions of dialogue with the above aims in view, with two groups of adults – white male industrial workers, one group from the mining industry, one from chemicals – attending courses on industrial studies provided by the Department of Adult and Continuing Education of the University of Durham. The results of these discussions are presented here in a way which invites yet further debate about how adult educators should themselves seek to understand the experience and interests of those whose learning they seek to facilitate. To anticipate the main conclusion: this small exploratory study highlights the critical importance for the value people place on their own education and learning needs, of the ways in which they arrive at interpretations of the social changes taking place in their lives. Differences here are major determinants of how people set their personal educational agendas.

The members of both groups were active trade union officials, pursuing extramural courses in industrial studies. There were 24 men in total. One group (11) worked in the chemical industry on Teesside; the other 13 were miners from both Northumberland and Durham. The miners were, on average, a slightly younger group concentrated in the age range 26 to 45 years. There were no chemical workers younger than 36.

Discussions took place separately with both groups during a morning session (three hours) of their course and were structured to a common pattern. The work of each group began with short general comments from me about social changes taking place throughout Europe and about the difficulties we all have in making sense of them. I explained that I wished to discuss with them how they themselves did so and whether they felt they were well enough equipped for the task. The individuals in each group filled in a short questionnaire which yielded some personal information about their education, their reading habits and clues about their involvement in both political activities and a range of voluntary associations in the community. It asked questions, too, about what they thought of the changes which have taken place in this country over the postwar years and their expectations for the future. The final questions concerned their personal plans for their own further education. My intention in asking people to complete the questionnaire, was not only to retrieve some basic information about them, but also to prompt them to think quietly and individually about the issues that would later dominate group discussions. Each group was then divided into four smaller groups, each with the task of discussing a particular but different question. The questions were as follows:

1.   Looking back to the end of World War II, how do you (and people like you) judge the changes which have taken place in British society?

2.   Looking back in time since your school days, what things have given you

the greatest personal satisfactions and what have caused you the most regrets? What, if anything, do you (and people like you) regret the most?

3.   What do you (and people like you) expect this country to be like in 25 years' time?

4.   Over the next 25 years, what do you (and people like you) personally hope for most and how confident are you your hopes will be realised?

Members of each group were asked to approach their question in the first instance from a personal angle and to share their views with one another. Having done so, the task was then to summarise the results and prepare to report them back to the larger group. No group was aware of the questions being discussed by the others. Following each presentation, a short discussion took place to assess whether the four groups as a whole shared in the views being expressed by each separate group. This was to check whether the views being presented were in any way idiosyncratic or specific to the men in the sub-group or to the way in which they approached the discussion among themselves, or whether they were, indeed, widely shared. My hope was that through this method, some of the shared, tacit, taken-for-granted assumptions of each group of workers about their world and the changes which have taken place in it, would be revealed.

       Following all the presentations there was general discussion and wide-ranging debate about how the answers given to the questions might be explained. By these means, dialogue took place which engaged people both personally and politically. It was a process which enabled all group members to contribute with confidence in an exercise aimed to clarify how those involved, and people like them, interpreted their world and judged their capacity properly to analyse it.

       The results of the discussions and debate, together with those of the questionnaire, provide some pertinent clues about what has shaped, and continues to shape, the personal educational agendas of male industrial workers in the North East of England, inviting comparison with other groups of workers – both men and women – in different industries, regions and, indeed, countries. Neither group could be presented as representative of men in the industry as a whole; they were active trade unionists and keen themselves to take part in courses like the one for which they had enrolled. Nevertheless, they are men with close contacts with other workers and they were asked specifically to comment on how people like themselves would answer the questions they were discussing. The glimpse their responses give into the attitudes and ways of thinking of men currently at work in the two industries, carries credibility.

Impressions, observations and bias

Interpretation of the results must necessarily build on three sets of observations: those made by the men in the questionnaires, the results of the group discussions and, finally, my own qualitative observations on the ways in which each group approached the tasks given them and the overall pattern and texture of the discussions.

To deal with the last first, if only to be in a better position to guard against it: the miners and chemical workers, though made up of active trade unionists supported by both their unions and employers to be on the course, seemed, as groups, to be very different from one another. Despite surface similarities of age, style of dress and attitude – both groups shared a joking, bantering, iconoclastic style in dealing both with me and with one another. Each group had a very different feel to it. Discussions with other tutors who worked with both groups lend confirmation to this impression.

The miners were relaxed and apparently much more inclined than the chemical workers to acknowledge that they knew one another well and valued one anothers' company. Above all, however, the miners seemed to possess a much sharper radical edge to their political views and a much greater commitment to the values of equality, community and fairness. They obviously possessed a much stronger sense of being a group together than did the men from Teesside. Care is needed, however, as the other tutors on the course pointed out, to distinguish, among the views expressed by the miners, those which they felt honour bound to articulate and those they might hold privately. With men for whom solidarity is a potent ideal, there is a real danger, in the public setting of the classroom, they would construct an idealised image of themselves and in talking about it affirm strongly the emotional force of the picture they were presenting.

The miners appeared, in comparison with the chemical workers, to be a group with much more secure convictions, confident of their traditions, trusting their sense of solidarity with one another and, as a result, able to be very open both with one another and with me, and not to feel threatened by such openness. These apparent differences did not show up quite so strongly in the responses of both groups to the questionnaire. Nevertheless, whatever the differences in their experience of their two industries and the communities which are part of them, miners and chemical workers share in a common, all-male popular culture, with its overt sexism and suspicion of foreigners. Only the chemical workers, however, expressed opinions which were obviously racist. Both groups are of the same generation of working people, reaching maturity within the traditions, structures and values of British society during the past 30 years and both had experienced considerable changes in their industry during the past decade. Neither group stands apart, therefore, from the materialism, the home-centred privatism and the pervading sense of powerlessness which have come to be such marked features of British society.

There were great similarities in the ways in which both groups of workers conducted themselves in the context of the classroom. It seemed in both cases that the unwritten rules were: do not be too serious unless it was necessary to be so and do not appear to be too well-informed or clever in any way. Competence and experience have to be tacitly acknowledged. Both groups valued a mildly cynical, worldly wise approach to questions and both insisted in a variety of ways that I should be able to demonstrate that I was a person to be trusted. The task, from my point of view, was much easier with the miners than with the chemical workers, though I had not previously met either group.

Lifestyles and expectations

The questionnaire results lend support to the following characterisation of the two groups: the miners were a slightly younger group. Almost half of the chemical workers had experience of further education whereas only one of the miners had. Most of the men in both groups were owner occupiers with partners in either full-time or part-time employment.

Questions about how men in both groups used the information sources of their society revealed the unstartling fact that all regularly watch television news and current affairs programmes. The chemical workers were much more likely than the miners to be members of a public library or a book club and to claim they considered themselves regular readers. Their selection of newspapers did, however, differ. Most of the miners (nine from thirteen) read the *Daily Mirror*. Only five of the chemical workers did so with six of the rest taking right-wing newspapers such as the *Daily Mail*, the *Daily Express* and the *Sun*. There were two *Guardian* readers among the miners and two *Independent* readers among the chemical workers.

How did they assess the value of the information sources open to them? For issues connected with the industries they worked in, both groups found trade union sources and the opinions of colleagues extremely useful and both identified the press and television as being not so useful to them. For the miners, however, trades union sources of information are valued most highly. This might well be explained by the different union structures within which the men worked and in particular by the ways in which these unions communicated with members. The National Union of Mineworkers has a clear political stance and has over the past decade felt the need strongly to pursue trade union goals by political means.

For general political information and opinion, there were some interesting differences in the way both groups ranked a number of sources. Both were in agreement about the high value they attach to their own opinions and those of their friends. The miners then listed the press and academic experts as their most valued sources; the chemical workers attached more importance to the TV and to professional political commentators. In neither group were there men who looked beyond these conventional sources of information for their ideas. No one mentioned that they read contemporary political literature and in neither group was there any trace of *serious* engagement with modern political ideas and perspectives.

Questions about the level of interest of these men in politics, community life and in their personal plans for education, revealed some small but significant differences of attitude and life-style between the two groups. The miners' involvement in trades union activity and politics, including their interest in current affairs, stands out in the questionnaire as being stronger than that of the chemical workers. Indeed, half of the chemical workers (seven men) as opposed to only one miner, admitted to little or no interest or involvement in politics. Miners appear, but only marginally, to have a stronger interest in community affairs with very few men in either group acknowledging interest or involvement in any voluntary associations or religious groups. Both groups, however, underlined a very strong involvement with their families and home life. The picture to emerge (from the crude figures of a simple questionnaire) is of men who, irrespective of their industry, lead essentially private lives as they keep a keen weather eye open on politics and current affairs. Theirs is a secular, family-centred world in which their strongest involvement, not surprisingly, as political actors, is with their trade unions.

A slightly more probing question about how men in the two groups assessed the world around them revealed some stronger differences between them. The miners were more likely to look back over their lives with a sense that much in their position has worsened or should at least have been much better now than it is. The chemical workers were more likely to cast a backward glance and see what they regard as gradual improvement in their lives.

Not surprisingly, given what has happened to their industries, when they look to their personal futures, chemical workers are more likely than miners to strike an optimistic note. Asked to reflect on the futures of their children, their country, their communities and the world in general, differences emerged between the two groups. Miners were much more worried about each of these than the chemical workers, though both groups expressed great concern. For understandable reasons most miners were worried about the future of their communities. They had, after all, experienced the worst industrial conflict of this century during 1984/85 and had fought behind the slogan, SAVE OUR PITS! SAVE OUR COMMUNITIES!

Educationally, most of the men rate their general level of education to be average and perhaps slightly better than that of today's young people. Neither group reports regular attendance at night classes and more than half of each group have never registered for courses at a college. Both groups, again as one might have expected, report frequent attendance at work-related courses or conferences. But, the majority in both groups expressed no current plans to improve their work-related qualifications or to take up courses at night school or college. Asked, however, whether they would take up opportunities for further study if they became available, the miners reported a twelve to one majority that they would. Only seven of the chemical workers said so and three said they definitely would not.

The difference between the plans of the two groups and the opportunities they feel they would take up if, in fact, they were really open to them, is an interesting and important one. The miners appeared to show a much greater willingness to study than the chemical workers. The questionnaire cannot reveal why this might be the case. The group discussions which followed did, however, help identify some of the reasons why the differences emerged. The essential one, to anticipate the argument, is that, given their experience of change in the recent past, the men in each group took different views of their own futures and the skills they had to survive it. The chemical workers would look with muted confidence to the long-term prospect of employment. This was not true for the miners; their job prospects are much more dependent on the politics of energy supply than their ability to acquire new skills. It was not surprising, therefore, that the perceptions of the miners were held in a much more explicit political frame than those of the chemical workers.

These comments apply to the situation of the men in 1991/92. Over a decade ago, as one of the tutors on the chemical plant courses explained, the results of this little exercise would certainly have been very different. Trade union studies at the chemical plant a decade ago were well attended and many of the men who came used such courses to escape the chemical industry and to enter further and higher education. Then the chemical industry was poised to enter its decade of shedding labour. The signal for those who could do so was to get out of it as quickly as possible.

Shared perceptions through group reports

Small group discussion provided an opportunity to reflect much more deeply on how people's aspirations are framed in time and in the social relations of their households and their community. Each group had its own task to complete and the results of their discussions can be reported under the main headings of the topics they considered.

Constructions of the past

Both groups of men have lived through a decade in which the numbers employed in their industries have declined dramatically. The collapse has been rapid and bitter in the Northumberland and Durham coalfield and experienced by miners as a serious threat to a whole way of life. This view of their past strongly coloured their views and their sense of their own future.

The groups asked to consider their views of how this society had changed since World War II both struck a gloomy note and emphasised a strong sense that much had declined or deteriorated. The question they discussed was designed to probe something of their collective memory and the narrative forms within which they interpreted the past.

The chemical workers noted that, in 1945, people had little, goods were rationed. Now, on the other hand, people took possessions for granted. In

1945, they explained, people worked in order to live. Now, they felt, as the rapporteur pointed out, 'people worked for luxuries'. Labour was once on an 'upswing' with a feeling of security; 'now there is decline and the prospects for manual workers were bleak'. When these points were opened up for wider discussion, two strong additional themes emerged: a belief that respect for authority had declined and that law and order was under threat. Their tone here was firm and foreboding, informed by the belief, typical of much popular thinking, that society and parents had become too lax in their discipline. One man, with his eyes fixed firmly on me, as if to press the point home, explained, with an air of knowing authority bolstered by the nods of agreement around the room, that 'when we were kids we did as we were told. We had to or else we'd be in trouble. Now they just don't care'.

The miners put their emphasis elsewhere: the early postwar period for them was marked out by the achievement of nationalisation of the mines and the setting up of the National Health Service. Now, they said 'it is all going backwards' – a clear reference to the prospect, with another Conservative government, of the privatisation of their industry. But it was more than that: present day miners are heirs to a great tradition. They perceive themselves as having been the vanguard of the Labour Movement. Their sentiments are drenched in a historical imagery which sets them above other groups of workers. They see themselves as having offered leadership to the whole working class in their demands for the nationalisation of the pits. The iconography of their struggle is woven into their banners and they are acutely aware that, throughout the British labour movement, the struggles of the miners have a potent symbolic force. The defeats experienced in the 1980s and the job losses threatened throughout the 1990s, are seen by these men as symbols of loss in a much larger struggle between the labour movement and the forces of capital and the state.

The Development Agencies of the North East of England have been spectacularly successful during the last decade in attracting inward investment from Japan. Nissan, Komatsu, Sanyo and Fujitsu are now household names in the region. With a humorous tone to it, one miner asked rhetorically, but with real seriousness and anger, 'Who won the war?' In the general discussion of the sub-group reports, other themes were brought out which amplified their sense of what was important in the past: the development of nuclear power, the employment of women and, on the international scene, the failure of communism and the growth of nationalism. One miner explained, with others in agreement, that 'the collapse of communism was a bad thing. Under communism they were all kept in tow. Now it's just chaos with nationalism and all that.'

The tone and feel of the group discussions was very different between the two courses: the chemical workers' perception of the past seemed a projection backward of their own material interests and anxieties about both job and personal security: the miners' construction of the past was much more clearly part of a political debate about public values and social changes and firmly held to a narrative line about the decline in the values of community, which have been so central to the lives of miners.

Looking back: the personal past

The question about personal regrets and hopes revealed a similar subtle difference in the way the two groups of men accounted for their experience of change. The chemical workers placed their stress on changes in standards of living; the miners talked about the quality of their lives.

Both groups regretted not having done better at school. The miners laughed in agreement at a description of themselves as 'We're just thickies now'. The chemical workers regretted their failure at school because it restricted their job chances. They felt they had been seduced, as one man put it, 'by the quick buck'. This sense of regretting their education was clearly deeply felt. One man gained general approval for the point that they wished they had 'listened more to their parents' advice about education and had taken 'jobs which would have given them more satisfaction'. The paradox is, of course, is that this is a feeling which does not necessarily translate directly into a determination to do anything about it. Miners, as the questionnaire revealed, were more interested in taking up educational opportunities if they were available.

Both groups said their greatest personal satisfactions centred on family life. The miners talked about being proud of their 'bairns' and were unanimous in the view that, with respect to their private lives, they 'wouldn't change a thing'. Lifestyles of miners in mining villages have a different pattern from those of urban workers who live on housing estates or, like some of the Teesside men, in rural commuter villages in Cleveland. This latter group were described by their urban colleagues as 'woolly backs', an obvious reference to sheep and rural isolation. A key difference between the two styles of life centres on the values attached to prevailing notions of community: for miners, the community remains an important ideal and frame of reference. Chemical workers do not use the term to describe how their lives inter-relate.

The chemical workers claimed satisfaction with their standard of living, with buying their own homes and cars and having holidays. They enjoyed their children, and, as they put it, 'their sport and their leisure'. They were proud, as one man explained, 'that they could give their children what they themselves hadn't had'. They noted, however, that it all depended on having wives prepared to go out to work. This was said in a way which suggested that their material gains had been bought at a very high cost and that their wives should not have to work if they did not want to.

My impression of the two groups on this point was that the chemical workers were much more focused on, and anxious about, their living standards than the miners, who seemed much more interested in the quality of their lives, which they did not measure in quite such strongly expressed material ways. One miner explained in a deeply felt way, which was acknowledged by the others to be genuine and to reflect their own feelings, that 'We didn't strike in 1984 for money. We went on strike for jobs, to save our pits and a future for our communities.' With great emphasis and in a way which had sombre support throughout the whole group, one man emphasised the point: 'It wasn't for money'. Such differences reflect the experience of people working in two very different industries. The chemical workers seemed much more concerned to defend a status quo, to keep what they had. The miners, on the other hand, felt strongly that, since their well-being was so precarious, a different future had to be defined.

The future of society

In their assessments of what the future of the country would be over the next 25 years, there were further subtle differences of emphasis between the two groups. The chemical workers feared growing disorder; the miners worried about greed.

The chemical workers predicted a united Europe with more nation states. The economic spiral, they felt, was still downward. Modern technology would reduce the demand for labour and there would be no recovery in the country's manufacturing base. High unemployment will be a permanent feature of the British economy. The quality of life would decline; inequalities would widen. They foresaw urban disorder of a kind already seen in the United States and an increase in racial tension. Their racism was expressed in the view that further immigration had to be stopped. 'Enough is enough,' they said, and some complained with virulence about Asians living in Middlesborough, who still speak their 'Paki language' and 'have rights and privileges denied ordinary folk'.

The miners shared something of this vision. They saw the UK as a 'lame duck,' a 'third rate society'. They felt, none the less, it would be a much more environmentally conscious society which had found a way to control and cut back the use of nuclear power. They predict a decline in educational standards, an increased brain drain. Incomes, they thought, would be much lower; they would be 'making buttons', they said, in twenty-five years time. They expected a 'greedy society' and, drawing obviously on their experiences since the 1984/85 strike, expected a 'split community' and a loss of feelings of solidarity with their fellow workers.

Hopes and anxieties: personal futures

It was in the way they articulated their personal hopes for the future that differences between the two groups emerged starkly. The chemical workers laid stress on the values of order and stability and improvement in their personal prospects. The miners focused more on public issues concerned with justice and equality.

The chemical workers hoped for a greater environmental consciousness, better education and health care and a 'better quality retirement'. One man received wide support for the noble sentiment that: 'There is only one world, therefore look after it'. They wanted to see a breakdown of class differences but were not confident it would happen. They looked to a future in which they could improve their current standards of living so that their present lifestyles would continue. A strong note was struck against 'do-gooders' who they hoped would realise their mistakes, if we all were to enjoy a safer environment free of crime and disorder. On the whole, however, they were not confident that any of these hopes would be realised.

The miners hoped for political stability, especially given the break-up of the Eastern Bloc, full employment, better education and greater democracy. They looked forward to a 'socialist government'. They wanted a more equal society which, through its government, did more to help the Third World. It was interesting that, although they had been asked to express personal hopes for the future, the miners did so without exception in collective terms. Their personal hopes emerged as being completely interdependent with those of a fairer society. When I pointed this out to them, they were quite clear about the reasons why: they came, they said, from communities where to help one another was the norm. Such values, they said, were part of their upbringing.

The rhetoric of their presentation – for such it is – has a powerful resonance in the North East of England. It is not used unauthentically; the views being expressed are deeply held and felt. How the men lead their daily lives is, however, another matter, something to be carefully explored in a different kind of study. It should not be forgotten that mining communities are still deeply wounded, struggling with the long-term effects of divisions among people in their attitudes to and actions during the 1984/85 strike.

Conclusion and implications

All adults are learning all the time as their lives and the world around them change. What should concern adult educators is how people come to make sense of these changes and consolidate what they understand. What resources do they turn to for help? And what kind of help do they receive? What kinds of explanatory narratives appeal to them? Are they in a position to analyse and joke about the stories that dominate their lives?

Both groups of men who took part in the exercise described here valued education. The chemical workers had a higher level of general education than the miners and probably felt more comfortable about their level of educational attainment. In replies to a question asking how they rated their understanding of a list of subjects (history, science and technology, literature and current affairs) miners were more likely to characterise their knowledge as 'not so good', particularly, but not surprisingly, in the area of science and technology. In neither group, however, was there any evidence of people attending classes (apart from those which they see as part of their work and union-related duties) to improve their education or correct what they took their weaknesses to be. Nor were there people with plans to do so. Critical reading was not part of their lives and most relied on the news media and the popular tabloid press for their information.

For both groups of men, initial education at school has been adequate for their employment, and work-related courses have provided them with the specialised skills they need. Their broad political education has been gained through their trade unions and their success to date in keeping their jobs and maintaining a lifestyle they are generally content with has not led them to feel ill-equipped to cope with their world. Both groups possess skills which take time to acquire, courage to use and live in settings in which they are valued and acknowledged. There is no reason, therefore, why education, as it is usually made available to adults, with its echoes of school and its paraphernalia of classes, teachers, books and reading, should hold any special attraction.

Nevertheless, the miners seemed more prepared than the chemical workers to step outside the prevailing assumptions of the society and the popular press. Theirs was a consciousness with a more radical edge, rooted, obviously, in their experience and collective memory of a century of industrial conflict and the systematic decline of their industry, for what they take to be political rather than economic reasons. A sense that there was little they could do about it and that there was no long-term future for the industry in the North East, might explain the stronger interest among the miners in taking up educational opportunities, if they were available.

We did not discuss what the terms of the availability of education would have to be for the men to take them up. The chemical workers would do so, I suspect, only if there were guarantees that their earnings would be improved. The miners would need reassurance their incomes would not decline, that the quality of their lives would improve and that new opportunities for employment and the development of their communities might follow. They would worry if education generated differences among them.

In the case of men from each of these industries, the provision of further education through well-designed public policies could be justified on strong economic grounds. Their future employment will depend on each improving their skills, their understanding, their adaptability and their levels of training. Adequate income support to make this happen would be a *sine qua non* for success. But that is only part of it; courses provided for such men would have to be based on a sound appreciation of how they currently learn, on how they routinely make sense of their experience and finally, how they balance the risks of new learning against the patterns of regret and satisfaction built in to how they live their lives.

What such provision might look like is something to be worked out carefully in close dialogue with the men themselves and an understanding of the constraints within which they lead their lives. Education could threaten the balance they have struck between their hopes and their current household strategies for earning a living and providing support for their families. Or it could simply be irrelevant. On the other hand, it could help these men improve substantially their job prospects, their earning power and the quality of their lives.

These men expect to be taken seriously. They are aware of the weaknesses of their initial education but value what they have come to understand through work, their unions and through their friends. Theirs is a sceptical, critical cast of mind. They expect their teachers to understand and respect them and to be able to enjoy and withstand the banter, the jokes and the fine-tuned common sense, which are the modes through which they make sense of one another and their world. It is a well-defended world they live in and they are careful in their assessment of the risks of changing their minds about it. Educators and the politicians who, through their officials in local authorities and colleges, might provide the learning opportunities for these men must understand the backgrounds against which the men themselves assess the worth of education. If they do, then there is much to be gained; if not, then everyone will be the poorer for it.

Postscript

This study was completed and published in 1992 (Williamson, 1992). Since that time all the miners in the group will have lost their jobs as Northumberland and Durham have virtually ceased to be mining counties. There are no deep mines left in County Durham. However, the heritage industry centred on mining does well. There are two fine museums in the region – Beamish Open Air Industrial Museum and the Woodhorn Colliery Museum in Ashington – which celebrate the mining past. The National Union of Mineworkers in the region is a spent force and the communities, in whose name so much was done in 1984/5, continue to struggle with high levels of unemployment, especially among the young, and all of the symptoms of decay and decline which scar the inner cities of modern society.

People from the ex-mining villages talk now nostalgically about a past which has gone and is irretrievable. The contrast they perceive between their present life styles and the collective mutuality of the past could not be more stark. Theirs is a world shot through with bitterness, anger, regret and they look to the future with foreboding. One writer, Mark Hudson (1995) spend a year in Horden, another Durham mining village, to find out what life was like there. The picture he paints is of a community in collapse without the inner resilience it once had to fight back, to organise or to imagine a better future. It is a landscape of unemployed men, women working part-time, of out of control youth, of incomers who cannot be trusted and of people whose facial expressions reveal what Hudson calls, a 'seeping fury'; their demeanour, he believes, carries the marks of 'internal bruising' and a 'festering compulsion to pass that bruising on' (1995, p. 257). Peterlee, the new town next to Horden, has a Save the Children Fund project. Local schools are regular targets for arsonists and vandals, as is the former colliery welfare ground in Horden. There is he believes a 'stoical cheerfulness', an 'unassuming generosity' to people, particularly some of the older ones, in Horden. It is, though, part of the past and stands now as something 'quaintly antique' (p. 302).

The future is a blank. Residual hopes that one day heavy industry will return to provide proper jobs are pure fantasy. East Durham is a development area whose authorities have had some success in attracting new inward investment from overseas, who promote small business, co-operative enterprise and training for the new information technologies. Former miners are trying to re-build their lives, re-interpret their past and come to terms with the challenge which faces them but which they, like everybody else, only dimly understand: how to rebuild lives and communities without regular and secure employment, how to keep the young at school and college and off drugs, how to rebuild civic institutions adequate to the task of improving the conditions of life in their communities, at their places of work and which offer them hope and pride. The task is not so different to the one their great-grandparents faced in the 1890s: it is to seek the ways to understand what is happening to them, to organise, to learn and to reduce the imbalance in those structures of power in society which had always worked against them and not for them.

The world they need to understand is not that of a burgeoining Victorian capitalism which needed their manual labour. The old categories of analysis which helped their leaders, well into the second half of the twentieth century, to explain that world and their place in it, will no longer do. A new account of history is required, a new 'reading' of the past. So, too, of the present; the people of Horden, Peterlee, Seaham, Dawdon – and of all other declining enclaves of industrial society which have been driven to the periphery of collective life and which bear heavily and unfairly the costs of social change – know what is happening to their communities. The challenge is for them to find the ways through the institutions which govern them, to make what they know known to others and to require change in the ways in which their lives are being ordered.

Part Two:

Contexts

5 Class, culture and adult education

Prudence is a rich ugly old maid courted by Incapacity.
William Blake, *Proverbs of Hell*

My mother used to say that she wasn't educated, that she wasn't clever, that she had only attended 'Basher's College' – the school of life and hard knocks. Like hundreds of thousands of other women of her generation – she was born in 1912 – she carried into old age the view that since she hadn't had much of an education, she wasn't very clever. In fact, she was one of the most adaptable, hard-working, skilful and essentially wise persons I have met. We could never persuade her that to be educated and to be wise were two very different things.

Her story is a unique one. What it reveals, however, are general issues about adult learning which are as relevant today as they were then, earlier in this century and during the interwar years, when my mother grew to maturity. Those issues cluster around the central theme of class inequality in British society and the destructive ways in which it erodes self confidence, holds people back, devalues their achievements and depresses the fuller development of society as a whole. They concern, too, the ways in which they can be challenged and their influence overcome. We can learn from it why some of the challenges to the divided society have failed; why some succeeded and through that what needs to be done in the future.

Learning opportunities for adults are structured in time. They are different for each generation, reflecting the kinds of demands people have been able to articulate and make of the educational resources of the society around them. In the field of secondary education, for instance, the issues of the twentieth century have concerned the access of working class children to selective schooling. That was until 1945. The problem then became one of how to retain such children in schools. That was the debate of the late 1950s. Throughout the 1960s and 1970s, the focus was on the academic performance of working class children. And in the 1980s, the focus switched to the content of the curriculum.

The discourses in terms of which the post-school education needs of adults have been discussed are different, but none the less constituted through the social and political conflicts of society. In the twentieth century, the focus of these discussions have been on education for democratic citizenship. That was in the era of the 1919 Report and the aftermath of World War I. For much of the interwar period and afterwards, the issues to dominate the discussion were the quality of life of working people and their capacity to take control of their lives. There was a radical political edge to much of this. Adult education was inseparable from the politics of the Labour Movement.

After World War II, the arguments shifted to debates about educational opportunity and to ways of compensating people in adulthood for what they had been denied as children. Community education – and within this, concern for issues like adult literacy and basic skills – became a prominent theme. Parallel to this there emerged within local authority adult education services, a somewhat depoliticised notion of adult education as constructive leisure activity.

Contemporary debates about adult education are structured around issues of access, employment opportunities, the educational needs of the socially dis-advantaged and the long-term reconstruction of the labour force to meet the needs of industry and commerce. At the centre of these discussions are the ways in which adult learning can be accredited within the currency of academic and vocational qualifications. The extensive critical debate around these themes has taken place, at least in the recent past, in a kind of political wilderness where those, usually on the left, who cling to a radical and sometimes socialist view of adult education, have struggled to recover some new vision of its possibilities – around themes like access, citizenship or cultural politics – while acknowledg-ing that its old concerns with the emancipation of the working class fade, like the class itself, into historical oblivion (see Westwood and Thomas, 1991; Taylor, 1996). Issues like injustice, social exclusion and poverty have not gone away; only the older frameworks for thinking about how they can be overcome have been shown to be inadequate. For the past two decades the answers to these questions – wrong ones, admittedly, have been provided by those on the Right of politics committed to free market dogmas and parsimony with the public purse.

These shifting sands of public debate are not moved around by natural forces. Their patterns change only when there is a shift in the distribution of power throughout society. The strident new vocationalism with its stress on education for work and its central belief that the only education that has any value is that which can be given a precise measure in terms of some scheme of accreditation, represents in public policy terms the dominant and desperate voice of employers in a failing economy. They distrust organised labour, high taxes, inflation and resent big government. Their ideas, however, in Britain and other European countries, find strong affinities in the experience of many ordi-nary working people.

The world they see around them, though, is an insecure one. Unemployment, crime, poor public services and slow economic growth seem to be all that is on offer. Increasingly, they turn to private solutions to the public issues they experience as intractable. Everything – including education and training – is judged in terms of personal utility and measured in cost–effect calculations. Learning comes to be valued in instrumental terms: does it lead to a job or to promotion, or does it not?

There are many parallels with the 1920s and 1930s and with the experience of my mother's generation. This same way of thinking held her back from what she could have really achieved. Tawney (1964) commented in 1931 on the effects of public expenditure cuts in education in scathing terms, emphasising that they were not just a matter of public finance. They reflected, too, a whole vision of how society should be ordered. 'Children are apt to think of themselves' he wrote, 'as their elders show that they think of them.' (1964, p. 142). Public schoolboys, he felt, were encouraged to see themselves as future rulers and were helped to acquire the values of 'arrogance, intellectual laziness and self-satisfaction'. The Elementary School pupil, on the other hand, was taught inferiority, though not directly. They were taught it through the facilities open to them – poor schools, large classes and premature employment. 'He is taught it,' wrote Tawney, 'by recurrent gusts of educational economy, with their ostentatious insistence that it is his happiness and his welfare which, when the ship of state is labouring, are the superfluity to be jettisoned' (1964, p. 143).

My mother's generation of working class children were denied educational opportunity in the interests of one version of political economy. Young people in contemporary Europe face very different circumstances. Their future, however, is uncertain. Those living in Britain face a system of local authority adult education which has been seriously depleted of resources. Between 1984/85 and 1993/94, adult education expenditure by local authorities in Britain has fallen from 10 per cent of total local government educational expenditure to 3.6 per cent. This represents a reduction of per capita expenditure from £22.90 to £11.70 and the trend continues downwards. (Data adapted from CIPFA Education and Finance and General Statistics.) During this same period, a century-old tradition of liberal adult education in higher education has quietly come to an end.

For those who have been denied a decent education, the collapse of a public service of adult education and the growth of a Byzantine structure of well-regulated modes of access and accreditation to all post-school learning is a mixed blessing. There is no doubt that more adults than ever before have better opportunities to gain access to education and training. The reality, however, is that for significant numbers of people, the new opportunities are fictional; for many more they are real but narrowly conceived and functional and as more people gain academic degrees, their value in the labour market declines. Meanwhile, the structures which routinely generate disadvantage and failure in modern societies remain unchallenged. Adult education as we knew it, at least in the period after World War II, was not in itself an instrument of radical social change. At its edges, however, it did provide a context in which radical ideas did flourish.

The boundaries of modern society have altered profoundly since my mother was a young adult. Today, the political struggles of British society are set in a larger European framework. Europe itself is a continent in flux. Its economic fortunes are set in a global market place. Its social and economic problems reflect those of the societies, some of them Third World societies, on its borders. And the values which shape its political life are increasingly those of a society in which older class divisions have disappeared. Workers have been incorporated into the structures of organised capital. The genie of high expectations for ever-increasing high levels of personal consumption has inspired everyone and lifestyles have become highly individualised and private.

It amounts to this: older models of class inequality and the politics which flowed from them, are no longer relevant to the circumstances of the modern world. The 'new times' demand new theories to explain them. The still relevant demand for improved opportunities for adults to secure an education which is lifelong and fitted to their needs, has to be articulated in fresh ways. To achieve that, we need new ideas, a new sense of possibility for people's lives, new theoretical perspectives, new kinds of dialogue and debate, new institutions and realignments of power. To achieve any of this we need an acute sense of history and a subtle, theoretical grasp of the ways in which personal attitudes, identities and motives both challenge and reflect the society in which they are nurtured.

Class, generation and place

My mother left school in 1926 at the age of 14 without a piece of paper to show what she had achieved. But she could read, write, play the piano, cook, sew and sing. She could clean, bake, look after both older and younger relatives and she knew the value of work. She insisted on truthfulness, trust, caring and respect for others and she had an easy way with people. She could talk fluently, discuss anything and showed an interest in everything. She was open to new ideas. She learned elementary bookkeeping to set up her own business and in middle age retrained as a hairdresser, attended night schools to do so, and had to learn some chemistry as part of her course.

Her world was none the less, throughout most of her life, a narrow, circumscribed one (see Williamson, 1982). Her father was a miner with the Throckley Coal Company, in Northumberland, who had started his working life at the age of 11. Theirs was not a home with books. She came from a large family – three brothers and two sisters – and lived in a small two-bedroomed house with very little privacy. Her village had an Elementary School and no tradition of secondary education. There was no library – except in the Working Men's Club – and young women were expected to follow their mothers into marriage and domestic work.

What she came to know about herself and her world was not something achieved through reading and study. It was built up through experience and what she learned from the people around her. For what she lacked in formal knowledge, she had ample compensations in her zest for life, the love of her family and her experience of real achievement in caring for others. Through this she gained real insight into and great sympathy for the difficulties people faced in their lives and established, early on, a firm moral foundation upon which to act and to help them.

Her childhood was perfectly happy and, by the standards of the day, normal. Her subsequent career as domestic help, shop assistant, wife, mother, shop assistant, hairdresser and grandmother was not in the least unusual. It is a story interwoven with personal tragedies, two World Wars and steadily rising standards of living. She looked back on it all with only a few regrets and died content that she had met the main obligations of her life as a daughter, wife and mother. Her story stands as one for her generation and her class. She was, of course, unique. It might even be said that she was bright. But she was not significantly different to other girls who lived in the street, or in the next village.

At the time she was born, infant mortality rates (at 135 deaths per 1,000 births) were as high in mining villages as they are now in many Third World countries. Although she lived to 74 years of age, her life expectancy at birth was closer to 45 years. In a very direct way, her life chances as a working class girl were set very low indeed. Women did not have the vote and secondary education was simply not on offer to the likes of her. Her ability to learn, and to continue learning and her potentiality to develop the talents she possessed, was never really tested or nurtured. Written off to remain in the roles open to her, she came to see her own self and destiny through the image which prevailed in society that others had of her and of people like her.

We can only speculate now about what she might have become, what she might have achieved and what her contribution to the society around her might have been. We have to judge, for her generation and for those that have followed, what determined the balance between opportunity and achievement. And we have to assess the balance of loss and gain, both for individuals and society, of the balance that was and is now being struck. It is a complex judgement to make for weighed in the balance are the complex and controversial questions of class, generation and personal, political identity.

The traditions from which the textures of my mother's life were woven, were set just as much by working people themselves as they were by the capitalists who employed them. The sensitivities of her life, its deepest meanings and the pattern of her values, were themselves fashioned in the context of her family, her village and of the ways in which, through both, she was connected with the broader movements of her class as a whole. The culture within which she built her life and her priorities, was a complex tapestry of actions, ideas, feelings, values, memories, hopes and regrets which themselves were anchored in the historical experience of her family, class and nation. Her connections with the cultural traditions of her world were not, however, direct or continuous. Her view of herself and the world around her cannot be read off or derived from general statements which describe the lives and attitudes of working class people of her generation.

Her uniqueness as a human individual has to be taken into account. So, too, does the uniqueness of Throckley as a village in the North East of England and the patterns of class and culture within the mining industry. Working class culture in general has to be explored with full attention to the myriad nuances of difference which distinguish working people in different industries, regions, generations and localities. Her family was not strongly political. Others in the village were. Her father had no real interest in books. Her cousin, though, had keen interests in music and conducted a male voice choir. Elsewhere in the coalfield, there were budding writers, politicians, trades unionists, painters, musicians, branch members of the WEA or the National Council of Labour Colleges. Even in Throckley there were members of the Club and Institute Union who borrowed from the club library. Jack London was a popular author in the 1920s and 1930s.

To understand her, we have to understand, too, the subtle patterns of difference within and among working class communities themselves. Her family was not bookish. But they knew and played and sang every popular song going. Their piano stool was stuffed with sheet music and in this way they shared in the wider currents of the popular culture of their time. And each day there was the relentless life lesson of the pit: its danger, its prices, its power. They learned much from that and the struggles associated with it, about the world they lived in and their place in it. The value she placed on her own educational achievements, were no higher, however, than those expected of her generation as a whole. In this way, her fate was sealed and her identity secured. What she valued most about her life – the warmth, the security of her family, the friendship, the hard, domestic work, her position as wife and mother – were the constraints which held her back. For it was only through her contributions in these areas that the society around her valued her at all.

The area of self-doubt and denigration, of blighted hopes, of failure and regret, which Sennet and Cobb (1972) once referred to as 'the hidden injuries of class', was in her case small. Paradoxically, it was all the more decisive as a determinant of her behaviour because of it. She accepted as normal the roles available to her and the limits they placed on her potential and on her hopes. Expecting little, she had little to regret. Her story, then, is not uniquely her own; it is a narrative drawn from a larger theme: the changing pattern of life chances and personal identities in a divided society.

How different it is for her granddaughters! They have been schooled to sixteen and beyond. They travel. They are confident young women who are determined not to let the limitations still imposed on women's lives, trap them into settling for second best. Not well-off, they nevertheless do not have to live their lives round the rim of the abyss of poverty or the Means Test. They are not complacent about this, however; the modern Welfare State, upon which each of them has, at one time or another depended, and from which each has benefited, is not as generous as it once was. Throughout the European Union there are thirty million people unemployed. European governments, pandering to the voting plans of the contented, terrified by world-wide competitive pressures, are trapped in the logic of holding down public expenditure, lowering taxes and protecting high levels of personal consumption.

This is what Galbraith has called 'the culture of contentment' (1991). It is a society in which the majority feel they have achieved their place in the sun and are unwilling to risk their personal success to benefit others. The majority embraces not only those who could be described historically as middle class; it includes, too, the fast-growing section of the working class who work in the new industries or who have climbed their way into supervisory and white collar employment. The 'new' working class is fundamentally different in its composition and attitudes to the 'old' working class, which fashioned throughout the twentieth century demands for a fair society and a Welfare State.

The 'old' working class sacrificed much for this society. In two World Wars they gave their lives for its ideals. Throughout the interwar years, they absorbed into their own poverty the failures of British capitalism to innovate and succeed on world markets. In the years following World War II, they suffered austerities to improve the public realm of the wider economy and the new Welfare State. They deferred their own hopes so that their children might have a better future. Through what they were denied, subsequent generations have gained. There is always a complex trade-off between the generations. The public accounting systems of the present cannot measure it. When we hear politicians tell us that goods like education have to be paid for, that the value of public expenditure has to be justified in current, cost–benefit terms, it is well to remember that bills have been paid in advance and the evidence is there in blighted lives, military graveyards throughout the world and in the immeasurable costs to society of the loss of talent from which we could have all been the glad beneficiaries.

It is one of the ironic tragedies of contemporary society, that the brazen new capitalism of the market place and the shrunken public sphere, is breeding socially corrosive inequalities which threaten the private affluence and security of the contented. Many older people now look back on the past quarter century with real regret and despair at the prospect of Britain ever again becoming a decent, caring society in which people find jobs and hope.

Class, culture and the politics of education

Talk of patterns within a culture can easily give rise to the false impression that attitudes and values, and the ways of thinking which are part of them, are social facts with a unique historical solidity. Far from it; in reality these complex patterns are the outcome of determined actions, of struggles, compromises and failures as different groups in a divided society seek to secure for themselves the wealth, income and opportunities to which they feel entitled. The meanings which are then conferred on experience, and the forms through which that experience is given expression, constitute their culture, and its patterns change through time.

The distribution of wealth and power and cultural capital in a society is a negotiated order, a precarious compromise which changes as the balance of power itself alters. The benefits some people enjoy in their lives in a divided society are bought invariably at the cost of others. The social identities people embrace, are themselves selections from a universe of possibilities limited by the roles and opportunities open to different groups of people within the society. 'All the world's a stage', said Shakespeare. But the roles available to people like my mother were limited indeed.

What some people are denied in their lives represents either a sacrifice or a subsidy from which others benefit. My mother's failure to gain an education suited to her potential, was not only a personal loss; it was a gain for other groups of people, whose educational life chances were increased because she was denied them. Through her failure, my mother, and people like her, paid for the apparent success of others. Her sacrifice of her opportunity to gain a decent education heightened the value of a good education to those few who secured one. Her failure, which was not in any way a reflection of personal deficiencies, strengthened the legitimacy of the claims of those who succeeded to possess abilities and qualities of mind which people like my mother were said not to have.

It is not only through inequalities in the distribution of wealth and power that a divided society blights people's lives. The denial of positive social identities and the failure to acknowledge that people have a potential for learning and achievement far beyond what they have realised, is one of the worst features of class inequality. In the face of educated opinion and educated voices, my mother could feel inferior. Much of what she did can be seen as an attempt to preserve her dignity against a thousand and one aspects of her life and status which threatened it.

Unfortunately, this aspect of class inequality is not something which the Labour Movement tackled directly. The Labour Movement in Britain, male-dominated and focused on the needs and interests of trades unionists, has always battled on the economic front in its campaigns against the structures of an unequal society. The fracture lines of that society which result from people not valuing themselves as they should, from devaluing what they are capable of and from their embrace of identities which confined their hopes to such a limited sense of possibility in their lives, is just as damaging to people as the brute facts of the economic exploitation of their labour power.

The solutions to this problem, however, are not coterminous with those that would redistribute wealth, income and power. Policies to combat economic inequalities are a necessary but not sufficient condition to achieve a society in which people have a soundly based self-respect and real opportunities to develop fully their abilities. For such a society to be built, people have to forge from their hopes a realistic vision of a different kind of future and have the confidence, knowledge and determination to secure it. These are qualities which only those who have had an opportunity to engage in serious new learn-ing can hope to acquire.

The village my mother grew up in was a mining village in the North East of England. Britain at that time – 1912 – was the 'heart' of a world Empire. That Empire was metabolised by coal. Coal powered its factories and ships; it warmed the homes of its urban workers and earned fortunes for those who owned the mines. The coal my grandfather cut was exported to the Baltic and to London. The ships that plied their trade to India and the Far East, to Australia, the Caribbean and the Americas, and the naval vessels which ruled the waves to protect them, were powered by coal. Yet my grandfather rarely travelled more than ten miles from his home and the life he and his family led in Throckley framed his whole world. It was in the context of the life of the village that he came to understand his world and his place in it. The divisions and identities of society in Throckley mirrored those of the society as a whole. The rich were incomprehensible to the poor and the walls built by working class people to insulate themselves, were as high as those built by the rich to keep them out.

My grandfather's class position at the time my mother was born is easily described. He sold his labour to a local capitalist. What he thought and felt about that was limited by the resources of understanding available to him locally. His sense of self, his hopes and fears and his sense of his family's des-tiny, were fashioned in a local context. He used to say to his children, 'See to your needs first, then your wants'. His own attempts to do so involved growing his own food, mending his boots, keeping his own chickens and being self reliant and fiercely autonomous in as many ways as he could. Without a wel-fare state to rely on, and determined he would never be demeaned by charity, he relied on himself and built his own networks for doing so in his family, his street and among his circle of 'marras' in the pit.

For each subsequent generation of miners in Northumberland, the local context of their lives became less significant. Those now who are redundant following the closure of the last pits in the county, know full well their fate was sealed by a determined, Conservative government, hell bent on opening up the British energy market to the full blast of world, competitive pressure. The cul-tural frames through which they make sense of their experience, are built up from ideas that are global in their reach, European in their political significance and national in their detail.

The history of their experience, the prevailing collective memory of their group (see Chapter 4 for further discussion), is radically different to that of my grandfather. Theirs is a world of regrets, his was of hope. He looked forward to the benefits of pit nationalisation. They look back to its failures. He lodged his aspirations in the prospects of Labour government. The ex-miners of the North East of England cannot credibly believe that a Labour government would significantly alter their plight. My grandfather saw himself as a miner and did not expect either himself or his sons to be anything else. Modern miners had different hopes and many of their children escaped the pits into white collar employment or higher education. They certainly did not limit the sense of possibility in their lives to the constraints of working in a pit or of living in a mining district.

It is the same for the different generations of women. My grandmother was content to be a miner's wife. My mother swore she would never have the insecurity of it. Young women in the coalfields today share in the wider aspirations of their generation. For this reason, the unemployment of their husbands is a cruel blow, for it denies them the prospect of possessing the goods they have come to associate with a decent life. Insecurity, regret and frustration are the prevailing moods in the mining areas of the North East. The point is this: the attitudes and values of people cannot be detached from the circumstances in which they have to live their lives. To understand the structures of feeling which prevail in any one generation, it is essential to grasp the interplay of local knowledge and the broader contexts which shape people's lives and identities.

The context for my mother's generation was one marked out by a number of critical trends in the British economy and in British society. From the last decades of the nineteenth century, the British economy had been subject to extreme competitive pressure from Germany and the USA. In the few years preceding her birth, British society had been wracked by industrial conflict and the early years of her childhood were dominated by World War I. In the vortex of these momentous changes, the Labour Movement flourished and there emerged in Britain a vision of a different kind of society. The years of my mother's childhood were those in which R H Tawney, Albert Mansbridge and others articulated a vision of education for working class people which promised to transform their social and economic circumstances as responsible members of a democracy (Fieldhouse, 1996). The socialist traditions of British politics were enlivened after World War I, though the circumstances were austere. The Labour Party grew in strength blunting the Marxist and syndicalist edges of British politics and the demand for a just society was an insistent though unrealised one.

The radical movement of ideas behind these developments did not, however, penetrate to my mother's family. They were touched by them, but only lightly, for the compelling pressures of their daily lives were too great. Their limited space for what Raymond Williams called 'affordable dissent' did not permit them to take active politics too seriously.

It has to be recognised, therefore, that for each generation, there is a gap between those who promote the most progressive and radical ideals of an era and the mass of the ordinary people who have limited access to them. The Labour Movement eclipsed the Liberal Party, but there is a sense in which it never wholly won over the working class. There is a difference between voting Labour and subscribing to a framework of thinking with a sharp radical edge to it. The Labour Party achieved electoral support but never really nurtured a radical outlook among its main supporters. This is not surprising. Raymond Williams (1977) once characterised the political culture of Britain in terms of three value systems: the dominant, the emergent and the residual. This was a way of describing the thrusts of change and resistance within society and to trace out the fracture lines of opposition, dissent, and re-assertions of the dominant order and its controls. For much of its history, the working class of Britain has been held within the assumptions of the dominant social order, whose power rested on the ownership of capital and its control of the central institutions of the state. At the end of the nineteenth century, the labour movement represented an emergent structure of feeling opposed to the old order and its inequities. From deep and tangled roots in much older traditions of radical protest, it gave expression to the idea of a new kind of society based on equality, democracy and justice.

The educational programme of the labour movement laid stress on schools for a common culture, equal opportunities for all and for a curriculum which would nurture democratic citizenship. In his brilliant essay, 'A National College of All Souls', written in 1917, R H Tawney demanded, as a memorial to those who had died for freedom, an educational system fit to reflect the values for which thousands of young men had been sacrificed.

The struggles to build that education system – from schools upwards to adult education services – took place over the next half century in Parliament, in town halls, university extension classes, Workers' Educational Association branches, in Ruskin College, the National Council for Labour Colleges, in Co-operative Society reading rooms, trades unions and working men's clubs. This was the Great Tradition of British adult education. It was never, however, a single, coherent tradition and it was never anchored in the life experience of all the different social groupings which composed the traditional working class. Its appeals were to the skilled, urban worker, though not to his wife, and its influence, though critical to the formation of labour elites, was not so significant for those whom they led. And, paradoxically, what it lead to in the period after World War II, was a state-funded system of education which provided working people with far greater opportunities than they had ever had, to join the ranks of their social superiors.

It was a success of sorts. It opened up ladders of opportunity to bright working class children which they might not otherwise have had, but through its own success, it helped consolidate a new dominant ethos in the idea of the meritocracy. But it did not, either in the ways in which it was organised or in terms of its consequences for those who passed through it, represent a challenge to the reconstituted order of inequality which was such a central part of British society after the war.

My mother was a fervent supporter of Grammar Schools, which had given her sons the success she had hoped for, and mistrusted the Comprehensive system which she served, for a while, as a dinner lady. The radical edge to the movement which had inspired the developments she approved of, but which she herself had not shaped except, perhaps, in a limited way through the ballot box, had become, by the 1960s somewhat blunted.

By the 1980s, some of the heirs to that radical tradition were looking elsewhere for new resources for their journey of hope. Raymond Williams (1983) is particularly significant. A lifelong supporter of the labour movement, an ardent educator and a man who, along with Richard Hoggart and Edward Thompson had done so much after the war in Britain to sustain a radical and critical consciousness, had to admit in 1983, that he no longer saw the organised labour movement as the vehicle to carry forward the ideals of socialism.

The attitudes, values and assumptions of the old working class were becoming, he felt, in some sense, 'residual' since they were fixed in a political problematic – the pursuit of individual self interest – which was set by capital. Capitalist thinking, he felt, had become dominant. The collapse of Communism had not happened by the time Williams had written this essay, but he hinted in it that the socialist project itself had been devalued by the failures of State Socialism in the East. All that was now on the agenda was a high consumption, market-led capitalism in which workers would struggle to defend their limited economic rights.

He sought for grounds for hope in the new, emergent movements of peace, ecology and the women's movement – none of which could be traced directly back to the institutions of organised labour, which were 'bonded' to the employment relations of capitalism and loyal to the institutions of particular nation states. The broad perspective of Williams' argument illuminates much of what has happened in the field of education throughout the century. The expansion of educational opportunities has been steady. But the cultural forms within which that expansion took place were not radical ones. The working class boys who got to Oxford and Cambridge Universities after World War II may not have experienced the anxieties and inadequacies of the scholarship boy so poignantly set out by Richard Hoggart (1956). But their education was not one which forged in them a new radical consciousness or a determination to build a new kind of society.

Within the Great Tradition of adult education, which experienced a state-supported re-birth after World War II, the central concerns were those of cultural improvement rather than radical social change. The extra-mural class and the night school were institutions to nurture the interests and sensibilities of individuals and not the solvents of an outmoded social order. This was, of course, simultaneously, a strength and a weakness. The strength lay in the assertion of liberal values and in forms of teaching which did respond creatively to the needs of many working class people. The weakness lay in its failure to challenge fundamentally the orthodoxy of the prevailing educational order which was, already by the early 1950s, functioning well to filter people into their allotted places in the labour market.

Sid Chaplin, one of the North East's most important, postwar literary voices, noted in his essay, 'A Tree with Rosie Apples' that he had been, through its extra-mural classes, a long-time student of the University of Durham, but that he had nothing to show for it. This wasn't a complaint. He had read literature, philosophy and political economy and benefited from it. He felt sorry for the full-time undergraduates who lacked the freedom he had had to explore his ideas to the full and went on to suggest that universities did not have need of extra-mural departments. It was the other way round. Each extra-mural department should take over the host university to ensure a proper education for the undergraduates.

Sid Chaplin would now have something to show for his studies. He would take exams, acquire certificates and, in Britain in the 1990s, probably be encouraged to take courses which would improve his chances of employment. The Great Tradition is about to come to an end, sacrificed to the interests of the economy, to the present-day needs of employers and the Treasury-induced pressure, which itself stems back from the fiscal crisis of later capitalism, to cut back on public expenditure. None of this was inevitable and it is still not set in stone. It is, however, inseparable from what has happened to the social structure of British society over the past 50 years. The dominant interests in British society, recast into a European and, through the multinational corporation, a global mechanism of economic exploitation, are based in finance capital. The residual interests of an older working class have been accommodated, at least for those in employment, by higher living standards than any other previous generation has experienced.

The education system of modern Britain has been reconstituted to be a better servant to the needs of employment. The European Commission articulates a vision of education in which students are meant to acquire, in addition to their degrees, occupationally relevant competencies in information technology, business and communication skills, to fend off Pacific Rim competition. Continuing education in these circumstances is less about recreating individuals than improving their economic performance. The emergent groups in the modern economy – the managers, technocrats, IT specialists and those who claim professional identities – the groups Robert Boguslaw (1965) once called 'the new Utopians', are winning the argument over the aims and methods of education suited to the needs of modern societies. Their commitment is to the view that all social and economic problems can be solved through the techniques of management planning. Whereas the 'old Utopians' – Plato, Sir Thomas More – believed a better world could be built only on the basis of better people, the 'new Utopians' rest their hope on better systems for managing them.

There is no humane centre to their vision, however. Theirs is a systems view of the world and they work hard to strengthen that rationality which, in its unintended outcomes, is corroding the whole social fabric of modern society. Growing inequalities, the emergence through its new social exclusions, of an urban underclass and a reduction in the quality of publicly provided services, are the consequences of the policies being followed. As always, a balance is being struck among the interests of different social groups and between the different generations. The balance is a complex, negotiated order in which interest are secured, identities settled and hopes are framed. There are winners and losers. Those driven to the periphery of this economic order – the poor, the unskilled, migrants – constitute in the minds of the contented a kind of civic threat to be contained.

Where, in these conditions, is the vision of a different future being defined? The dominant mode of thinking is clear: it is the ideology of technocratic, market-capitalism with strong support in the modern state systems of European and other advanced societies. There is a no nonsense, right-wing radical edge to it all as well as an underlying fatalism that the world is as it is and cannot be otherwise. The emergent structures of feeling have both radical and deeply reactionary potentialities. Raymond Williams rested his hopes on the peace movement, on the women's movement and on the green movement. That was in the early 1980s. The Cold War has ended eroding active support for the campaign against nuclear weapons. Electorally, the Greens have not been a threat, though there is a much stronger environmental awareness now among people in the developed industrial societies. The women's movement continues, though whether the term movement is an apt descriptor can be debated. At the edges of the prevailing political culture of contemporary Europe, there is a deeply worrying, xenophobic, neo-fascist potentiality, fuelled by fears of immigration. Theirs is the world of racist attacks and within it they deny the historical reality of the Holocaust and see in immigration the corrosion of their national heritage and pride.

What potential is there within the still remaining central traditions of political culture, with their roots in a longer past and their hopes reflecting the aspirations of the mass of ordinary people in modern society, to define a different future? The answer to this question has to be always an open one. When Sid Chaplin reflected on his deepest convictions, in his essay, 'A Credo', written in 1964, he sensed that the old working class, the one he came from, the one my mother came from, was fading away. He noted that 'the future lies in the cities, great masses of roads and houses and factories, great masses of newly affluent people' (Chaplin, 1987, p. 179). The millions in 'Coronation Streets' and multi-storey flats constituted for him 'a great unexplored continent' so far as fiction was concerned. At the time that essay was written, this comment was true, too, in sociological terms.

We know more now. The sociological portraits of the new working class highlight the social mobility that many have experienced, the continuing poverty of some, the sense of desperation among inner-urban communities and the relief some feel of having escaped it all into private housing.

The political reflexes of the older working class were sharpened in the pit, the factory, the trades union lodge and the internecine struggles of the Labour Movement, each having a strong local context. Those of the new working class have their source in the factory, the office, the private housing estate and in the media brawling of the main political parties, playing sound bites to mass electorates on a European political stage.

In the realm of ideas, radical discussion now takes place in the press and mass media, the universities, among members of the political class who control party political power and, not least, among writers and artists. Radical thinking has escaped the older political frames which held it. What is not clear is how it can be made more generally accessible and turned into a programmatic vision of a new social order.

However, it was just as uncertain in 1919 and in 1945, the two moments of profound change that altered the life chances of people in the old working class. The old working class secured its Welfare State after 1945. The new working class has experienced its dismantling. Within the political traditions of the old working class, Britain gained an framework of adult education – in university extra-mural departments, the WEA and in local authorities – which nurtured a distinctive civic culture and held out the hopes of a common culture. It is a framework being dismantled. Its demise is not inevitable but it is explicable in terms of the shifting structures of feeling and power within British society.

The framework to replace it is not a pre-ordained one. There is no compelling necessity for it. The vision of society it reflects is not the only one on offer for modern Britain or for modern Europe. Adult educators have always understood that their educational aims were inseparable from their broader social vision. The urgent task is to debate what the current vision is and to find the ways to broaden out the discussion of it. It is not just a matter of policy. It never was. It concerns, too, the way society is constituted, the identities that are offered to people and, through them, the hopes they carry through their lives. These are questions, simultaneously, of class, of culture and of education. How they are understood will determine how people are approached, how their learning is facilitated, how they are valued as people and what goals they will achieve. These are matters of curriculum, of values and of how adult educators relate to the people they hope to help.

For each generation there is a calculation to be done: Who joins in? Who is excluded? Whose experience is valued? Who is ignored? Whose view of the world is valued? Which interests predominate in the provision of opportunities for education? Who says what is to count as education and how it should be paid for? How do people assemble meaning and significance in their lives? What are the resources open to them to articulate experience into thought? From what materials can people forge an identity for themselves?

The choice is between allowing these questions to be decided in the course of the ordinary political struggles of the society and, therefore, without any coherent plan to them, or to anchor them in a broad, rational and creative debate about the possibilities in people's lives and the futures open to us in modern industrial societies. Either way, adult educators cannot avoid the need to analyse critically what they do against a hard-won understanding of how this society works and how it changes.

My mother used to say that she 'was born in a bottle and never got further than the cork'. Her sons escaped the bottle; so, too, did her granddaughters. For each subsequent generation the realm of freedom expanded over the realm of necessity. None of this was inevitable and it is not hard to imagine that the cork might one day be put back in the bottle. Had she chosen to do so, my mother could have gone along to adult education classes to discuss these matters. She did not. But it is not now a choice open to her grandchildren. Their options are simultaneously wider yet more restricted and certainly just as vulnerable.

6 Education and community regeneration

The bird a nest, the spider a web, man friendship.

William Blake, *Proverbs of Hell*

Criticised for its imprecision, its backward-looking nostalgia, its lack of a radical political edge and for the paradoxical way that, while pursuing the opposite, it actually generates social exclusions, the idea of community is none the less still very much alive and doing stalwart work. The recent report to UNESCO (Delors *et al*, 1996), *Learning: The Treasure Within*, submitted by Jacques Delors, makes much of the idea of community as the context in which people can learn to live together. The idea that the community is a resource for learning has, in the idea of the learning city, become a potent source of new ideas for cultural policy, urban regeneration and social change (NIACE, 1996). Some writers – and politicians, notably President Clinton and Prime Minister Blair – have found in community a radical political concept to rebuild their societies, strengthen the sense of social obligation that people have for one another, and reclaim the moral high ground from the radical Right whose ruthless individualism had corroded the moral sensibilities of modern societies.

The radical versions of community are alive, too. In the theory and practice of community development and social movement politics, community is a guiding idea of change with a sharpened, radical edge. The politically animated community becomes both the means and the end of radical change, a tool to expose the inequalities and social exclusions of societies which claim to be much more open, democratic and inclusive than they actually are in practice. It becomes the foundation of an enriched model of democratic citizenship (Smith, 1994; Usher *et al*, 1997). In social science, the term community has both supported a vast range of research into how human beings actually live and has informed the thinking of politicians and planners about how they ought to. Today, those writers who are trying hard to define a new public morality in the wake of the moral anarchy of New Right policies in the 1980s – writers like Etzionni (1995) and others like Philip Selznick (1992) who are searching to ground moral precepts in a clearer understanding of how contemporary society actually functions – are turning afresh to the idea of community.

For Selznick (1992), a credible theory of community should be both descriptive and normative. It should describe what is and what it should be. In pursuit of this, he identifies seven dimensions of community life which interact with one another to define an ideal version of community. These are as follows: historicity, identity, mutuality, plurality, autonomy, participation and integration. Each provides a way to describe aspects of the structure and functioning of different communities and each represents an important value in that a 'fully realised community will have a rich and *balanced* mixture of all of these seven elements' (1992, p. 364). In the case of this writer, the good society is one in which people can be valued, their autonomy respected, their interdependence acknowledged and their differences tolerated. It is a society whose institutions nurture these values and in which rights and obligations complement one another and where there is a strong prevailing sense of the common good. From this angle, community is a fundamental element of the good society. The mutualities and interdependencies it nurtures, are the foundations of civil society itself.

The common good is, however, elusive. For all its power as concept of social inclusion, the idea of community can be very exclusive. The urban geography of any modern city includes both social areas and groups of people – in slums, ghettos, dump estates and wine alleys – of people who have been systematically excluded from mainstream society. The boundaries of belonging to any dominant social grouping can be tightly drawn to exclude the old, the weak and the chronically ill. Racial and ethnic minorities are as they are because they have been predefined as people who do not belong. The Jew, the Gypsy, the Immigrant are all imposed identities; each the product of a dominant group's attempt to define itself and secure its domination of those it seeks to exclude.

The warm mutuality of the ideal community often turns out in practice to be, for the excluded, an experience of harassment, violence – on racial and sexual grounds – and of isolation. As a resource to support and inspire people, communities can too often do the opposite. They can set severe limits on human aspiration and hope, throw up impenetrable barriers to higher levels of achievement and personal development. When the boundaries of *gemeinschaft* become too tightly drawn, as Richard Sennet (1978) pointed out, it can become destructive, unable to bear the weight of expectation that the closeness it promises will solve all the problems of the human need for love, recognition and support.

In an interdependent world, the concept of community has to be extended beyond its immediate localities to its global limits. The world we all live in now is one. There are structures within it – states, multinational institutions, companies – which operate in a global framework and which can and do easily override in their actions the needs and interests of people living in particular localities. Community life in many developed societies depends on the private motor car. The oil companies' search for oil, on the other hand, has too often been at the expense of the welfare of local communities elsewhere in the world who have suffered terrible environmental damage.

The rhetorical force of such terms as 'the European Community' which lends justification to economic and legal co-operation among the countries of

Europe, or notions like 'the international community' which has been so decisive in legitimating multilateral aid in disasters, war crime tribunals (as in
Bosnia), as well as military interventions into world trouble spots – Somalia,
Bosnia, the Gulf – is clear. They stretch the concept of community to include
world-wide contours of belonging and identity. UN troops can be 'our boys',
whoever we are. Such communities of belonging are, of course, as 'imagined' as
any other and not in any way benign. The imagined communities of the Islamic
Umma or the People's Democracies of the former Soviet Bloc or those of the
Free World, confer (as explained more fully in Chapter 10) social and political
identities which fuel political violence throughout the whole world.

Community is a concept therefore which cannot be avoided. It is no longer
clear what it describes. It means different things to different groups of people. It
is deployed rhetorically to justify a very wide range of different kinds of actions
in urban planning, public welfare, education, law enforcement, international
relations and the radical politics of social movements. At the centre of most
accounts of what it is to lead a human life – and to many now the source of all
morality – communities nevertheless can become pathological. They can provide the justification for the worst kinds of harassment, social exclusion and
violence of which humans are capable.

The aim of this chapter is to set out the view that the idea of community
has to be at the centre of all political debate and hope. Communities are the
means and ends of social change and there is no greater challenge in the modern world than to find the ways to enable the underlying mutualities and interdependence of all communities to be acknowledged, understood and acted upon
in ways which enable people to live together in a sustainable way in peace. But
no wishy-washy model of community will do and actions justified in terms of a
theory of community have not only to be very clearly conceived and focused
but also rooted in a sound understanding of all the forces that are at work on
and within them.

A theory of community

Sometimes the decisive forces at work in a community are intensely local, and
even, as Colls (1995) described it, in a piece reflecting on the nature of working
class communities in the North East of England, they are at the level of the face
to face encounters between people. At this level of interpretation, communities
define themselves through their loyalties, antipathies, memories, their dialects,
symbols and their rituals. It is a territory difficult for outsiders to enter and, as
Colls says, 'you have to be there, daily, to understand how it works' (1995, p.
14). A second level of interpretation is described by Colls as 'associational life'.
'At this level,' Colls writes, ' "community" was a broader encounter' (p. 14). It
was an encounter with a wider trades union and labour movement. It extended
(for middle class people) to embrace 'civic' institutions like literary and philosophical societies, libraries, parks, museums. In Coll's account the final level of

community is regional 'which interprets itself only in contradistinction to what is "national" ' (1995, p. 16).

The thrust of Coll's argument is that at each level, the capacity of communities to maintain their identities and define their own futures has been radically reduced by the cold winds of economic competition and market logic. In the North East there are industrial wastelands and collective endeavour has been badly corroded by economic and social insecurities. Despite this, at the level of the national state, community is alive, a concept to carry forward the public policies to establish the flexible labour markets, inward investment strategies and community enterprise initiatives which are meant to 'empower' local economic and communal regeneration at a time when local government has been emasculated and market logic determines the value of every public service.

This is a powerful analysis of recent history in Britain and a richly suggestive view of the meaning of community. It underlines why the community is not the appropriate level of analysis or action for the solution of problems that are national or international and which arise from the workings of a whole economic and social system whose contours are global and whose operating logic is impersonal and bureaucratic. The areas of industrial decline in the North East of England or in South Wales have their counterparts in Northern Europe – in the Ruhr, Belgium and northern France. The collapse of the Soviet Bloc has left whole swathes of Central and Eastern Europe – in Silesia, Slovakia, Romania and Bulgaria – bereft of the smoke-stack industries that once constituted the backbones of their economies. Each case is different; each region and the communities they sustain, is unique. In each one there is a distinctive cultural profile of regret, of hope and feelings of powerlessness which nurture new identities and fears. What they have in common, is an inability to respond with new industry and new ideas to the changing circumstances of the global economy. And beyond Europe, in the Middle East, the Far East, in Africa, Latin America and the Caribbean, those same global forces are at work altering the balance of success, failure and interdependence among the national economies of the world.

To achieve the understanding of communities we need, therefore, we need to think historically. We need to see where communities have come from and how they define themselves historically. We need to see them in relation to one another and trace out their interdependence across regional, national and international boundaries. And we need to check how people in particular localities comprehend that interdependence and how they perceive the world beyond the confines of their own immediate lifeworld. We need to know how the boundaries of belonging are drawn, who they include, who they exclude. Only in this way will we gauge how far sympathies are stretched, how far people are prepared to help one another or act in concert.

It has to be acknowledged that communities are not in some ways 'natural' but are constructed (Williamson, 1982) and 'imagined' (Anderson, 1983); that they are as much about social exclusion as inclusion; that to be part of a community is to be someone who has learned something about what it means to be part of that community, and knows how to enact its rituals and live in the patterns of its ordinary daily routines. People become members of a group by coming to share its values, acknowledge its symbols and construct pictures of their world, both its past and future, and of their own place in it, by drawing on the myths, images and prevailing ways of talking through which a group defines itself. Communities are the imagined elements of lifeworlds (see Chapters 1 and 4).

From this angle, communities cannot be seen as static and essentially pre-occupied with their own perpetuity. They are, in fact, vehicles and resources of change and in some moments of their history capable of bringing about pro-found changes in society and personal identities. Newly imagined communities continually make their appearance in history – the Working Class, the Workers Of The World, the New Nation States, the Muslim Brotherhood, the United Nations. Each in its own way forges new identities and fashions new hopes, redefining the past and building alliances for new futures. Community politics and community development spawns action groups, alliances, identities and movements that transcend the physical limits of particular places and bring people together in new relationships which define new kinds of societies.

How these shifting identities become stabilised into societies, power blocs and political groupings is for historians to explain. New communities emerge, old ones die out; some face the future with confidence and hope, others with despair; some are centrally connected with the networks (Castells, 1996) of power and authority that define the modern world; others are marginal, discon-nected and excluded from them. The fate of a community is not, however, predetermined; the changes which take place within them are not in some way natural. They are the consequence of political action among different groups each with different aims, ambitions and hopes and each possessing different capabilities to achieve their ends.

Community, learning and education

The idea of community sets educators a number of challenges: to understand the ways in which communities condition the ways in which the people who live in them think and make sense of their world. This is a necessary precondi-tion to the next challenge: to clarify the ways in which people in communities can learn more about their world, take greater control over it and develop themselves, with and through others, to greater levels of well-being, under-standing, freedom and sustainable growth.

Communities are contexts of learning. Communities teach, whether they believe this is what they do or not. Membership of a community presupposes some acceptance of how the community defines itself, of how its structures become part of the taken-for-granted world of everyday life. The structures of a community – those defined by its location, whether the country or the city, those which define the particular meanings of gender, ethnicity and class, of generation and nationality – all have to be learned so as to be understood.

Through such learning people come to know their place; they acquire a sense of who they are and where their responsibilities lie. They learn to define the boundaries of their belonging, their sense of interdependence and mutuality, their quality of hope and their sense of their own purpose, agency and possibility in their lives.

The community is a series of overlapping cognitive frames from within which people interpret their experience. Those frames can and do change. How they change depends on whether the initiatives for it arise from within or from without. The liberal tradition of adult education valued community as the vehicle of a common culture; its radical offshoots in left-wing politics, the women's movement and the groups set up to combat racism, have seen it as the driving force of social and political change. Much that is said now about communities from the perspective of adult education is concerned with such narrow agendas of seeing them as vehicles to promote the access of the socially disadvantaged to education or to the kinds of training which will lead to employment or seek to solve some of the recurring social problems of modern society.

The currently fashionable idea of the learning city, for example, promoted actively by the OECD (1992) and through the European Lifelong Learning Initiative (ELLI) has a community agenda at the heart of it. The city is seen as a context to co-ordinate adult learning, improve the access of people to learning to improve their access to training and employment, strengthen partnerships to match skills with labour market requirements, engage in 'high culture' those communities who have traditionally avoided it, and promote citizen participation in community affairs (NIACE, 1996).

The radical agenda in the field of community development has a much wider remit than this: it is to empower communities to seize their own fate and to mobilise the poor and disadvantaged to challenge the inequalities that blight their lives. The pursuit of this strategy is, however, beset with the dilemmas of compromise. Publicly funded anti-poverty projects under European Union regeneration schemes, invariably require community involvement in the management of local initiatives. The paradox is that the institutions behind the initiatives reflect the needs and interests of a social order whose routine functioning produces the industrial wastelands, the insecurity and collective decay which have blighted the communities of many working people. Community participation in urban regeneration does not in these circumstances threaten the kind of society which produced the decay in the first place.

At the same time, however, it has to be acknowledged that modern societies have nurtured, through private and public initiative, a dense network of cultural resources of a kind barely imaginable only half a century ago. Culture itself has become an industry of urban regeneration and, frequently, as many examples from Continental Europe show, a vehicle of political mobilisation and change to replace those of labour movements which had simply run out of steam and imagination (Bianchini and Parkinson, 1993). Cultural policies have developed to promote the image of different cities to make them attractive to new investment. Cities like Paris, Frankfurt, Rome have projected themselves

through cultural policies as 'global cities'. Glasgow tried to lose its older industrial image by declaring itself a 'city of culture'; Liverpool has attempted to
create jobs through the arts and cultural industries and to create opportunities
for the young and the long-term unemployed. There is a danger of course that
such initiatives do not always benefit the people for who they were primarily
intended. Franco Bianchini and Michael Parkinson (1993, p. 168) have suggested that prestige projects of the sort Liverpool has promoted may not benefit
socially disadvantaged groups.

Nevertheless, the cultural geography of almost any reasonably sized town
in the developed societies of the world, is a mosaic of galleries and theatres,
concert halls and libraries. Access to radio and to TV is universal and there are
more events, exhibitions, shows and concerts than most people could visit in a
lifetime. *The Northern Review* – the monthly entertainment broadsheet of
Northern Arts – which lists only the cultural events it is informed of, listed in
February 1997, for the North of England alone, the range of cultural events in
Table 6.1.

Table 6.1 *Cultural events, Northern England, February 1997*

Type of event	Number available
Performing arts	82
Events – miscellaneous	76
Visual arts	48
Classical music	41
Jazz and Blues	32
Folk and Country	44
Rock and Pop	67

The performing arts category covers everything from Opera to one-act shows,
the Royal Shakespeare Company (who spend three months each year in
Newcastle) to local drama groups performing everything from Arthur Miller to
Roald Dahl. The events category includes painting workshops and creative writing courses. Enthusiasts of steam trains to Brahms symphonies are catered for.
Computers are linked to poetry and there are exhibitions covering photography
to quilt-making. The venues are church halls, museums (of which northern
England has 76, Yorkshire and Humberside Museum Council advertises 150),
concert halls, theatres and universities.

In County Durham alone, there were during July and August 1997, two
major theatre productions, 25 concerts (covering all musical tastes), seven exhibitions, five festivals and countless events from lectures to cake-making demonstrations. The County Council promotes its heritage to attract tourists and lists
five specialised gardens, six castles, nine museums, five industrial heritage sites,
two Roman sites, 21 churches, a world heritage cathedral, 16 countryside sites
and 60 miles of cycling track.

Such activities, nurtured by local government – and reflecting, therefore, some aspects of a community's concern to promote itself and develop its amenities for cultural tourism, education and leisure – has to be set alongside other provision, some by central government, others by the private sector, for education and training. Universities and colleges, voluntary associations, employers and broadcasting authorities all offer opportunities for people to acquire new skills. Behind each activity, particularly in the local arts field, we have to imagine an organising committee with its chair and secretary, monthly meetings, annual reports and related fund-raising activity.

The learning society is an emerging reality to provide a context within which to nurture learning regions, learning cities, learning communities, learning organisations. A public realm of rich cultural opportunity is emerging to complement those structures of 'civil society' – the parties, trades unions, voluntary bodies, charities, sport and leisure clubs, churches – which enable citizens to participate more fully than ever before in the decisions that affect their lives and which guarantee their essential freedoms against the Scylla of the market and the Charybdis of the state. Through participation in these activities people learn new things, sense new possibilities in their lives and stretch their understanding of themselves and their world.

As the boundaries of belonging break free from work-based communities, they extend to embrace wider constituencies of interest and obligation. Community is then set free from locality, identity and opportunity from place. In practice, for three main reasons, it is not as easy as this. First, the kinds of developments mentioned which have transformed the public sphere of modern societies, have not affected all groups of people in the same way. Access to culture and new learning is regulated tightly still by the structures of social inequality and exclusion in society. Second, the growth of dense networks of civil society has not promoted a new sense of civic responsibility, commitment and concern or renewed what many people remember as the bonds of community. The opposite (as discussed in Chapter 9) has happened. People participate in a wider range of events and institutions for reasons that are essentially private and personal.

In Britain, for example, average TV viewing is 25 hours per week and this is still the most popular home-based leisure activity (HMSO, 1997). Only 4 per cent of the population belong to a political party and there has been a steady decline in trades union membership over a period of 20 years. Reading is a popular activity. Evidence shows that 59 per cent of men in Britain and 71 per cent of women are regular readers of books. Nineteen per cent of men and 34 per cent of women are regular borrowers from public libraries. The top authors, however, are the popular fiction writers – Catherine Cookson, Danielle Steel, Dick Francis. Britain has a long tradition of newspaper reading. Twenty-six per cent of men read the tabloid, the *Sun* (compared to 19 per cent of women) and only 3 per cent of men (2 per cent of women) regularly read the *Guardian*, a broadsheet newspaper.

The use of the cultural resources of society reflects factors such as age and social class. While one third of all adults visit the theatre with some regularity, only 9 per cent of those over 60 years do so compared to nearly 50 per cent of people aged 25 to 34 (HMSO, 1997). When household expenditure on leisure goods and services is examined, the data reveal a clear social class gradient to spending.

Table 6.2 *Household expenditure by social class of head of household (1995) Average weekly expenditure in £s*

Social class	I	II	IIINM	IIIM	IV	V	Retired
Leisure goods	24.86	20.46	12.70	15.79	13.46	9.69	8.62
Leisure services	65.52	51.16	34.43	30.73	25.53	19.60	20.05

Note: Leisure goods includes books, newspapers, TVs. Leisure services includes cinema, theatre, holidays, etc.
Adapted from: Family Spending: A Report of the 1995–6 Family Expenditure Survey (HMSO, 1996).

The same national survey indicated that the income group comprising the lowest 20 per cent of the population, spent £7.25 and £11.71 on Leisure Goods and Services respectively, compared to £30.70 and £80.84 per week for members of the highest 20 per cent of income group. There is a clear gradient here of expenditure and opportunity linked directly to social class. People who are better off spend more on Leisure Goods than those who are not so well off. Poverty studies indicate clearly that people who are poor have little or no money for social activities so that isolation and exclusion are key features of their lives. People from poorer homes watch more TV and have few or no opportunities for travel beyond their own localities (Oppenheim and Harker, 1996).

Class inequality which in Britain, as in Europe, has increased over the past decade, is not the only structure of social exclusion which limits the access people have to culture and learning. Closer inspection of the poverty data reveals that women are more likely to be poor than men and that racial discrimination in the markets for jobs and housing is a major determinant of poverty in Britain. The effects of such discrimination on unemployment, job security and income levels are not mitigated by the way in which the system of social security operates to lower the relative value of benefits to dependent households. The outcome is that for many people from ethnic minority backgrounds is social exclusion. For too many it is compounded by racial harassment and violence.

Since people interpret the world through the filters of their own experience, the prevailing perceptions of how it works, of what forces are shaping their experience, are built up from rather narrow perspectives and information. The boundaries of their private worlds are tightly drawn to limit the kinds of communication and dialogue they can have with people from other communities. The paradox is that as the means of communication have expanded, people have less and less to say to one another, know less about each other than they need to if there is to be any chance of reasonable collective solutions to the problems all communities face.

Community regeneration through dialogue and learning

The learning society requires a civil society to nurture it. The groups and communities that constitute civil society can either be supported in their work by the wider climate of public policy or turned off by the magnitude of their impossible tasks. The problems of social exclusions of some localities are so severe it is hardly surprising the response of people who live in them is one of hopelessness and resignation. The capacity of some communities to regenerate has been so depleted that there is very little hope for them. The knowledge of how to rebuild is missing. Neither the official gatekeepers who manage the resources of communities or local people themselves have the understanding or the means to think radically about the future. Compared to private companies and multinational corporations (see Chapter 2) the R&D capacity of many communities in both the developed and underdeveloped world, is negligible.

Although not necessarily. The world is an increasingly complex place and increasingly difficult to comprehend. The knowledge of how particular localities work and of how they might work differently does, however, exist – or, at least, can in principle be discovered. There is no mystery about how this can be done. People can be helped to articulate what they know, express their concerns and work together to achieve collective solutions to their problems. The learning society can be built to enable them to do this more effectively. But it must be built from below; the challenge is for people themselves, particularly those who are systematically excluded, to find ways to demand more of their legitimate share of collective resources. To do that, they must take careful stock of how their worlds are being shaped now – by whom, for what purpose, through what means – and of the ways in which their own prevailing understanding of it needs to alter and develop.

Communities are constructed and they construct themselves. The balance between the two is what describes the structure of community life – its textures, mutualities, opportunities and hopes, as well as the capacity to think fresh thoughts about the future and press legitimate claims on public resources. It is an unstable balance.

Some communities can, in some moments of their history, be victims of how others define them. They can, indeed, be constructed and controlled as to brook no dissent, no opposition, to think only the thoughts of their masters. The history of industrial paternalism in nineteenth-century Britain was a history of elementary education: employees were taught to know their place and to desire no other, to entertain no prospect of different arrangements to society.

The history of colonialism is one of domination of one group of people by another. Its most pernicious feature, as Third World intellectuals have forcibly pointed out, was the colonisation of the mind nurturing among those it controlled a feeling of worthlessness, dependency and, as Freire pointed out, silence. The colonised could not protest; they did not understand their own repression. Even the educated among them experienced what Remi Clignet (1971, p. 303) once called a 'double alienation'. They were alienated from their own culture and background by exposure to western education, but alienated from that because of their own ethnic origins and dependency. Franz Fanon (1973) evoked it all vividly in his image of the colonised as people with 'black skin and white masks', as people who had in some way internalised the white man's image of them as being inferior.

The history of the labour movement in Britain, Europe, the United States and, indeed, throughout the world, has its parallels in movements for colonial freedom or for national independence. Both were animated by a strong sense that the world could be a different place. Through struggle against oppression, they both deepened and extended their knowledge of how their societies worked and how they could change to realise a different set of values. Both movements drew deeply on the skills, understanding, commitment and sense of belonging to one another which existed among members of oppressed communities. Both helped ordinary people think about themselves and their world afresh.

As the twentieth century draws to a close, struggles for justice, decency, self-determination, continue in both the developed and the underdeveloped world. As Apffel-Marglin put it, 'Political decolonization has not meant the decolonization of minds' (Apffel-Marglin and Marglin, 1996, p. 12). The older forms of the struggle have been transformed and the exploitation of people by other people has broken free of its older forms of colonial domination or industrial paternalism. The exploitation is now global, impersonal and, at least in the developed societies where the affluence of the employed conceals the misery of the excluded, its consequences are muted and manageable. In the underdeveloped world the exploitation is open and savage. The world itself is being managed in terms of a particular rationality which is scientific, western and ruthless. The 'dominating knowledge' which drives it is western. Stephen Marglin (1990) has characterised it as a model of development which is environmentally destructive, which generates meaningless work and what he calls 'spiritual desolation' which closes down thinking about alternative pathways to sustainable development. Other ways of knowing, living, hoping, feeling and being are devalued and many indigenous cultures have simply been destroyed by it. For Marglin and his collaborators (Apffel-Marglin and Marglin, 1996) the task facing the world is to decolonise knowledge and through dialogue (discussed in detail in Chapter 11), generate new forms of knowing and acknowledge the understanding rooted in the cultures of non-western societies.

The struggle to decolonise minds exists in the developed societies and the challenge is great in some of the most socially disadvantaged communities to break free of the dominating knowledge which is currently applied to them. The two issues are connected: the global economy runs as it does because the dominant industrial societies work in the way they do. If both are to change, there has to be a shift in consciousness and awareness which can only come from below, from those whose lives are blighted by the routine operation of the modern economy succeeding in engaging in new kinds of dialogue those who seem to benefit from it. It is in no one's long-term interest that economic growth of a kind judged to be successful should presuppose failure for large numbers of people and global instability for millions more.

The central issue to be considered is the capacity of communities to make sense of their world, the problems in it and to be able to articulate solutions to address them. It is a problem that can be compared to the Research and Development (R&D) capacity of companies. The more successful companies in the knowledge economy are those that think ahead, research new products and markets, develop new ways of solving old problems and invest in brains. Communities which strengthen their capacity to think, to plan, to organise, to acquire the resources they need and if necessary, to protest are the ones most likely to combat exclusion and improve their opportunities.

It was no misty-eyed hope which informed the labour movement's historic commitment to extend education and learning to the people. They knew that 'Knowledge is Power' and that they had to acquire the means to gain it. The tragedy, of course, is that this impulse, this need to learn has, in the twentieth century, been incorporated into the dominant frameworks of public education where it has become for many an experience, not of the joy of learning and of feeling empowered by ideas, but of failure and of a determination never to return to study again. The culture of many working class communities is ingrained with a hostility to education and everything it represents.

This is not surprising. Education has functioned well to select people well for the unequal roles they are to play in society. Many people's jobs demand little of their intelligence or creativity and certainly offer few opportunities for further personal development, education and training. The market-led leisure open to people too often requires of them only passive involvement as consumers of experiences designed by others. The daily business of paying bills, of working, maintaining homes and families leaves little space for creative dissent or new learning. The realm of necessity is pitiless with those who do not keep up, who lose jobs, who cannot pay bills. For generations of women, the realm of necessity has been the home and its compelling demands. It has been a long struggle for women to achieve the same citizenship rights as men and although they have broken through into employment and established their rights to gainful employment, the cards are still stacked against them limiting their chances for promotion, training and job security. They have yet to break through and destroy those male-dominated perceptions which confine women to a separate sphere and identity. The irony is, of course, that as the new century dawns and the effective power of the old institutions of organised male labour decline, the people best placed and able to carry forward radical agendas for change in their communities are women and perhaps, too, other marginalised social groups – ethnic minorities, the young, the old.

It is no longer sufficient to assert the value of education as a means of improving the capacity of communities to transform themselves. Knowledge does lead to power but not directly, not without organisation, analysis, action and evaluation and certainly not before the barriers that prevent people realising their potential are understood and overcome. We know what some of these are and we know, too, they are a complex interaction of social, psychological and political factors, each with its own history and unique local expression. They can be represented as in Figure 6.1

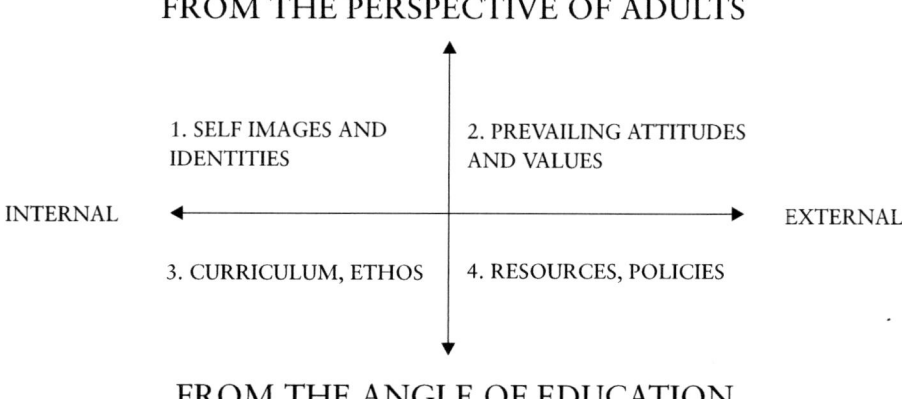

FROM THE PERSPECTIVE OF ADULTS

1. SELF IMAGES AND IDENTITIES	2. PREVAILING ATTITUDES AND VALUES

INTERNAL ⟷ EXTERNAL

3. CURRICULUM, ETHOS	4. RESOURCES, POLICIES

FROM THE ANGLE OF EDUCATION

Figure 6.1 *Constraints on Learning*

What prevents many adults returning to formal learning is the image they possess of themselves and their sense of who they are. It is the value they place on themselves and on their ability to learn and take initiatives for themselves. There is a dominant discourse about learning which justifies it in terms only of helping people to get jobs. Social researchers have shown, however, that those adults who do return to learning often do so to heal some doubt about the self; they are people who, in adulthood, take the opportunity to realise something in their lives that earlier circumstances had prevented them from doing (West, 1996).

How people see themselves is inseparable from the prevailing patterns of thinking in the groups to which they belong. For this reason, for example, many working class men will not countenance a return to learning on the grounds that it is not for them, that education is only for the young, that they are too old to learn or that it is in some way effeminate to do so. There was once a strong tradition of self improvement among working men. Working Men's Clubs in the North East of England, as in South Wales, possessed libraries. In the 1920s, Jack London was a popular author among such men. The Workers Educational Association, Ruskin College, The National Council of Labour Colleges, the Trades Unions, all promoted and reflected a deeply felt need for education for collective improvement.

The society which nurtured these developments, like much of the educational provision it spawned, has passed away. Secondary education has for half a century been available to all. Working class education in the twentieth century achieved much to combat the experiences and the lack of opportunities which denied working people their right to learn and to improve the quality of their lives. Yet it never went far enough; too many remained outside it (see Chapter 5) so it was never really able to challenge fundamentally the cultural bastions which denied working people a decent education and which sealed in their indifference towards it. Those who remain resistant to new learning pay a heavy price in terms of lost job opportunities and their communities which include some of the most socially disadvantaged and troubled, lose the ability to challenge creatively the sources of their distress.

It is not just the social backgrounds of people which hold them back. Formal education itself (as explained in more detail in Chapter 7) has built into its ethos, its patterns of resources and its curricula, arrangements which unintentionally deny people the kinds of learning opportunities they need and could best respond to. Universities and colleges are changing rapidly, but they find it very hard to adjust what they do to provide flexible course designs tailored to the needs of part-time students and minority groups. For too many ordinary working class people, formal education still represents a bridge too far; it is still something beyond their sense of the real possibilities of their own lives. It is still not for the likes of them.

The new managerialism of further and higher education which, throughout the developed world, expects education to dance to the often dissonant tunes of labour markets and to do so as if they were businesses in their own right, compounds these problems of access making it more difficult for colleges to meet the needs of those who really cannot pay. The story is the same everywhere: those who are poor, socially excluded and vulnerable to the worst excesses of the market economy, who are most at risk of crime, ill-health, of being poorly housed, poorly educated, those who are vulnerable to the drug pusher and the loan shark, are the ones least likely to seek solutions to their problems through education and new learning.

The intractable problems of modern society are at its periphery, not in its centre. Affluence and economic growth has delivered to those in employment material benefits their grandparents could only have dreamed of. Secondary education is taken for granted as a universal right and in the developed industrial societies higher education has finally reached the masses. Yet the benefits of all this have not quite 'trickled down' in the ways expected and the economic forces acting on modern economies are so ruthless in their treatment of weakness and failure, that increasing numbers of people find themselves powerless, exposed and poor and too often victims of the criminal economy – in drugs, violence, theft – that has grown up in their communities and which offers their young such positive role models.

Much, though, is done in their name and on their behalf and herein lies an important historical shift. While the institutions of the labour movement, public bodies like local authorities and the great offices of State were the key players in the public realm of politics which worked – sometimes together, supportively and often in conflict with one another – to find solutions to collective problems inspired by some shared values and with agreed notions of how society should develop, the agencies which are now decisive are much more devolved, market-led and responsive to sectional needs and interests. The global economy is essentially anarchic and local communities, wherever they are, too disconnected from one another – are, indeed, often in competition with one another – to bring any collective order and focus to their common interests.

Public support for communities which is intended to enable communities to help themselves more effectively, can compound this problem. They do so in two ways: first, by short-circuiting the conduits of collective learning and by maintaining the fiction that the solutions to local problems are to be found locally, by encouraging the perception among some groups of people that their problems are unique to them. The use of the term 'community' in many locality-based initiatives to solve problems or achieve economic regeneration, is wholly misleading for it maintains the fiction that local problems have local origins and local solutions. Second, since many local initiatives are centrally inspired – by national governments and, increasingly by international agencies like the European Union – they fix in people's minds a false rationality which justifies the belief that there are solutions to be found if the right procedures, methods, consultations, initiatives and evaluations are carried out by well-qualified people who know how local systems actually function.

It is difficult to question such assumptions for they have come to form part of a taken-for-granted view of the world and of urban regeneration. The careers of economists, planners, consultants, community developers and local politicians depend on the widespread acceptance of these models of urban change and their encoded rationalities. There is a whole industry of regeneration and of community education and development at work to maintain the fiction that it is through the work of communities themselves that real change can be found to combat the exclusions of the modern economy.

Newspaper job advertisements are telling examples of all this. They reveal the shape of the public realm of our society. From the breakfast table, readers of newspapers like the *Guardian* can see, each week, in an instant, how different agencies and communities perceive the solutions to the problems they face. Behind each advert (there are 300 or so each week in the *Guardian* alone) for a public sector job there is a reading of a need and the hope, endorsed by committee, of a solution. Behind the adverts are real problems – of homelessness, poverty, fear of crime, drug and solvent abuse, racial harassment, chronic sickness and dependency among the old, the mentally ill, the handicapped; there is delinquency, crime, vandalism, environmental pollution and a bottomless pit of anxiety, stress and depression demanding counsellors and care workers galore to offer help and support.

The senior staff required to manage these projects are well-paid professionals who work in directorates for development, support agencies and strategy units. They are expected to be good motivators of staff, to be themselves possessed of drive, energy and strong negotiating skills. They must be able to plan, evaluate, be customer-led in their work orientation and able to generate funds from private and public sector sources. One advert asks for 'proven skills in operational, financial and performance management'; another demands 'a strong personal belief in open and empowered organisational culture'. These innovative, high-level achievers with excellent communication skills are the 'very model' of a modern manager whose identity, purpose and language has been fashioned in the past 20 years in the board rooms of Japanese-inspired manufacturing companies.

The people they manage – occupational therapists, mental health teams in multiethnic city centres, HIV workers, counsellors, drug awareness workers, welfare rights officers, tenant participation workers, environmental conservation workers, social workers, family therapy workers, equal opportunities managers, drug-befriending co-ordinators, dementia outreach staff, resettlement workers, safe routes to schools workers, inspectors of residential care, consumer advice workers, homeless support workers, local economic development officials and co-operative development workers – are the front-line troops of a society collapsing from within. Theirs is a world of poverty and bleak urban landscapes of hopelessness and despair insulated from the affluent mainstream by high boundaries of mutual incomprehension.

The workers are expected to have 'an ability to evaluate complex situations', 'excellent communication skills'. They need to be able to shape and plan, have 'energy, commitment and flexibility'. One sums it all up:

> Do you want to be at the sharp end of developing new services to
> vulnerable people in the city centre? Will you enjoy the challenge
> of helping some of the most vulnerable people in society – the
> rough sleepers, the heavy drinkers, the drug abusers and young
> people at risk in access to housing, employment, training and
> health and social provision? Are you willing to work in the
> evening and at weekends?

This was an advertisement by the City and Council of Cardiff for outreach workers. Poor communities throughout the country are subject to the same kind of attention. They provide work for health care workers, community educators, advice workers, youth and community workers, social workers and the police. It is as if these communities have been invaded and have become a mess of initiative, ideology and intrusion. The term community dances like a vision of hope in urban environments which are soullessly bleak and imploding and where other architects are at work setting the shape of things to come: organised criminals, drugs cartels, loan sharks and anyone else determined enough to prey on the weak and vulnerable. The key architects of the public realm, in housing departments, schools, employment offices, the voluntary sector, defend a thin line between minimal levels of decency and security and hope on the one hand and despair on the other.

Their difficulty is that the resources available to them are insufficient, too transient and uncertain. A dynamic then emerges – which no one intends – of initiative fatigue. Portfolio funding of community initiatives has resulted too often in short-term job contracts for community workers, high levels of turnover of staff and for members of the target groups affected, in cynicism and mistrust of public efforts to help them. The management of urban space and resources in Britain is fragmented across local authorities, Training and Enterprise Councils, Urban Development Corporations, Government Departments. The funding flows are from tax payers, European Programmes and often particular Task Forces set up to tackle single issue problems. As the streams of funding dry up, so, too, does the work they sustained. The process can be visualised as in Figure 6.2

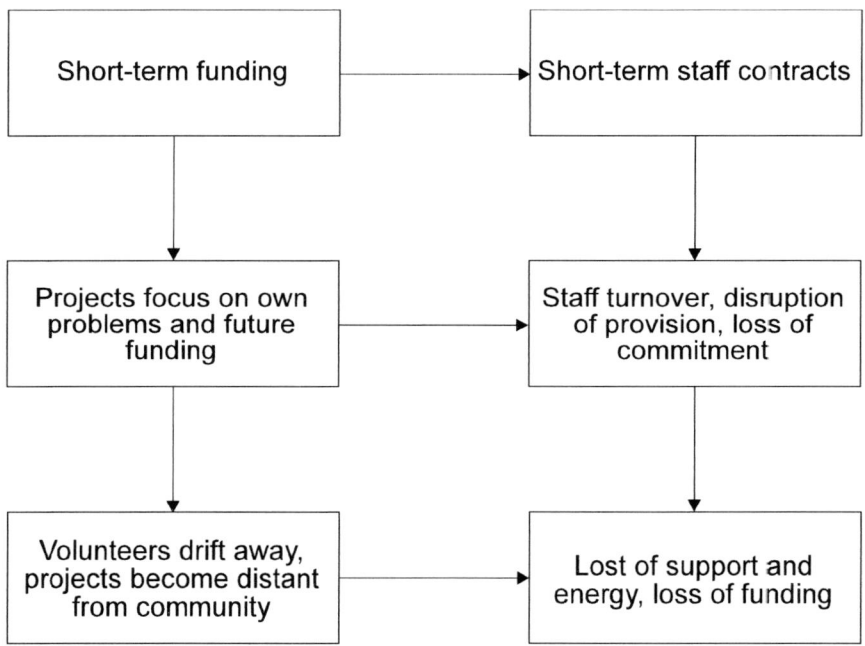

Figure 6.2 *The dynamics of initiative fatigue*

Community development practice provides endless examples of projects which have failed on grounds like these. For groups in the community well able to cater for themselves this is no problem. The vulnerable, the inadequate, those driven to the periphery through poverty and its associated threats of insecurity, do not have the confidence or the organisational capacity to cope with the uncertainty or to re-frame their understanding of it and challenge it at source. Unconnected with the political bodies that could help them do that, they remain effectively powerless, citizens without a voice.

The record of community development does, however, contain other messages, as does the experience of those engaged in 'pioneer work' in community education in socially disadvantaged communities. All such work, as Ward and Taylor (1986) noted, reflecting on their experience of it, requires time, careful preparation, high levels of participation in and control of projects by members of disadvantaged communities themselves. It requires, as Ward later noted (1997) careful negotiation, relevance and partnership. The education on offer has to respond to the expressed needs of people and must lead to the development of ongoing structures for the development of partnerships which will last. Ward writes about the role of a relatively permanent institution – a university – working with tenants groups and community groups to maintain community education initiatives. Even here, however, funding changes can undermine the capacity of the 'mainstream' institution – even when it has a commitment to work in this way which many universities do not have (see Chapter 7) – to maintain its contact with local communities.

At the level of community education practice, we know enough now to realise that good work – work which promotes personal development and public participation – and the very best work – which enables people in particular localities or communities to generate new knowledge and ideas – requires dialogue, joint interpretation of evidence and experience and is rooted in a value commitment to enable people to work together to build better circumstances in which to live their lives (Smith, 1994). It requires educators able to listen, to make contact with people and who are not trapped in didactic modes of helping others learn. They are people who can nurture a sceptical outlook in others and help them participate creatively in a group. They are people who act on the deep understanding that all knowledge is, as Smith has put it, 'situated and shared' (1994, p. 81). Given this, it is vital that people are enabled to reflect on what they know, that their views are respected and that the work of learning groups is in some way consolidated, passed on into practice and embedded in the institutions of the local society.

Such work, then, has to be informed by a strong sense of the dialogical nature of knowledge itself and a moral commitment to other people that is far removed from the premises which inform current public policy in many of the advanced industrial societies. Community initiatives in education, training and community development have to be justified in terms of their impact on the labour market, on improving job-related skills, higher levels of employment and through that, sustainable economic growth. These are not aims to scorn, but the means through which they are achieved – through the top-down initiative, the short-term programme, the narrow focus on limited competencies – are as likely to turn people off as turn them on and they certainly do not solve the underlying structures of inequality and exclusion which are at the root of the problems many communities face.

So many particulars, so many questions: towards a conclusion

There is a real danger that, in trying to explore the limitations to development work focused on communities, the real achievements of such work is devalued and the efforts of those engaged in it will not be recognised. It is certainly very easy to describe the changes ripping through the institutions and communities of modern societies as if they were inevitably and necessarily destructive and unstoppable. Yet this is clearly not the case. Bottom-up community regeneration is clearly possible if those involved are committed to it, know what they are doing, are well-organised and able to build on the public resources available to them to achieve new goals.

The regenerative capability of communities is, however, related to their own internal capacity to discover new knowledge and ideas, to create new visions for their own future and on their ability to strike up strategic alliances with others to achieve their ends. The circuits of communication to enable this to happen have in some respects never been more extensive but they are distorted in their patterns of use. Those without power in modern society are those unable to understand how their world is being shaped and who are therefore unable to articulate their grievances, needs and interests. Their communities are constructed by others over whom they have little control or influence. The belief that there are those who know what is best for them is both naive and crippling for it leaves people in a state of dependency.

We have learned enough now of dependency status in the underdeveloped world to know that its most pernicious feature is the way in which the ideas, knowledge, values, lifestyles and identities of dominated peoples are devalued. Their needs and interests are not reflected in the education they are given. Their culture and creativity is not acknowledged as being of value or is valued only because it is innocuously traditional. Those who are dominated are denied the resources to gain access to the culture of the dominant group. Their knowledge of medicine, environmental management, farming, animal husbandry and of the need for balance in economic development, of what it means to work and to be a human being in relationships with other human beings, is devalued and swamped by modes of knowing which are scientifically rational and bureaucratically technocratic. Possessed by experts, the dominant way of knowing brings with it the structures and the institutions of the dominant society setting the constraints within which people actually think and sense the possibilities open to themselves. Knowledge, in short, becomes colonised (Apffel-Marglin and Marglin, 1996). As a result, the dependency of people on the skills, knowledge, power and resources of the developed industrial societies is secured.

At the core of all successful anti-colonial struggles and of civil rights movements, for example of American Blacks, is a counter-cultural claim which asserts the authenticity and the value of the culture of the oppressed. This central claim has been expressed in all the struggles of the labour movement to assert the dignity of working people and the value of their cultural achievements. The dissident movements of Eastern Europe celebrated national cultures to fend off Soviet hegemony. The Czechs, Hungarians and Poles took *their* poets, *their* novelists, *their* musicians, *their* history and *their* language very seriously as a way of countering what they took to be the imposed Sovietisation of their minds. Ethnic minority groups throughout Europe assert the value of their own cultures and their traditions as a way of preserving identities in a world where mass culture and standardised modes of thinking threaten to wash over them, turning them all into the anonymous units of production and consumption in a global economy dominated by the experts who make the corporate and political engines of the global economy work.

The labour movement in the nineteenth century and in the first half of the twentieth was animated by a sense of the importance of class and of the struggle between different classes. The colonial liberation movements of the twentieth century, adopting the language of their oppressors, were driven by a sense of nation and the belief that nations should be free and independent. Development policies to counteract poverty and social exclusion are everywhere justified in terms of the needs and interests of communities. In each case the underlying mutualities and solidarities were different. The labour movements of Europe, of the world's major colonial powers, railed at class distinction but fell victim to nationalism and racisms which eroded their solidarity with, respect for and understanding of the colonial people's leaders their own societies exploited. The exclusions based on nationality, on race and ethnicity which have informed so much of the politics of the modern world, have been tragic in their consequences.

The exclusions which are based in doctrines of community threaten to be no less dangerous, for the solution to problems which are essentially global require mutualities and solidarities which go far beyond the cultural boundaries of nation states. Communities are socially constructed entities symbolically realised in the ways in which people think and feel about one another. If the boundaries are drawn too tightly around them – boundaries of region, locality, gender, ethnicity or class – then their capacity to work together at different levels – locally, regionally, nationally, internationally – is eroded. Unchallenged, the impersonal structures of power, control and inequality and the modes of thinking they nurture, will continue. They will erode in the name of the majority, though in global terms the few who are well-off, the collective security of all.

This is not an argument to deny the importance of communities or policies aimed to improve their lot. Rather it is an argument that neither class nor community constitute in the modern world an adequate basis on which to build programmes of social change. Both class and community are concepts which emerged in the early political struggles of modernity to deal with the problems of liberty and equality which a new kind of society spawned. The challenge for the new century is to move beyond both and work out the new politics and policies of an inclusive concept of citizenship robust enough to capture the complex inter-dependencies of global modernity and to nurture the mutualities upon which all effective action for change rests.

Communities play a role in this; an improved quality of the life of people in communities – of better living standards, of greater tolerance, of personal fulfilment and development, of wider opportunities for learning and access to culture – all have to be the ends of public policy. The means to achieve these goals are only partly in communities themselves – and in some, the most excluded of them, hardly at all. If the poor had the community development skills of the rich and the kind of access to information, ideas, culture and learning (much of it subsidised through public funds) the well-off simply take for granted their life chances would be significantly better. If the institutions of the public sphere – the schools, colleges, theatres, libraries, national parks, museums – worked better to meet the needs of the disadvantaged, things would be different. Such power is not, however, in their hands and therein lies a challenge.

The current climate of concern about social exclusion and about the need for far more effective strategies of lifelong learning is one full of promise. As learning opportunities escape the frameworks of formal education and extend outwards to the worlds of work and community, the prospect of a new and richer model of citizenship is within reach. Ideas like that of the learning city and of the more inclusive learning society, are there to be used and built upon. Both, however, must be informed by a strong moral imperative and neither can develop into successful practice without the involvement of people with local knowledge and experience. The challenge is to find the institutions through which new learning and new forms of dialogue and action can emerge to strengthen the foundations of a much more open, democratic society. Communities, like knowledge, can flourish only in the context of an open society where people have the skill and confidence to understand their world and to enter into debate with others beyond the boundaries of their own narrow belonging, and when they realise that their own welfare – as well as their fun and enjoyment – is dependent fundamentally on that of others, most of whom are and will remain, unknown to them but whose lives, nevertheless, enrich their own.

7 Institutions and power: the archaeology of educational organisations

> The road of excess leads to the palace of wisdom
> William Blake, *Proverbs of Hell*

Preamble

The motto of the University of Leiden in the Netherlands, founded by William of Orange in 1575, is *Praesidium Libertatis* – Bastion of Liberty. The Senate chamber of the university is an austere room with stained glass windows. One of these celebrates an act of defiance for which the university remains intensely proud. It commemorates the day when, during the German Occupation of Holland in World War II, Leiden professors resigned their posts to protest at the action of the Germans in dismissing a Jewish professor. Staff, students and alumni of the university, wherever they are throughout the world, celebrate each year the memory of this. In doing so, the university asserts that if institutions like it are to stand for anything in modern society, it is freedom.

The liberty they should protect is for people to study, to think, to question received wisdom and to be able to express themselves fully and confidently. The freedom of those who work and study in universities is, however, fundamentally dependent on the freedom of others and on the society in which they function being founded on firm, democratic principles. Without the open society, universities cannot develop new knowledge, for the danger would then be great that their work would be distorted to meet the needs and interests only of those with power in society.

Introduction

Notwithstanding their vast resources of information, ideas and specialist skills and their technological capacity, at least in principle, to make all these accessible to anyone who needs access to them, higher education institutions in modern societies remain exclusive. They ration educational opportunities, define curricula and control the ways in which learning is evaluated and accredited. Some institutions are geared to open up opportunities for learning; others, in defence of what they take to be academic standards, seek to restrict them. In some societies, student numbers are tightly regulated by the state as part of a plan to link higher learning to labour market needs. This was the case, for example, in the former Soviet Bloc countries of Eastern Europe and remains true in some developing countries. Elsewhere, for example the USA or most of the countries of contemporary Europe, the supply of higher education opportunities is regulated more by student demand. In many developing countries of the world, student demand for higher education is so great it is unmanageable and dissatisfied students are a source of political instability.

Some academic institutions, often in line with the laws which define their constitutional status, define their mission in almost exclusively scholarly terms to undertake research, scholarship and teach students. Others have a strong commitment to serve a wider range of needs and interests and seek to engage more directly with the localities and regions they serve. In doing so they seek to reflect in what they do some of the broader, though central, values of a cultured and democratic society. The thrust of this chapter is to suggest that these are not contradictory goals; neither the utilitarian rationale of service to the economy or the scholarly mission of higher education, can be defended without a strong and open-ended commitment to democratic values and to the principles of the open society. These guarantee freedom of expression, tolerance of different ways of thinking and believing and they celebrate objectivity and critical dialogue. In the open society, everyone is free to investigate their world and to test out the ideas of others, especially those with authority and power.

Throughout the advanced industrial societies, universities are under pressure to change – to become more accessible, to be more effectively managed, to have stronger links with industry and commerce, to cost less, to be innovative in how they teach and research. Those who have worked in higher education during the past two decades have had to live within a maelstrom of contradictory demands on their professional lives, expanded student numbers and, everywhere, lower real levels of funding. Some look back on this with regret because the golden years of academic autonomy – of what has become known as 'donnish dominion' – have passed; others are excited by the prospect of new futures and radical agendas for change in how knowledge will in the future be gained and passed on.

Throughout the world, each within the constraints of its own traditions, politics and resources, governments are pursuing policies to change higher education. A new kind of society is emerging which is global in its reach, market-driven, socially and culturally fragmented, individualistic in its moral commitments and powered by the technology of an information revolution (see Chapters 1 and 2). Higher education is everywhere being 'repositioned' in its relationship to it (Coffield and Williamson, 1997). The success of such policies – to make such institutions, at reduced costs to the state, more accessible and responsive to the needs of fast-changing markets for labour – is dependent not only on the political will of those pursuing them; they depend, too, on how far the inertia of educational institutions can be overcome so that they can respond to the new agendas for change. This chapter focuses on one aspect of the problem in higher education: the past, and on ways to move institutions beyond its grip to define a new future for themselves.

The need to do so is clear. If institutions of higher education are to contribute creatively to meet the changing needs of complex societies for knowledge, research and lifelong learning, and to continue to draw heavily on the public purse, they themselves need to be responsive to new circumstances, new kinds of students and new forms of study and research. They themselves must be able to engage in the critical debates about values and public policy which the democratic polity itself presupposes of its citizens. They must be a resource for new ideas and enable citizens to articulate different versions of what their collective futures might be.

Universities exist, however, in time. Their institutional forms – structures of government, forms of teaching and research – stretch back in time to periods which were not democratic in any way at all. They must build on the past and its achievements and consolidate the best of them, but they cannot be held in its thrall. To do so, however, those who manage them and work in them and students who seek to study in them, need a critical understanding of how they function and of how they can be changed. It is a question of knowing the past in order to build a new future.

Developments in new information technology which enable new kinds of distance learning, new modes of study and new forms for the development, control and dissemination of knowledge could be a real threat to higher education as it currently exists, for universities and colleges can no longer lay claim to having exclusive bodies of knowledge or skills in teaching. Commercial and government-led research has broken the universities' monopoly of research – except, perhaps, though not inevitably, in the field of basic research. The frameworks of the 'new production of knowledge', as Michael Gibbons (Gibbons *et al*, 1994) and colleagues have pointed out, are global, transdisciplinary, applied, flexible and just as likely to be in the private sector as in the public realm of higher education. Universities which do not adapt to these circumstances are likely to find themselves marginalised and unsupported.

All institutions of higher education are being repositioned; the challenge they face is to reposition themselves. The thrust of the argument in this chapter is that they can only do so if they pay more attention to the social, economic and political conditions of their own success and engage themselves actively in promoting the continuous democratic development of the open society. Alan Tuckett (1996, p. 51) captured it vividly when he said:

> It is an important dimension of the function of higher education
> in a learning society that the social institution which enshrines
> intellectual liberty should play a role in fostering active democratic
> citizenship, the right to dissent, and the securing of a plurality of
> views.

Only when these conditions are secure can the members of a society look confidently to a future in which new, creative solutions will be sought for old problems. The challenge in this is a universal one, but the different social and political conditions of higher education in different parts of the world provide their own unique twist to it. The universities of the developed societies are uniquely privileged; they still function in a political climate which is supportive of their claims to academic freedom and institutional autonomy. There are many regimes in which is not the case, underlining all too clearly that both institutional and academic freedom need political support from a wide democratic constituency. Universities cannot simply rely on it being there; they, too, must nurture it.

The past in the present

Archaeologists study the stratigraphy of their research sites to uncover the ways in which the history of previous occupations set the constraints on how subsequent generations of people were able to occupy a particular place or building. The uncovered layers reveal the continuities and discontinuities which have shaped the structures of the archaeological record. The excitement of it all lies in the clues excavators reveal of the decisions people, now long dead, have made about how they wished to live and what their priorities and preoccupations were.

Those who study how modern, complex organisations function, have much to learn from archaeological methods of research. For the compounded layers of assumptions and priorities which have been integral to the history of all organisations, leave their traces in the fabric of the modern institution. Those traces can be revealed. The facades of organisational life can be peeled back to reveal the ways in which previous generations have left their mark and continue to set a framework within which contemporary attitudes, values and priorities are shaped.

In the fabric of their architecture, the construction of their curricula and in the ways in which they draw their boundaries to define who shall belong to them and who shall not, educational organisations reflect the assumptions of the past. Just as dead stratigraphy can be interpreted to show up the patterns of dominance and the real conflicts and discontinuities of the societies whose traces remain in the soil, so it is with complex organisations. They encode in their structures the residues of the systems of authority and power of a society as well as the conflicts and the changes which have shaped them. In the case of universities, such residues can be seen, for example, in the institutions of their governance – university governing bodies, courts, academic boards – and in the ways in which they are managed. There is a struggle within higher education between collegiate and managerial modes of control in which claims to academic freedom and autonomy have to be balanced with those of management control and accountability for the ways in which resources are used.

This particular balance touches on the nature of the relationship between the universities with both the market and the state. It either preserves the independent status of universities or erodes it to the point where state control could become – as it did in the totalitarian states – absolute. Were market-led managerialism to take over, universities would respond only to a narrow range of needs and interests. Even in systems – such as that of the USA – where higher education institutions are private and independent of the state, there is still none the less a framework of law and opinion which underwrites and requires them to preserve values like academic freedom and to maintain standards of critical scholarship and professional teaching and to maintain their place in a public realm where they exercise their rights with responsibility. To do otherwise would be to risk the loss of public support upon which a healthy system of higher education ultimately depends.

To secure a strong position in society for higher education is not something that can be left to chance. Universities have been hi-jacked in the past. In the case of Germany, this was not too difficult to achieve. Jarausch (1982) has shown that illiberal sentiment, anti-Semitism and nationalism were well established in the German universities before the Nazis, who were able to take them over without resistance. The 'co-ordinated' (*gleichgeschalteten*) universities of the Third Reich or the state-run institutes of the Soviet Bloc, destroyed academic freedom – and with it, serious scholarship – in the interests of a dominant ideology. Universities in some of the Islamic states are compelled to teach in ways which affirm the truth of the Holy Koran. The 'Godless civilisation of the West' then becomes something to reject, even to abhor. The danger in this is that students are expected to put their religious faith before their reason, to be more ready to obey those in authority than to question them.

In the more liberal regimes of the West, mass higher education has just about preserved its freedoms but could hardly be said to have catered for the needs of diverse student constituencies. Higher education has been the preserve of the privileged groups in society – the young offspring of middle-class families pursuing their studies on a full-time basis. The research undertaken in universities has reflected the needs and interests of those who have paid for it and has been particularly beneficial to industry, commerce, the professions and the state itself. Dependent on the patronage of the powerful, universities have not been able to claim a real independence of the state and they still have not realised that this is their greatest weakness.

The development of ideas which challenge in fundamental ways the dominant discourses of public life, is not something for which universities are famous so their 'co-ordination' is something which could happen again. Universities need the protective support of a civil society which celebrates social and ethnic differences, which encourages dissent, tolerates different ways of thinking. With such support they could constantly seek out new solutions to old problems, both within themselves and in the societies they serve. Constant change which broadens out the basis of their social support is a requirement of their survival.

Each new generation has to negotiate its own position against the constraints of the old and finds in the stratigraphy of the organisations they work in, the attitudes, values and ways of thinking which once were part of a dominant discourse. These structures of thinking describe the underlying images of the organisation which its members carry in their minds as templates against which to evaluate change (Morgan, 1997). Some of these images promote change and flexibility and value innovation; others are backward-looking and value more the achievements of the past. It is the shifting balance between the two which determines how an organisation will change. That balance is very much affected by the quality of leadership within institutions and whether those in leadership roles are prepared to help others reframe their thinking, their goals and priorities.

Those who lead universities are unfortunately among the least likely to want to do this. They achieve their positions of leadership through being successful, often as leading academics themselves, within the prevailing models of the university. The generation of Vice Chancellors in Britain who managed the expansion of higher education during the 1960s, were men educated predominantly during the interwar years in Oxford and Cambridge and who had acquired deep respect for and understanding of the values associated with these institutions. More than half (54 out of 90) of Vice Chancellors as late as 1974 were educated at either Oxford or Cambridge (Wakeford and Wakeford, 1974).

The attitudes Vice Chancellors bring to their task and their views on the nature of leadership, have been researched by Middlehurst (1993). What she found was that their priorities and success criteria 'were seen in terms of academic achievements and institutional positioning, the development of internal morale, and the maintenance of financial viability' (1993, p. 93). While these are not aims to scorn, it can hardly be said that they encapsulate a strong desire to promote a wider, democratic agenda which seeks to engage the university with the central questions faced by the societies and communities that pay for them.

Stability, change and crisis

The archaeological record covers a number of different patterns of change in human societies and organisations. Some are long-term evolutionary changes with evidence of continuity of practice and belief over great stretches of time. Others are catastrophic. The record reveals those moments when change was possible from within and when it was imposed from without, for example through invasion. There is much to be learned here for those who manage change in the here and now. If the future is to be secured for organisations of higher education and learning, there is a need to know about how such institutions have typically changed in the past.

Universities, colleges and schools are all examples of complex organisations and have this in common: they all have a history. That history stretches back a long way. The universities of Europe are part of the history of European civilisation and of the ways in which European nation states, from the sixteenth century onwards shaped the modern world. The development of capitalist society transformed world societies. Through colonialism, imperialism and, later, through their dominance of the global economy, the developed capitalist states of the West exported their cultural institutions to the rest of the world.

In the course of this they secured global affirmation for a particular view of the nature of knowledge and of a particular style of human cognition. In this view, Apffel-Marglin and Marglin (1996) have argued, the most valuable forms of knowing follow those of the rational, analytical science. Theoretical knowledge is valued more than practical wisdom. The 'objective' understanding of facts is valued more than forms of understanding and insight which rest on other ways of knowing such as insight, experience, 'tacit knowledge' and practice. The consequence is that traditional ways of knowing – in agriculture, fisheries, environmental management and other areas of essential human practice, such as medicine – which put much more emphasis on the wholeness of creation and of forms of understanding based, for example, on stories, are as the British physicist, David Peat (1995) noted in his study of 'indigenous science' among native Americans, devalued. The practitioners of these different ways of knowing lose out as western knowledge and ways of doing things are imposed on their societies or, worse, as information they hold for example about medicines, is extracted from them and repackaged into saleable commodities by western companies.

The university is the institution above all others to promote such a view of knowledge, to codify its 'subjects', define the gradations of its 'experts', and confer high status and prestige on those at the top of its hierarchies. This is the model of the university which defines the meaning of higher education throughout the world. The demand from within Third World countries for higher education is essentially one for the kind of education on offer in the developed societies. The demand from overseas students for higher education is at its greatest in those institutions which are perceived as having the greatest prestige and status. An important aspect of that status is a claim to be part of a long tradition, to be old and well-connected with the high-status groups of society which conferred their respectability to begin with.

In defining their goals, institutions can strike different attitudes towards the past. Some celebrate it and preserve its symbols and rituals. The older universities of Europe have always made a special effort to preserve their connections with the past. In their architecture, rituals and iconography, continuity with older scholarly traditions are a key element of their claim to status and public support. The new universities of Eastern Europe, freed of state control and the stifling effects of Communist Party rule and ideology, have actively embraced the pre-communist past as a way of facing a non-communist future. Degree-giving ceremonies, for example, even in 'new' universities and throughout the world, are modelled precisely – in their ritual pomp, music and sartorial style – the practice of the medieval university which frees the symbolism of the event from the politics of the present and establishes an ancient legitimacy for the degrees of the awarding institution. And any institution worth its salt will maintain an alumni list of its great and good graduates and enshrine its past in institutional histories specially commissioned for the purpose.

Other organisations regard the past as a constraint to overcome. The polytechnics of Britain, set up in the 1960s, saw themselves as innovative, modern institutions unconstrained by traditions that they saw as educationally exclusive and conservative. Yet it was not too long after their foundation that some commentators complained of 'academic drift' as the new institutions sought to emulate the old. When the new institutions were accorded university status in Britain, it was a richly ironic experience to note the alacrity with which they quickly acquired the accoutrements – the titles, gowns, the rituals – of the older institutions to whose legitimacy they aspired.

The Open University in Britain was, *par excellence*, a modern institution exploiting the new media of mass communication for educational purposes and free of all the bureaucratic baggage of older institutions. Two points to note, however: the first is that in the structure of its academic governance it followed precisely the model of the older universities and, second, despite its determination to be accessible, the social profile of its students was little different to that of other universities. The Open University innovated with the medium of instruction of higher education, not with its message.

Elsewhere in Europe, parts of the past are being systematically erased from higher education. In the universities of the former People's Democracies of Eastern Europe, communist-appointed teachers have been sacked, their departments closed down and curricula have been completely rewritten. It will be intriguing to see how they develop from now on in. Demand for higher education is high in East and Central Europe. Knowledge matters in career terms and cultural capital is more important than economic capital in defining social differences in those societies. The orientation of students and young scholars is towards the West and they look to higher education as a vehicle to complete the social and economic transformation of their societies.

In other parts of the world, for example the Middle East, the secular, western model of the university is being challenged by people who believe that Islamic values should prevail within them. In Turkey, Islamic students insist on dressing in ways which assert their religious identity and question the secular basis of the Turkish state. It is a way of saying that the 70-year history of the Turkish republic has been a distortion of the Islamic destiny of the country. Similar trends are also observable in Egypt, and in Algeria religious fundamentalism is one of the elements in a dangerous and violent wave of protest which has all the hallmarks of a civil war. Throughout the Maghreb, there is a tension between those who interpret the past in secular and those who view it in religious terms and this tension reveals itself in fundamental disagreements about the values of modern education and the role that universities should play in the life of their societies. None the less, right across the same region, and the story is the same in much of the developing world, the demand is beyond satisfaction for university places – and not places in technical colleges or training schools –

for it is a higher education which opens the door to modern employment and social status.

Institutional autonomy in higher education

No institution can escape the past, for what an educational organisation becomes is not simply a question of how its leaders define its mission. One of the more facile beliefs of modern management is the illusion that their realm of freedom is as wide as they care to make it. It might be true of some business organisations; but educational institutions are keyed into a culture. They are part of a much wider framework of values, expectations and relationships which constitute the arrangements through which a social order is reproduced through time.

Higher education institutions have a particularly special role in the continuous building of social institutions, for they are the centre of the process of discovering and teaching people new knowledge. Yet universities are, however, intrinsically conservative institutions. Those who work in them have a duty of care to the traditions of scholarship and enquiry to which they are the heirs. Those traditions are alive. They are revealed in the ways in which people talk about their lives, explain their purposes and account for their experiences. They are part of the repertoire of narratives in the terms of which people find coherence and continuity in their work, order their priorities and assess the changes taking place around them. They constitute the deep structures of understanding and perception within the institution. Those who would like to change academic institutions so that they achieve new ends, have to confront these narratives and the deeply interiorised, older models of the organisation which are held tenaciously by different generations of staff.

The deep structures of academic institutions often bear little resemblance to their public manifestations. What is said by academic leaders to one audience may not correspond to how they talk among themselves. Because university staff are in possession of a unique commodity, that of specialised knowledge, and have, through that, a strong professional identity, it is very difficult for outside bodies to determine precisely what goes on within the academy. Professional bodies – in medicine, law, engineering and social work – and governments, through their control of the resources of, for example, teacher education, can and do specify what must be taught if students are to gain professional recognition of their degrees. Universities retain, however, considerable freedom to determine how they will meet these criteria and in non-professional areas their freedom to teach as they see fit remains sacrosanct, limited only by the availability of students to take their courses. It is difficult, therefore, to engineer from without, real change in academic institutions.

Only under exceptional circumstances involving the totalitarian use of force, is it possible to co-ordinate the academy to the purposes of the state. This was achieved in Nazi Germany and the Soviet Bloc societies of Eastern and

Central Europe. But even then, particularly in Eastern Europe, it was never complete. Academics found ways to retain their intellectual integrity while seeming to follow the party line. And the system created by the totalitarian states turned out, in the end, to be unsustainable and inefficient.

Current policies in Britain to fashion higher education to the purposes of an employer-led economy, meet, among some academics, as Prichard and Willmott (1997) have argued, a quiet resistance and scepticism. So, too, do the populist demands from government that universities should widen the basis of their recruitment of students. This has been achieved over the past decade, even with a steady erosion in the unit of resource made available to the universities by the state. But it has not been a universally welcomed development. And it has not affected all faculties in the same way. As with the parallel agenda of promoting continuing education, the subject areas which have proved most responsive to the access agenda are in the social sciences, humanities and business studies areas. It is as if educational innovation and the pursuit of radical educational values – in, for example, the extra-mural tradition of British universities – is something which has always taken place only at the margins of the academy where, in a real sense, it could be tolerated, for its impact on the main institution was minimal.

The older bastions of academic privilege remain intact. The historical memory of many academics is a filter through which the past is seen as superior to the present, as a time when academic standards were higher and institutions had a serious academic purpose. Even in the world of mass higher education and unitary higher education systems which seek to collapse the distinction between universities and other forms of higher education such as polytechnics, teaching training colleges or *Fachochschulen*, the subtle hierarchies of distinction attached to the old models reasserts itself. No amount of egalitarian change and widened access to higher education in Britain will, in the foreseeable future, knock Oxbridge off its perch. Indeed, there is, in the new global economy, an international hierarchy of institutions to which the elite students of the world's universities aspire: Oxbridge, Harvard, MIT, the Grande Écoles in France. In the world of business Education, there is a real global market now in students and a proliferating range of elite-validated distance learning programmes followed by students all over the world.

At the heart of all this is a distorted image of the ancient academic excellence of the older universities. Prewar universities in Britain were not power houses of intellectual creativity. After World War II, as servicemen returned to pick up the pieces of their education, universities embraced a much wider spectrum of students than they were later to recruit during the expanding years of the 1960s. Despite the social changes of the postwar years, some universities remained steeped in the older values, a sort of *Brideshead Revisited* time-lock of eccentric dons, beer-swilling students – who were predominantly male – and *angst* about the democratic drift of modern society.

This is clearly a caricature, but it makes a point, at least for Britain: it was an older system of higher education which expanded in the 1960s. It is the

1960s expansion which frames so much now of how academics conceive their past and the values they believe were central to it. It was during these years that new institutions embraced the culture and practices of very old ones, sealing in academic aspic attitudes and values much more suited to times past than to the future.

This is not to claim that higher education institutions are changeless. Far from it. There has been a subtle shift in the government of institutions. Academic management has become professionalised. Collegial government has given way to a new, cost-conscious managerialism. Some writers (Prichard and Willmott, 1997) have compared the changes that have taken place to those that have transformed the fast food market: it is as if, they claim, the universities have been *MacDonaldized*. The 'MacUniversity' has become through its modular courses, pre-packaged curricula and flexible staff (many of whom, especially on the research side, are on short-term contracts), the very model of a post-Fordist industrial organisation. Despite this and perhaps, even, because of it, the system of higher education has both diversified and strengthened its links with different constituencies of interest in society and has become much more attuned to the need to market its products professionally.

In so doing, however, they have become victims of their own success. They now must continue to appeal to a political constituency which expects the university to be the vehicle of its upward social mobility and to funding agencies, both state supported and private, which expect them to pursue research on topics they define as important. The critical autonomy and academic freedom, which, in the older model are the core values of higher education, are seriously under threat in a society that increasingly expects universities to service the state and the economy.

The danger for students in all this is that the experience of learning will be mechanised and unchallenging. Ronald Barnett (1990, 1995) has been insistent that there is a real danger that under the new regime of higher education, students will not have the chance to develop a critical awareness of the subjects they study. Academic subjects have become highly specialised; knowledge has been reduced to its smallest elements. Disciplinary boundaries – which reflect, as Becher (1989) has shown, more the social bonds among and identities of academic bodies than the intrinsic structures of different bodies of knowledge – remain strong and the honours degree is a seriously overloaded programme of study.

Nor is the experience of higher education for students a uniform one. Mature students are still the Cinderella's of the academy, though they now outnumber the young ones. Their needs – for child care, flexible opening hours in libraries, flexible hours of teaching and learning – and their interests, eg in having their prior experience of work acknowledged in some way as an element of their academic assessment, are not really met. Despite the universality of the title, 'university', it is also well-known and understood that there is a hierarchy of institutions differing in status which reflects back on the academic identity, social position and self-confidence of their students. Students from working class and inner city backgrounds pick up a strong sense of their position at the bottom of the academic pile (Brown and Scase, 1994).

R H Tawney once noted that it is only those institutions which touch the imagination that are loved. As secular servants of the state or of employers, universities will not be loved. They stand some chance of preserving their cherished values if they change the ways in which they connect with the societies they serve. Their failure to do this convincingly is at the heart of their vulnerability and it is a failure embedded in a false notion of what their best traditions are and what preserved them.

Institutions which have allowed themselves to become specialised in the education and training of the young and in research terms to the needs and interests of business and the state, have forfeited their right to a wider support from society as a whole. Universities cannot ignore the demands of their paymasters. But they can neutralise their effects and seek support from a wider constituency. They will do that to the extent that they meet a wider variety of education and training needs. And they will reduce their vulnerability to the state if they are seen to have a unique place in the cultural life of society as a whole.

The more narrowly they define their purpose, the more vulnerable they are. The more determined they are to preserve older traditions of an elite university system, the less they will secure the support of wider constituencies of opinion and interest in society. Their future, in a real sense, is within; it is in their hands to secure it. Modern society needs universities as it has never done before; they are critical to the future of any successful modern state. The great danger at the moment, is that there is a failure of imagination and possibility within universities that prevents them from defining their own agendas and priorities for the future. That failure is rooted in the values, habits of mind and social exclusivity of higher education itself.

Change generates conflict. The balance in the archaeological record of what has been preserved and what has been destroyed, reveals which groups prevailed over others. What we continue to conserve is not our heritage, but what we select as being worthy of conservation in it. The distribution of structures and sites is not, therefore a random one; it reflects decisions taken in society in the light of values and priorities. The curricula, teaching methods, educational goals and distribution of resources within and between educational institutions, can be seen as a negotiated order in which different groups within society secured for themselves the conditions they deemed essential for the realisation of their longer term educational interests. Change within education is, therefore, always contentious and invariably difficult. Radical innovation is rare and perhaps only possible at the margins of the life of the institutions. The most significant changes have come, invariably from without.

Learning, experience and identity

For those who have experienced higher education – staff and students – the experience is unforgettable and profound in the way in which shapes a distinctive sense of self. Higher education confers status; it remains, despite expanded numbers, a major factor predicting for those who have it, higher lifetime earnings and career advancement. To have had a higher education is a mark of distinction; it is to have had access to ideas, experiences and people which enable graduates to think critically and to dare to doubt received wisdom. Indeed, they are encouraged to be iconoclastic, critical, to seek evidence in support of arguments and to have developed a competence to argue persuasively and with confidence. They are expected to have acquired the skills to take their learning further and to be capable of independent judgement.

Universities are not factories; they cannot turn out uniform products. The kinds of graduates they produce reflects differences in the social backgrounds of the students they recruit, the subjects they study and the kinds of preuniversity preparation they are required to have. To such differences have to be added those deriving from different patterns of study offered by institutions as well as the widely acknowledged differences of quality – of the level, intellectual vitality and challenge of the courses and the skills and commitment of teachers – among different institutions. There are wide institutional variations on each of these dimensions and they all change through time.

Different groups of students make use of the academy in different ways. In the older, extra-mural tradition of British universities, especially during the inter-war period, students used universities to sharpen their political wits, improve themselves or to advance the aims of their class. Mature students now, research has shown (West, 1996), are deeply committed to their studies because they are, through their studying, realising a new sense of self. Some work hard to compensate for earlier failures or to prove a point about their ability to partners or parents who they once believed undervalued them. Part-time students often use the academy to gain job-related qualifications. For the majority of young students, university is a privileged opportunity to experience a new realm of freedom away from parents, to entertain new ideas, identities and to grow up. What they all in different ways acquire, is an ability to think, to question and to question authority. They are qualities which employers value and young graduates know that a higher education improves their chances of finding a rewarding career.

In this way, a university education both opens up opportunities for individuals and marks out clearly the ways in which they differ from those without such an education. Focused on the development of individual talent and ability, however, a university education can often mask the fact that such individual achievements are the result of collective endeavour and that the freedoms on which they rest have been bought at great cost.

This is not to deny that those who achieve their degrees have had to display talent, hard work and critical qualities of judgement. The best of them acquire in addition skills in communication, in working in teams and in problem-solving. Students, however, cannot be seen apart from the society in which they live or outside the structures within which they are taught and learn. Too often a higher education is devoid of any sense of real critical challenge to received wisdom. Too often students are taught by the institutions in which they study that their role is to accept received wisdom and the authority of their teachers; that knowledge is something the experts possess. Not having been helped to acquire a knowledge of how to learn, too many students remain dependent on experts and dare not develop ideas of their own. Students are typically not encouraged to develop an insight into the philosophical foundations of their subjects or, indeed, of the university's claim to be the guardians of scholarship and research.

Having little real say over the ways in which universities themselves are managed – though they have more now than ever before, especially before the groundswell of change in student life in the 1960s – or over how courses are developed and not, therefore, having had the experience of negotiating their own curricula or modifying the modes of teaching and learning they are subject to, students are typically denied any understanding of the politics of knowledge or of higher education. Modes of learning which go beyond the classroom and the laboratory and which require work with and through bodies outside the university – in industry, public service, the community – are still at the edges of a higher education.

Towards a democratic future

All over the developed industrial world the student radicals of the 1960s challenged the structures of the university and demanded greater representation within it. These were the protests of an elite and without doubt the university became a focal point of social criticism because they were seen to be implicated in a wider injustice – the failure of governments to protest strongly enough against the Vietnam war, to respond to Third World agendas for freedom and development, to work for a more equal society in which people were not alienated and repressed. As bodies well-equipped to cut through cant, universities were criticised for their complicity in helping maintain the ideological foundations of a social order which had built a military capacity capable of destroying the world itself, which rained napalm on helpless children and which seemed out of democratic control.

Today, it is hardly conceivable that students would become a vanguard of revolutionary social change. Their realm of freedom has been circumscribed. Their needs and interests have become sharply focused on getting their job tickets. Students demanded successfully greater rights of representation in academic government. In the past 20 years their status as consumers of academic courses has been substantially improved. Throughout the developed world, governments have worked to improve the quality of courses and the accountability of institutions. They have 'empowered' the student as a consumer and made the university more accessible.

Universities have become tightly aligned again with the agendas of government and of employers. The radical criticisms of the universities from the 1960s now seem naive. They imagined that an old institution could be changed to challenge the inequity and oppression of a wider social order. The changes envisaged in the society were clear enough; what was missing was an alternative model of the university itself. The world-wide expansion of higher education in the past 30 years has to be applauded. It is irreversible. But it has left the model of the university intact. Look closely at it and what one sees is enormous variation among institutions and nations. Even similar institutions in the same society differ profoundly in their ambience, attitudes, schemes of study, capacity for innovation and change. Each university is an academic micro-world of its own, with its own politics, loyalties and problems. Stand a little further back, however, and these differences are ironed out and the model remains with all its historical accretions and continuities and assumptions.

Louise Morley (1997) wrote recently, reflecting on the fact that, although universities have opened their doors to new groups of students, their own structures remain deeply inegalitarian. There are few women professors. All institutions claim equal opportunities policies but the evidence is that less than one third have clear implementation strategies to achieve their mission. Few have strongly anti-racist mission statements or policies to improve the educational life chances of ethnic minority groups. 'A central obstacle,' she writes, 'to cultural change in academia is the belief that knowledge is decontextualised, and constructed and communicated with impartial power and authority' (1997, p. 232).

There is a problem, then, which lies deep in the structure of the institutions themselves and in their own inwardness. It is not one they can solve by themselves. They need help to define a new mission for themselves. Over 30 years ago, Sid Chaplin (1969b), the novelist from the North East of England, detected a problem in the University of Durham. Noting the university's lack of real connection with the community – apart, that is, for the 'Extra-Mural men and two or three generations of archaeologists' – he compared it to a 'a vast velvet padded treadmill with rows of young men and women wearily lifting and putting down their suede or stiletto-heeled shoes, looking neither to the left or the right but awaiting only the day when they can opt out and vanish without trace, without even a shade of nostalgia let alone grace and gratitude' (Chaplin, 1969b, p. 88). Chaplin's problem was that he felt it should be very different. 'I sometimes feel', he wrote, 'a pang for what the University could have given, or what it could be in the distant future, if only somebody cared. A tree with rosy apples ripe for the picking is better than all the old nostalgia in the world' (p. 91).

We are now in that distant future and there is a bountiful harvest of rosy apples to pick. Has Durham, or any other university for that matter, realised Chaplin's hopes? Has it been able to alter profoundly the nature of its engagement with the region, with diverse student communities? Has it helped the North become what Chaplin believed it could be, a 'citadel of learning and culture'? The answer is in the question. In 30 years, however, the questions have also changed because modern societies themselves have altered profoundly. The production and dissemination of knowledge is the *sine qua non* of economic success. But the economic success of modern societies has done little to guarantee their continued ability to generate new ideas or to cope with the consequences of global economic change. Stuart Ranson and colleagues (1997) have recently argued that there is a need to take our ideas about the learning society further, to embrace the notion of a learning democracy.

This is a society which has secured the material conditions of democratic life – justice, a fair distribution of reasonable incomes, health care, decent housing and living conditions, education – but which goes further to engage people in democratic practice. This, they have argued, requires an enriched public domain which challenges the fragmentation, the privatism and sectionalism of modern society and political life and engages people, in association with one another – not as solitary learners – in discussion in their own schools, their own localities about the problems of building that society. It is a society based on trust and co-operation and which finds new ways to solve old problems and resolve differences and which acknowledges the myriads of ways in which all lives are interdependent.

The idea of a learning democracy subsumes that of the learning society. It holds out the promise that public domain institutions like schools and universities can function differently. Such institutions must be open, accessible on a lifelong basis and confident enough to be critical. Their academic freedom has to be secured against their responsibility to the wider public domain. It is an agenda requiring new kinds of institution with new kinds of systems of governance reflecting a wider range of interests: those of a much more diverse student body, communities and regions, as well as those of academics and the professions.

The university of the future must embrace the agenda for lifelong learning and to do so requires a new kind of academic leadership, one much more clued up about the changes taking place in society and determined to shape the direction of such change in democratic ways. It means that universities have to become much more critical of themselves and of their old ways of doing things. The paradox to overcome is this: universities are organisations which facilitate learning, but they are not learning organisations; they have not been good at defining for themselves the ways in which they must change or of learning the lessons of their own past.

Democratic values have to become a much stronger part of how staff in universities manage themselves, their courses and their students. Such values have to inform how knowledge itself is generated, tested and applied. Universities are institutions of the world and must seek to engage what they do with international developments in scholarship and research and be ever-vigilant about the values of academic freedom as it applies to others as well as themselves. But they exist, too, in particular places, in particular regions and they have a responsibility to contribute to the development of them through their scholarship, research and teaching and to do so in ways which meet the needs and interests of much wider constituencies of students over much longer periods. Vice Chancellors should not sleep soundly until they feel sure that, faced with another round of financial cut-backs or any threat to their academic freedom, they could confidently expect street demonstrations when members of the public, inspired by the love of learning, carry banners saying 'Save Our Universities'.

Part Three:

Experience

8 Learning and creativity

What is now proved was once only imagin'd.
William Blake, *Proverbs of Hell*

People cannot live in the world as it is. They have always imagined alternatives to it or created new, fantastic worlds beyond it. They have always been incapable of just reproducing that which is given and of accepting their place within it. Through art, religion, music, literature, dance, drama and fantasy, they have tilted their imagination against the oppressive givenness of the present and the compelling routines of their daily lives. Through their creative work they have changed the world and the history of the forms of human, imaginative expression is the history of human civilisation itself.

Modern industrial societies have given this process a distinctive twist: they have programmed it into the workings of their economic and political institutions. Through massive Research and Development (R&D) budgets, great schemes of public works, from dams to space travel, through scientific work geared to commercial ends and public support for the Arts, the political and commercial leaders of modern societies have channelled the imaginative powers of people to discover new knowledge, develop new ideas and to do so as a matter of routine as part of the daily requirements of their jobs. Creativity has been thoroughly tamed and *disenchanted*. Its ultimate sources in the human mind may remain still a mystery, but that does not matter as long as sufficient numbers of those minds are hard at work producing new ideas, products, images, experiences and solutions. Without a developing capacity continually to improve in this way, no modern society, or any organisation within them, is safe from the challenges of intense, global competition or from forces that threaten the freedoms their creative vitality rests upon.

It is surprising, therefore, that in the main systems of social and political theory which have shaped the modern world – in Marxism, Socialism, Utilitarianism, Conservatism, Liberalism, Fascism, and in most contemporary varieties of sociological theory – themselves a product of human imagination – little was or is said about the phenomenon of human creativity itself. A major consequence of this is that we lack not only an adequate theory of social change and of history, we have also only an impoverished sense of the creative possibilities in every human life.

It is the purpose of this chapter to explore this proposition and its implications. The questions pursued are these: how can the imagination and creative powers of adults be understood, nurtured and celebrated? How can people contribute more effectively to the building of a better world? How can the imagination of people be nurtured so that they approach all the problems they face in their communities, in their places of work and in the societies they live in, in fresh ways? The answer to be explored is this: people can be helped to be more creative but only if there is a change in the prevailing cultural models of creativity itself; only if people are enabled to see themselves and the creative possibilities of their own lives in a different light.

For that to happen, we all need a better understanding of creative activity, how it is possible, the forms it takes and, at least for the purposes of this chapter, of how people typically construct their own ideas about what it means to be creative. The chapter presents some data which illustrate how five different groups of people (a total of 72 individuals – 47 men and 25 women) – all of them meeting to discuss creativity – viewed the nature of creativity itself and how they assessed their own creative potentialities. The data were not collected to be in some narrow sense scientifically credible. The study was undertaken to illuminate the typical ways in which creativity is understood in this society. It was to explore the prevailing cultural models of creativity tacitly embraced by people and through which they made judgements of their own creative possibilities and the achievements of others.

The groups were not randomly selected but emerged from the teaching programme of a university department of Adult and Continuing Education. Each group, following well-tried methods of syndicate work and group discussion (see Jarvis, 1992; Williamson, 1992) was helped to articulate the views of its members about creativity. The groups were as follows: miners (8), nurses (14), manufacturing managers (12), manufacturing supervisors (19) and part-time adult education tutors (19). The individuals covered an age range from the early 20s to over 50s. The members of each group filled in a questionnaire which explored aspects of their own individual creative activity and each group, through small group work, discussed several aspects of the problem of creativity to establish an overall perspective on it which they could agree with. The method is a good way to probe the views of people. While the data cannot be held to be representative of the prevailing views of people in the society as a whole, the interpretations they sustain have a credibility beyond the immediate context of the study and certainly open up questions for further debate and research.

The key proposition to be explored is this: if people can be helped to a better understanding of the creative process and to recognise their own creative potential more clearly, then they will be able to develop their abilities, their contribution to their societies and reach forward towards a new sense of themselves and of the possibilities of their lives. What people do understand of these issues is not something they arrive at by themselves. They draw upon prevailing ideas within the culture which identify for them the people whose works, ideas and achievements are exemplars of creativity and genius. The stories they hear about such people, in whatever domain of achievement, provide the narrative frameworks upon which to build their understanding of creativity itself. Those stories are embedded in a wider discourse that encodes prevailing psychological and sociological assumptions about how people are able to change the ways in which they think about the world.

In this sense, the prevailing, taken-for-granted models of creativity within a society, which enable people to judge themselves and the achievements of others, reflect the terms of whichever discourse is dominant. If we can understand this, then we can think of new ways to release the full creative potential of everyone. The tragedy for millions of people – which becomes a collective tragedy for us all – is that they hold such a diminished sense of the creative possibilities of their own lives that they never realise their full potential as human beings.

Social theory and creativity

In Marxism, history, by and large, just happens; it evolves through a sort of mechanical process of unfolding contradictions, not much dependent upon the conscious action and imagination of sentient human beings. 'Men make their own history,' proclaimed Marx, but then added, darkly, 'but they do not make it just as they please; they do not make it under circumstances chosen by themselves, but under circumstances directly encountered, given and transmitted from the past' (cited in McLellan, 1971, p. 61).

From the materialist perspective which is the foundation of Marxism, all kinds of human, creative achievement – in art, philosophy, law, religion – are merely part of the ideological superstructure of society, and a complex reflection of its economic base. It is not even clear how the revolutionary class consciousness of the proletariat, which in Marx's theory provides the catalyst for the demise of capitalism and the vision for the future, communist society, would be formed. That it could come into existence is surely a reflection of the power of human beings to think new thoughts and to anticipate in their hopes, new futures. Marx provides no satisfactory account of how this can happen.

It is one of the tragic consequences of this that, in Leninism, the vision of the new society had to be imposed by the revolutionary vanguard. Russia became, as did the People's Democracies of Eastern Europe, a kind of prison of the soul which stifled both revolutionary politics and all forms of human creativity. Of course, the suppression could never be complete. Creativity cannot be contained. Soviet art and music, science and technology and, of course, literature, spawned some of the greatest achievements of the twentieth century. No one can ever know, however, how much more might have been achieved in a less oppressive regime. The historic irony is that the Party's attempt to control creative work for ideological ends created the dissent among artists and writers which undermined it.

In what Marx called bourgeois political economy, a tradition of economic and social theory from Adam Smith and Ricardo to modern writers, in which we would now include Hayek and Milton Friedman, history happens impersonally through the logic of markets giving shape to human behaviour. The related tradition of evolutionary social theory – in the work, for example, of Spencer – history evolves in a Darwinian frame of chance, in which selective advantage is conferred on those random adaptations which led to some groups being privileged over others. Looked at from this angle, creativity – and, therefore, change itself – is an impulse of evolution but random in its origins and consequences, something literally which is a matter of chance and of individual endeavour and achievement.

For some writers, Max Weber, for example, whose views on this matter echoed those of Nietzsche, history is given momentum and meaning through the pursuit of power in which individuals and groups of people struggle for domination over others. How they imagine what they will gain by this or what vision of the future they hope to realise is not made clear. It is as if power was an end in itself and not merely the means to some other anticipated or imagined end.

Among the writers on the extreme right of the twentieth century, the authors of Fascism, with its nationalism, anti-Semitism and racial biology, history came to be conceived as an inevitable struggle for survival between different races of people, its driving force mystically flowing through the blood of a culture. In none of these views of social change is any special attention given to the ways in which human beings come to think in new ways or imagine new worlds. Indeed, the main thrust of them was to justify the suppression of creativity and to promote only those forms of it which in some way dignified the state itself. Soviet realism and Nazi art had this in common: creative artists were expected to promote the dominant ideology of the State and the Party.

There has been much written in social and political theory about the ways in which different world views, ways of thinking and expressing ideas, can be shaped and influenced – by ideology, religion, mass communication, the actions of competing classes struggling for power – but no convincing account of the social processes of creative thought itself. Western social theory has thus given us history without imagination and a theory of social action which strips from people their capacity to learn new things and think new thoughts.

Contemporary social theory has not overcome the limitations of its classical origins. *Homo sociologicus* was indeed a pale shadow of a human being, trapped in the roles he or she is required to play, socialised to know no others and held in the iron grip of deeply internalised structures of rules, perceptions and modes of understanding the world. Cast now to the winds of postmodernist uncertainty, modern men and women no longer have faith in the old 'grand narratives' of their culture – religion, science, progress, reason – but that does not make them any more capable of thinking fresh thoughts. It just leaves them uncertain and ready to believe almost anything. John Rundell (1994) captured the ambiguity nicely introducing a collection of essays on the imagination. He writes that 'The cultural constellation of (post) modernity appears to swing between the experience of open-ended creativity and the parade of manufactured images consumed by a voyeuristic, privatised public' (p. 2). This is, of course, just a version of the old mass society theory with its implicit division of the social world into creative (and sometimes very dangerous) leaders and the dull mass of the people they so easily can dupe and lead.

Even to those modern social theorists (see Crossley, 1996) who build on the insights of philosophical phenomenology and attribute to human beings a capacity to think, to create symbols and build a shared, meaningful and essentially *intersubjective* universe in which to live, the really important changes in the development of knowledge, culture and society, are the result of the work of the few, of artists and intellectuals, and not of the many who remain trapped in already-existing imposed constructions of social reality.

Within all these traditions of social theory, it was always recognised that people were capable of Utopian thought, but in the main, the Utopias they imagined, were dismissed as mere ideologies, of no special significance in themselves except in so far as they mystified the more fundamental search for an objective understanding of social realities. Even within the traditions of Utopian thinking, there is scant attention paid to the processes of imagination which enable people to conceive of the different worlds they aspire to. Utopias are therefore imaginative new worlds which have to be created for people to behold; it is as if it was not in their power to create them for themselves.

None of these traditions, therefore, contain a credible theory of imagination and creativity. Yet they all require one, for in each case there is an attempt to understand how thought and feeling relate to action and how the cumulative outcomes of the actions of millions of people shape the patterns of society and of human experience. Without imagination and a capacity to hope and to invest our thoughts with feelings, in ways which confer meaning on existence and stretch the range of all our emotions, human beings would be indistinguishable from animals. The importance of a clear understanding of the processes of human imagination can not, therefore, be understated. It is the key to our understanding of the past. Without a theory of the imagination, we shall not understand how people experience their lives – their joys, sorrows, hopes and fears – or appreciate beauty or sense the sublime. And the exercise of the creative imagination – in art, science, politics and, indeed, in everyday life – is, both from the point of view of the quality of life for individuals and for the development of society as a whole, what all our futures depend upon.

Without a cultivated capacity to conceive of different ways of organising our societies, we would be condemned to live the lives set for us by dead generations past and we would, literally, have no future. Without the means to experience ourselves and our world in fresh ways, to enlarge the range and depth of our feelings, to enjoy the creativity of others, our lives would be dulled to a bored insensitivity.

One of the consequences of the industrial division of labour at the heart of the modern economy, as Adam Smith well understood, is that the lives of millions of people are reduced to the narrow limits of their undemanding work. Fantasy, rather than creative effort, then becomes the vehicle through which they escape it, and fantasy itself, packaged as accessible pleasures to be bought in the market place, is relentlessly commoditised.

But not necessarily; the other side of what can be a very gloomy picture, is that the imagination always wins through; that millions of people are engaged in creative work – in their leisure, in their homes, in their communities. Millions more, through the media which can trivialise their dreams, have become aware of possibilities in their enjoyment of art, music, drama and in their sense of the possibilities open to them, which are far richer than anything available to previous generations. What, then, is this capacity that people have to transcend themselves and to create?

Imagination defined

Imagination, which is the basis of all human creativity, is a universal quality of human minds. It is a process of thought and feeling in which people explore the contours and boundaries of their consciousness, extend them and give expression to the new thoughts and feelings which arise in doing so. It is an inescapable, lifelong activity of the minds of each unique human being. The brain is its biological substrate but not its source.

The forms in which ideas are expressed, however, and most of the resources for their expression – in art, language and science – are essentially social. They are part of the cultural order of a society and are altered and changed through time. The process at the root of all creation – *thinking* – is, as a prominent neurologist (Edelman, 1992) has noted, 'a skill woven from experience of the world' (1992 p. 174). 'The acquisition of this skill,' he writes, 'requires more than experience with things; it requires social, affective, and linguistic interactions' (1992, p. 174). It follows from this, therefore, that a theory of imagination which is adequate to the complexity of the phenomenon itself must go beyond the insights of biology and psychology and embrace those of history and social theory.

Since the ability of people to exercise their imaginative faculties is limited or enhanced by their education and experiences and by the kinds of lives they lead, there is an essential sociological and political dimension to its development which cannot be ignored. Václav Havel (1991), now the playwright President of the Czech Republic, reflecting on his own creativity while imprisoned in Czechoslovakia for dissident activity in the 1980s, was clear about two things: first, that although he had unlimited time for thinking, he had not come up with a creative idea in months. 'Mental activity,' he noted, 'needs outside impulses' lest it become stunted (p. 58). Above all, however, he explained in another letter from prison, 'creation is related to freedom' for without that even writers become trapped in the joylessness of being and lose their sense of their own creative horizons and possibilities.

The starting point for a theory of imagination and creativity, has to be, however, with the fundamental ontological question: why have human minds become organised in ways which enable people, through the exercise of their imagination, to transcend the limits of their immediate environments and past experience, to be able to conceive of ideas which enable them to alter their world? The question is part of another: why do humans have culture? For culture is the resource which enables people to generate new thoughts and to express them in novel ways.

The evolutionary answer has to be this: through the development of culture human groups have, over millennia, enhanced their adaptive capacity to their environments. Through an ability which is essentially linguistic, humans have been able to consolidate their knowledge in memory and to communicate it through the generations, and have therefore, increased their chances of survival through being able to capitalise on the knowledge and experience of others.

In this way, human beings do not need to learn from their mistakes; they have the mistakes of others to inform them and this is of profound evolutionary significance. For it means that individuals do not have to repeat the experience of their elders in order to come to know the world in which they live and understand its dangers.

It also means that human beings can develop specialised activities within the groups in which they live. They do not need to know everything in order to survive for they can depend on others to know it. This confers on human beings a capacity to work together, to acquire what Kropotkin called, 'habits of mutuality' on the basis of which, human society became one of the most complex and productive mechanisms of the whole of creation. Such a view, though analytically powerful, is still, however, limited. For it ignores a key element of human culture: that cultures constitute systems of meanings and symbols with a capacity, achieved through the minds of unique individuals, to generate new symbols, meanings and ideas and through that, to reflect back into the processes of thought and imagination. Culture in this sense is self generating, the property not of individuals, but of groups, whose cultural identities transcend those of their individual members.

It is this self organising, regenerative capacity of human cultures which has enabled *homo sapiens* to achieve, as a species, its evolutionary success. The biological residue of the process is the human brain, an organ capable of fantastic computations, insights, feelings, ideas and possessed of a completely unpredictable but vast capacity to generate new ways of thinking which are different to those acquired by people in the course of growing up. Because these ideas and new experiences can be communicated, human beings can incorporate into their private worlds, the experience of other human beings, both living and dead, so that the capacity of individuals to think, or to dream, is constantly renewed and refreshed. Human consciousness, as a consequence of human culture, is open and attuned to seek out new experiences.

So far so good; but the ideas just set out only help explain the development of human strategies of survival – in finding food, defending themselves against predators and developing their technologies to live in their environments. It says nothing about other features of the human imagination: its playfulness, its non-utilitarian delight in novelty and its search for significance in experience.

The search for meaning in the events of birth, death and catastrophe, may be at the root of the universal, human phenomenon of religion. But culture is not just a reflection of serious issues: it reflects, too, the sophisticated – though in this case not exclusively human – capacity for play and forms of expression which celebrate joy and delight in completely non-utilitarian ways. Dance, art, music, sexual pleasure, narcotics, laughter and playfulness certainly have recognisable functions in all human societies, for example in binding people together into a common identity, or to release tensions, but they reflect, too, a human need to search out the new, to live beyond the present constraints of their world so as to understand and change it. This human need is one which must be met both by individual people and by human cultures themselves, for it is linked to the overall adaptive capacity of the group and its ability to respond to changing circumstances, both from within and without.

This cultural–evolutionary view of imagination gives us an account of the human need to be creatively innovative and of the capacity of the healthy, human brain to enable us to act in that way. Furthermore, it leads to two more fundamental questions, whose answers, insofar as there are any, define the scope of the field of the study of imagination. The first is this: why do different societies, cultures and epochs differ from one another in the way imagination is expressed? Second, why are individuals, each endowed with brains with this phenomenal capacity to create and to learn, so different in the use they make of their creative and imaginative potential?

The first question is about the forms and content of human creative expression and the historical and socio-cultural traditions which, over hundreds of years, have shaped them. The second can only be answered through an exploration of the ways in which people are constrained in their personal development by their position in the social order of the societies in which they live. The constraints which matter most are those which are woven into the arrangements of economic and political life and which are reinforced by the prevailing views in a society about how the creative possibilities of all human beings are understood. Some societies – modern Japan is a good example – plan, through long-term investment, to succeed in industrial and commercial innovation and have found ways to engage the employees of companies in the continuous improvement of their products and services. In many other countries, commercial and industrial innovation is left to the chance of the market place or to individual initiative. At the root of such differences are differing views of the creative process itself. It is to this that we now turn.

Cultural models of the creative process

Two linked themes need to be considered: how does the creative process work and, how do people in different societies and cultures believe it works? What model of creativity and of the imagination prevails in a culture? It is vital to know the answer to this question, for we must understand what beliefs and values constitute the prevailing view of human potentiality in a society. Such fundamental beliefs shape how people are valued and how they value themselves. Ours, unfortunately, is a society built around what Pierre Bourdieu (1974) once called, 'an ideology of giftedness', in which it is held as a matter of scientific fact, that those who succeed in the educational and cultural realm, do so because they possess unique gifts, which the majority of people do not have and cannot acquire.

It is this tacit, yet misleading belief, which, historically at least, has shaped attitudes among teachers, psychologists and politicians and set the agendas both of psychological research into human abilities and public policies in the fields of culture and education. Together, these traditions of enquiry, belief and action, have culminated in the view that the kinds of social inequalities which exist in modern society which stifle initiative and creativity, are not only inevitable but are, indeed, legitimate. It is not a universally accepted view; it is a highly contested one about which each generation raises new questions. At the root of them all is the underlying question: what is the nature and source of human creative potential and expression?

In Greek thought, these questions were raised through the study of epistemology and poetics. Throughout the Middle Ages and the Renaissance, human beings were thought merely to imitate in some way the patterns of and forms of Nature. God was held to be at the centre of his creation so that there was necessarily a divine inspiration behind all forms of human creative expression. Faced with an empty canvass, medieval artists said a prayer. The eighteenth-century philosophers placed reason at the centre of the imagination. Romanticism sought out the creative spirit and the poet's muse. The Victorians searched scientifically for the roots of genius and twentieth-century psychology has fully secularised the issue of creativity as a particular feature of human cognition to be studied in its relationship to different patterns of social organisation and communication.

In the closing decade of the twentieth century, we still struggle with the legacy of these interpretations. It is becoming clearer, however, that creativity is not confined to the arts or to science but that it is generic to all of the contexts in which people live and work and, in principle, at least, to everything they do. This generic model is not widely understood; it does not yet provide people with an account of their experience or open their eyes to the creative activity going on around them. It does not yet supply people, both those in authority – in work, politics or the community – and those struggling to change their world in various ways, with a model of practice from which could flow new ideas, solutions, practices, sentiments and hopes. The older models which too readily tied creativity to artistic or scientific work and which gave it therefore a rather narrow and highly individualistic frame, still hold sway. The emerging, generic model which embraces all that people do and is built on a strong collective frame to understand and support the creative endeavour of individuals, are becoming clearer but do not yet sanction profound changes in the ways in which we organise work, politics and community life.

The psychology of creativity

John Keats, reflecting in 1817 on the nature of artistic achievement, wrote (in a letter to his brothers) that the quality decisive to it was 'Negative Capability' (1988, p. 539). He defined this as 'when a man is capable of being in uncertainties, Mysteries, doubts, without any irritable reaching after fact & reason.'

Modern psychologists who study creativity have much to say about the qualities of creative individuals are in agreement with him. One summary of this research by Tardif and Sternberg (1988) sets out their conclusions as follows. Creative individuals are said to display four key *traits:* intelligence, originality, verbal fluency and a good imagination. The are held to posses a number of cognitive *abilities*: to be able to think metaphorically, to be flexible in decision-making, to show independent judgement, to enjoy novelty, to think logically, to visualise problems, to escape conventional ways of thinking and to search for order in chaos. The style of their thinking is thought to be characterised by a questioning attitude and they are as interested in what is not known about something as in what is known. It is claimed, too, that they are willing to take risks.

Creative work builds upon a sound training in a particular domain and rests on hard sustained work. Howard Gardiner (1993) has researched the creative achievements of Freud, Einstein, Picasso and other great men, including T S Eliot and Gandhi, and claims to find that their creativity is related to their childhood experiences when most of them displayed the qualities of the explorer and the innovator. Creative individuals, he claims, organise their lives to heighten the prospect that they will achieve a breakthrough in a particular domain or field of enquiry. Creative individuals, argues Gardiner, are 'self confident, alert, unconventional, hardworking, and committed obsessively to their work. Social life or hobbies are almost immaterial, representing at most a fringe on the creators' worktime' (1993, p. 364).

But their achievements are not merely the outcome of their special qualities as thinkers or human beings. Each needed the support of others, both in terms of personal intimacy and professional acknowledgement and each was fortunate in that their placement in time was fortuitous. Picasso and T S Eliot both worked among a circle of fellow artists who were themselves at the edges of creative endeavour in painting and poetry. Of great significance for Picasso was Braque and for Eliot, Ezra Pound. They lived at a time when the main traditions of their art forms were at an end and avant-garde work was valued.

Thomas Kuhn (1962) has made a similar point about scientific creativity. Breakthroughs come when a scientific tradition – a paradigm – can no longer solve the problems of research and an entirely new approach is required.

What happens when the creative breakthrough occurs? What has changed? The answer is clear: patterns of thinking and feeling change. The frames through which people perceive the world (or, at least, that part of it in which they are working) alter and new questions arise in their minds. Old approaches to problems appear inadequate. The cumulative outcome of millions of people achieving such breakthroughs in their way of thinking is that the patterns of understanding within a culture alter, transforming the ways in which people interpret the world around them and, through that, change their perception of themselves.

From this perspective, creativity is a process which must be viewed in its psychological, social and cultural complexity. While no one would claim to be able to pick out the next Einstein or Mozart there is an emerging consensus among those who research this field that there are ways to enhance the creative potentiality of individuals, that elements of the process can be taught and that social organisations – companies, parties, pressure groups, schools and colleges – can be changed to enhance the creative capacity of the people who work in them. To do that, however, requires a shift of perception from within both the organisations themselves and the people in them; both have to acquire a new sense of the possibilities before them. Whether they do that depends upon the kinds of understanding of creative work tacitly at work among them.

Models of creativity

How do people view the creative process? What is the prevailing model? These are empirical questions and in searching for answers to them I followed a well-known practice in the world of adult education of asking student groups their views on the matter. In a series of structured dialogues, we made an attempt to clarify what individual people felt their creative potential to be and to explore how people in this society viewed the creative process itself.

As already explained, six groups were engaged in the dialogue. The groups were made up as in Table 8.1:

Table 8.1 *Groups: gender*

Group	Male	Female	Total
Miners	8	0	8
Nurses	4	10	14
Managers	11	1	12
Supervisors	16	3	19
Tutors	8	11	19
Total	47	25	72

Each group had come together to follow a different course of study and agreed to take part in a half-day session to explore aspects of creativity. Following a short introduction about the purpose of the meeting and their agreement to take part in it, members of each group were asked to complete, individually, a short questionnaire which probed several aspects of their understanding of their own creativity and of the issue of creativity itself. The questionnaire was designed to help them focus their thoughts on a range of issues which would later be subject to open discussion.

Data from the questionnaires indicate a group of people who, whatever their occupation, are quite active in their leisure time. They visit libraries, concerts and plays; they watch television, cook and do household repairs. Five miners claimed to be involved in writing as a creative activity though none attend classes to develop this interest. Eleven of the nurses had, as adults, performed on the stage and five had written poetry. Similar patterns emerged with the other groups. From a list of 18 activities, for example writing poetry, designing buildings, dreaming up new recipes, performing on stage or organising people to do things such as raise money, protest or strike, the top five categories to emerge for the group as a whole were: helping people solve problems, home decoration, writing and telling stories, cooking and creative photography. While music appeared as something people would like to be able to do, very few had attempted to be creative in this field in any way. Nurses and tutors showed an interest in public performance. The group as a whole contained a large number of people who are clearly organisers in their communities and work place. But their creative activity is by an large private and concerned with home-based activities.

One of the questions asked members of the groups to rate their capacity to solve problems and think about new ways of doing things. They were encouraged to answer in respect of any area of work or activity, including their normal employment. What the replies indicated was that both men and women have a positive view of their own problem-solving, creative abilities. The responses to the questionnaires suggest that there are no significant differences between men and women in this respect or between the different groups in the study.

Table 8.2 *Perceptions of creative ability: gender*

	Very good	Good	Not bad	Not so good	Poor	Total
Men	9 (19)	23 (49)	13 (28)	2 (4)	0	47
Women	5 (20)	13 (52)	5 (20)	2 (8)	0	25
Total	14	36	18	4	0	72

Figures in parentheses are percentages

Members of all groups had clear creative ambitions. Each was asked to ist three things they would like to do but at the moment do not do. These were classified into six main groupings as in Table 8.3.

Table 8.3 Creative ambitions and hopes

	Society and politics	Practical work	Education and writing	Music	Painting	Leisure
Miners	1	7	5	5	2	2
Nurses	0	15	15	3	1	1
Managers	2	8	4	10	5	5
Supervisors	4	13	11	6	7	10
Tutors	4	4	17	11	8	4
Total	11	47	47	35	23	22

Neither the world of work or the public realm of politics figures highly on any group's list of creative hopes. Under Practical work, people listed activities like building design, home decoration, landscape gardening. There was a strong interest in writing and in music making. The picture emerges of people nurturing hopes that they may extend themselves and achieve new levels of personal cultural enrichment. These hopes are private, they exist in the realm of freedom rather than of necessity. We can only speculate whether there is a widespread perception in this society which confines ideas about creativity to the realm only of the individual.

One question asked people to list the names of six people, dead or alive, who are thought of as being famous for their creative achievements. A large number of different names were listed with a few standing out on nearly every list: Einstein, Mozart, Picasso, Brunel, Faraday, Leonardo, but also modern figures like Bill Gates or Stephen Spielberg. I classified the names and logged those mentioned by each group. The results are presented in Table 8.4.

Table 8.4 Number of creative people by group

	Engineers	Scientists	Painters	Writers	Entertainers	Politicians	Musicians	Architects
Miners	2	8 (2)	5	4	9 (1)	4	3	1
Nurses	7 (2)	7 (2)	3	10 (1)	9	6	3	1
Managers	9 (2)	8	5	2	13 (1)	4	9 (2)	1
Supervisors	18 (1)	16 (2)	10	4	11	7	15	2
Tutors	9	9	15	26 (1)	17 (2)	8	13	0

Figures in parentheses indicate rank order

Entertainers were the most frequently mentioned group of creative people followed by writers, with engineers and scientists and musicians close behind. Politicians do not figure highly in these lists. There is a hint in these data that people tend to identify creative people in their own domain of interests and that the lists are influenced by the level of education of the group. Miners high-lighted entertainers well known in popular culture: Gary Glitter, Phil Collins, Michael Jackson, the Beatles. Tutors in higher education singled out writers and highlighted names like Shakespeare, Hardy, Dickens. Manufacturing super-visors mentioned engineers and scientists.

Debates among researchers about creativity raise questions about whether the abilities of individuals are genetically determined or substantially shaped by education and training. The members of these groups were asked to comment on this and a strong view emerged that although genetic factors had some significance, the importance of the early social environment and of education and training were far more decisive. There is little support among these people for a genetically determined model of creative gifts.

This point was reinforced by their answers to questions about themselves. The creative gift model would lead us to expect that people would look back over their lives and see themselves as having been most creative during the early years. It turns out not to be the case. In each group, without exception, people reported that they felt they had been at their most creative in the recent past. Some even said their best was yet to come. These are positive observations suggesting that people do see room in their lives for change and improvement and deeper creative fulfilment.

When they were asked about the factors which inhibited their own crea-tive ability, both men and women highlighted the limitations of time, opportu-nity and ability. Shame or the fear of failing to complete a task were not significant factors holding people back. Several of the miners felt that the absence of money held them back from being more creative and this contrasts with the nurses who felt the key constraint was time. Such differences of viewpoint are a reflection of the cultural orientations of different social groups, especially dif-ferent social classes. Access to the realm of freedom for miners requires money; for nurses, managers and tutors it is time that is in short supply.

Each group was asked to break up into smaller groups to consider a number of different questions about creativity. These concerned the character-istics of creative people, how people can be helped to be more creative, whether or not different civilisations or periods of history could be said to be more creative than others and what would have to change in their personal lives for them to be more creative. These 'grouplets' generated lively discussion. The results were reported back in plenary session and further discussion followed. The exercise enabled some of the tacit assumptions people have about creativ-ity to become explicit. They also revealed something of the prevailing catego-ries and ways of thinking about these issues which exist in this society. If we listen to the language used to discuss a phenomenon, we can gain some insight into how that problem is constituted within a culture.

All groups agreed that different civilisations could not be ranked in terms of their creative achievements. The groups who discussed this were emphatic. There was no sense of a glorious past – 'The splendour that was Greece, the Glory that was Rome – to inform their thinking here. They could acknowledge that some creative achievements had universal cultural validity and importance but comparison was impossible. Each culture was unique with its own evolving capacity to be creative. One group captured this in the comment that 'The Greeks were human; the twentieth century is a product of the machine'.

The qualities they all identified that describe creative people included the following: energy, persistence, dynamism, risk-taking and passion. They saw creative individuals as people acutely conscious of their own individuality with a willingness to be unconventional, critical and able to live with tension in their lives. The nurses group highlighted qualities like imagination, curiosity and open-mindedness. The miners highlighted confidence and played down the importance of hard work or education as important factors in the lives of creative people. The managers had acquired from their course some additional ways of conceptualising creativity. They saw creative people as those able to 'step out of the frame' of conventional thinking, to be able to initiate a 'paradigm shift'. The tutors, not surprisingly, place some emphasis on the skills and education of talented people; without a solid background in an area of enquiry, people could not innovate within it.

One question asked people to comment on a number of occupations and rate them in terms of the capacity of people in them to solve problems in fresh ways and to be innovative. In all groups there was a remarkable consensus: politicians and civil servants, particularly the latter, were rated very poorly. It is as if the public realm of politics was run by unimaginative bureaucrats, a telling little glimpse into a facet of British political culture and social imagery.

All groups were agreed that creativity is something that can be released, if people are helped and given the right opportunities. The manager group were clear on this: if certain barriers were removed – guilt, inhibition, fear of being undervalued – and more opportunities were opened up, through time, investment, encouragement and reward, most people could achieve more and think new thoughts. The miners made telling comments: as might be expected from a group whose own school achievements were poor, they did not see education as the vehicle to catalyse creativity. One was very emphatic. 'People confuse intelligence with creativity' he said but noted, 'some people can be thick as bricks but still be very creative'. Their concern was about opportunities to be creative – mainly money and time – and they felt strongly that if more of both was available to people then they could achieve much more in their lives. They took a dim view of the education system insisting, as one put it 'a lot are being left behind' and 'it's going to get worse'. The tutors, on the other hand, saw learning, work with others and participation in creative activity as the elements of creative success.

There are hints here that people perceive creativity through the subtle constraining lenses of their education, their experience and their class. There are gender differences at work, too, though they are not as strong as some might have expected. Both men and women have a positive view of their creative potential. They share a very similar view of the factors that inhibit them. From their discussions, it might be said that the miners placed more emphasis on money as a constraint than did others, particularly the nurses, who were more concerned at their lack of time for creative work, but the issue needs much deeper exploration. The tutors' responses reinforce the strong impression that in this society, class and education are good predictors of a willingness to be creative, especially in the areas of personal expression and the arts.

What was lacking in all groups, and perhaps most surprisingly of all among the managers and supervisors, was a strong, work-based model of creativity. Their perception of creativity was very much framed within the prevailing cultural model of it which clearly has roots stretching back into nineteenth century Romanticism. It is about personal development, individual creative talent and achievement and it is highly focused on activities outside the world of work. This may be a typically British phenomenon where the cultural divide between work and non-work is clear and a reflection of other distinctions bound deeply into the class structure, history and sensibilities of the society as a whole: the two cultures of science and the arts, the distinction between manual and mental labour, the hierarchy of artistic achievement from the merely popular to the serious and a strong undercurrent of individualist philosophy, often with a radical edge, which defines a strong boundary between the worlds of the public and the private. There is certainly something unique in the absence of any sense of creativity being tied to public political discourse.

Towards a conclusion

There is much to be optimistic and excited about when the creative potentiality of people in modern society is considered. Modern societies are dynamic. Industrial and commercial innovation, tied to the relentless growth of new knowledge is one of the hallmarks of economic life. In the global village, cultural diversity can be celebrated and more people can learn to think about their world in new ways than ever before in human history. The arts have become thoroughly secularised and made accessible to millions. More books are being written, sold and read than ever before. In the developed industrial societies secondary and higher education are now a birthright. Modern organisations, both private and public, are structured to generate innovation and change. Millions of people have been freed from the drudgery of mind-destroying work and are now able to celebrate that freedom and indulge themselves in whatever creative fancy turns them on.

Yet there is a paradox. Millions of people still live dull, programmed lives and feel unable to act to change the circumstances of them. In the world of work, there is a relentless pressure to reduce jobs to routine tasks, to control those who do them ever more tightly and to remove from people the guarantee of secure employment. Insofar as the modern economy breeds both inequality and high aspirations, it necessarily nurtures in those who do not succeed, a sense of failure, resentment and hopelessness which lead on inexorably to a sense of powerlessness. Just at the point when the realm of freedom could expand for everyone, the realm of necessity (as discussed in more detail in Chapters 5, 6 and 7) has become ever more restrictive.

The people discussed in this chapter – with the exception of the miners who were about to lose theirs – all had jobs. They all display a rich quality of hope and are possessed of a strong sense of the creative possibilities in their lives. Their hopes were, however, highly individual; their sense of what creativity was did not really embrace the public realm which, were it to be different, could offer more of them the opportunities and the encouragement their further development required. Those in work complained of their lack of time to develop their creative interests further and few saw the realm of work as the arena in which they would realise their dreams.

It seems clear that both the ability and the will exists among ordinary people to be more creative in their lives. Yet they feel constrained in ways which do not allow them to develop their potential. The model of what it means to be creative that they carry in their minds is in no way inconsistent with what social scientists have found out about creativity. They hold to no false theory of giftedness. They acknowledge that people can be creative throughout their lives. They know people need support and encouragement to be creative. How then can their creative potential be fully realised? How can society as a whole benefit more from the resources of innovation of people?

The problem is one of balance, between necessity and freedom, creativity and constraint (see Figure 8.1).

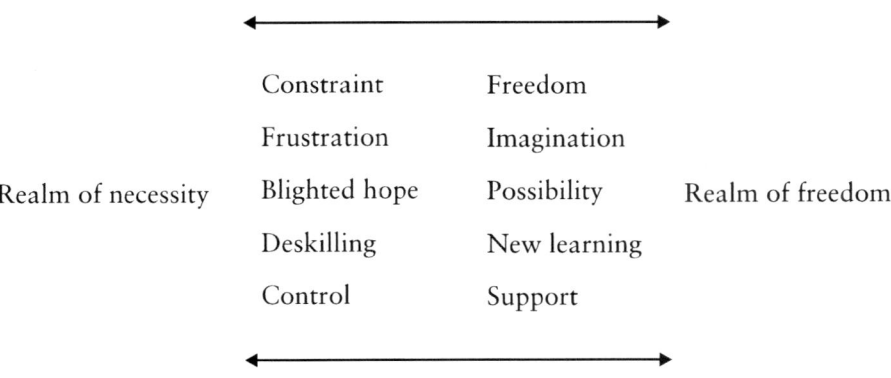

	Constraint	Freedom	
	Frustration	Imagination	
Realm of necessity	Blighted hope	Possibility	Realm of freedom
	Deskilling	New learning	
	Control	Support	

Figure 8.1 *Freedom, necessity, creativity*

It is as if there are contradictory pulls in the society that people experience in the immediate contexts of their daily lives and which, over time, shape decisively how people come to see themselves, the opportunities before them and their own creative potentiality.

In Britain there is a distinctive twist to this tale. The balance between the realm of freedom and the realm of necessity is a changing one. More people than ever before experience their lives as open possibilities. They have found ways to free themselves from the older controls of class, gender and place and through increased income, education and leisure are able to attend more to their own personal development. There are more books, libraries, learning opportunities and in every town and city more films, plays, dance troupes, concerts and exhibitions than there is time in a normal life to see.

From these angles, Britain and other modern societies like it, would have to be described as lively and creative opening up to all who want them, opportunities to be creative in any way they dream of. People are strongly disposed to join clubs and societies so that the networks of what Gellner (1996) has called 'civil society' are dense and vital. There are horticultural clubs, art groups, poetry societies, book clubs, birdwatchers, rambling associations, model engine societies. There are keep fit clubs, youth clubs, women's institutes, ex-servicemen's associations and evening classes galore. There are churches, pressure groups, environmental groups and parish councils. Educational television has opened up a nocturnal zone of learning to give people access to almost any subject they ever dreamed of.

The opportunities within all this for personal development and change, (and for discussion of these themes, see Chapters 3 and 10) for the development of new skills and competencies and creative abilities has never been better. The problem is that none of this activity engages with the creative challenge of changing the society itself, its institutions, structures of power and the predominant modes of organising its economic life. It is the constellation of constraint in these realms of necessity that limit what people can actually do. By the same token, of course, once this is known, acknowledged and acted upon – in work, in the public realm of government, in education, in communities (discussed in Chapter 6) – much could be done to release the creative energies of everyone and expand their realm of real freedom.

The central challenge which many have taken up in the field of community development and community politics (see Smith, 1994) is to enable people to reflect on what they know, share ideas, engage in creative dialogue with one another and learn their way out of the problems they face. Had the people who participated in the discussions which have informed this chapter been drawn from the worlds of community politics or radical political or environmental movements, their models of creativity might have been different and perhaps less individualistic. The paradoxes would still remain, however. People are creative. The modern, global economy is driven hard by the creative energies of engineers, designers, marketing managers, financiers. The world they are creating is none the less one in which millions of other people are denied the opportunity and resources to exercise their creative potentialities. People can realise their creative dreams. But the society around them has to change to enable it to happen.

9 Moral learning in the moral maze

The most sublime act is to set another before you.
William Blake, *Proverbs of Hell*

Adulthood is typically seen as a period of maturity in which people are expected to have acquired their basic values, their sense of purpose and a stable view of themselves as individuals. With adulthood comes a clearer sense of responsibilities and obligations. The judgements people make about how they should organise their lives are expected to be much more rational and considered. It is a period when personal development takes place within clearer guidelines and usually without sudden transformations of identity.

Yet many people experience in their adult lives crises which challenge all their old certainties. In societies which are changing as rapidly and as profoundly as ours, this is inevitable. The life projects which seem credible and realisable when people are in their twenties are unlikely to fit the circumstances of their lives in their thirties, forties and fifties. The values which once seemed so important can often appear irrelevant or contradictory. For many people there are no certain answers to the question: how should I live?

The problems associated with such uncertainty in the life course have been extensively discussed in the contexts of economic change as well as in respect of the status transitions related to ageing. In the former, great stress has been placed on the fact that few people can now expect a job for life; that people can expect to have several significant changes in their careers in employment or, as is the case with Europe's 20 million unemployed, no work at all.

In respect of the latter, it has been well observed by Hockey and James (1993) that ageing is a social process in which people acquire and sometimes have imposed on them new age-related identities. In societies like ours ageing has a strong negative connotation which is part of a socially constructed discourse of dependency. One of the consequences is that too many old people find themselves in positions of powerlessness and abuse in which their moral integrity as adults is denied them. Older people who find themselves in such a position have every reason to look back on their lives with regret and with a sense of having been cheated. They might wonder what changes have taken place in the moral order of their society that this could have happened.

They would not find satisfactory answers to their questions. The changes which have taken place in the moral universe of adults and in the ways in which people construe their moral obligations to other people have not been so well explored. Psychologists have tried to identify the different stages of moral development in adulthood. But how people arrive at a sense of the moral values by which they should live their lives is an empirical question without clear answers. It is one which must be anchored in a sound understanding of the changing historical contexts of people's lives and of their attempts to make sense of those changes. This chapter aims to chart the moral contours of adulthood and to explore how adults adjust to changes in the circumstances of their lives. As Peter Jarvis (1997) has argued, learning is a moral activity, but morality, too, has to be learned.

What the account shows (and the theme is further explored in Chapter 10) is that the attempts of individuals to create moral meaning in their lives has to be related to changes in the public discourse about morality on the one hand and the nature of their life experiences on the other. Both the public discourse and private experience of individuals are bound up with the structures of power and social inequality in society and both change through time.

The importance of understanding these issues cannot be overestimated. In all domains of public and private life, morality matters. The success of modern economies presupposes, as Fukuyama (1995) has argued, values like trust and loyalty. Democratic political institutions require a respect for individual rights and freedom. The recently installed Bishop of London, the Rt Reverend Richard Chartres, in an interview with the *Guardian* newspaper (25 January 1996) made the same point. 'It needs to be said again and again in words of a few syllables,' said the Bishop, 'that market capitalism and democracy presuppose moral conditions.' Personal relationships of a creatively supportive kind are built on values like respect, care for the needs of others and love. The caring capacity of communities and the ability within the institutions of the modern state to care for people in different states of social dependency, is something determined by the underlying structure of moral sentiment within society.

Such values can no longer be read off from the codes of a traditional morality. There are no longer any moral absolutes. Nor can moral codes be defined and imposed. Indeed, as will be seen, the whole notion of a code of morality is unhelpful. To imagine such a code exists and that it can be described is to misconceive the nature and meaning of moral choice. The thrust of the argument developed here is this: moral choices are tied to social contexts. Morality is both learned and situated. Moral learning is continuous throughout life and the understanding of morality people arrive at is related directly to the structures of their lifeworld. Put differently, morality is bound up with the life of institutions and the kinds of experiences people have within them. In the private domains, the forms of life with families and communities is decisive in shaping the moral outlook of individuals. So, too, is the world of work and the public realm of citizenship.

Each domain has a history in which the sedimented moral discourses of the past exert themselves on the present. The moral contours of a divided and fragmented society are structured through the inequalities of power, reflecting the wider inequalities of class, gender and ethnicity. Within these, the subtle gradations of status, age and dependency, exert a further influence shaping moral sentiments and understanding. There can be therefore no overarching morality, no universal moral code, at least not in societies which remain open and differentiated. The peculiar circumstances of the Soviet State, or the radical Islamic Umma, as Gellner (1996) noted, brought together the dominant version of truth – and for the purposes of the argument being developed here, morality – with the structures of power of the state itself. Even with such an apparatus of control, however, there was and is no way of stopping heresies and apostasy. In open societies there will always be open and critical debate about moral values. In divided societies it is also inevitable that some people will acquire such a limited sense of what it is to be moral that the precarious moral frameworks of public life will always be threatened and undermined.

There is no reason to despair in the face of this. Relativism, fragmentation and pluralism may be the central feature of post-modern morality (Bauman, 1993). Modern societies may well have lost a capacity for moral discourse (MacIntyre, 1986). It is, however, better to acknowledge this, to understand its implications and to be clear about how morality can be studied in these circumstances, than either to bemoan the loss of some imagined moral order in the past or to believe there are ethical absolutes to be revived and enforced. The Christian image of the tablets of stone with the ten commandments written on them remains a potent symbol of moral authority. But it is misleading; in a secular society no such tablets exist or can exist. Even if they did, the rules they contain could not provide a guide to action in the moral circumstances of modernity where moral choices people are required to make in the real circumstances of their fast-changing daily lives, are inevitably ambiguous and contradictory. If we can understand better the situated nature of moral sentiment and attitudes, we can debate more effectively the social changes needed either to strengthen or to change them.

The argument developed here is that to achieve such understanding, we need to situate morality in time and to understand the changing nature of moral discourse in modern society. This requires historical analysis. Secondly, morality must be studied as it is lived and learned by adult members of society. Too often discussions about moral learning are centred on the experience of children. They can learn moral precepts but it is as adults they experience the contradictions of their moral choices in the real settings of their relationships and their lives. It is in these contexts – in the private sphere of the family, in the public worlds of work and citizenship – that adults acquire their moral personae, their deepest sense of their values and obligations to others. It is here that the moral contours of modernity need to be studied and in which the detailed ambiguity of moral choice reveals itself.

When this is done a stark fact stands out: there has been no moral decline. Indeed, the whole idea of decline is subjective and without real meaning. What has happened, however, is that, as the boundary between public and private morality has become blurred, the full diversity of moral attitude and action can be more clearly seen. Behind the facades of conventional morality we can now see the deviations, ambiguities and weaknesses of the powerful and the respectable. The realm of the private has been exposed to public scrutiny in ways which reveal great diversity, uncertainty and complexity in moral attitudes. There has been, to borrow a striking phrase from Victor Kiernan (1989, p. 93) 'a widening of the moral franchise'. All can now join in debates about what is right and wrong.

There are no grounds for despair in this. As the situated nature of moral understanding becomes much more explicit, the real moral dangers of modernity can be more clearly identified. They are in the structures of power and opportunity and in the kinds of expectations of people which are woven into the fabric of the institutions in which they work and live. It is these features of how society is organised that shape the experience and, therefore, the moral learning and personality of people. This is a profoundly hopeful proposition. If it is true, then situations can be changed and so, too, can the lives of people in them. They will not change by themselves alone, however. Change requires understanding and an awareness of new possibilities in the social organisation of collective life. That can only come through learning, reflection and dialogue. The resources to enable people to join in the debate are not, however, equally distributed. The real moral challenge of modernity is to further democratise moral discourse and broaden it to cover all aspects of how citizens experience the demos of their lives.

This complex interplay of history and structure, of experience and action, becomes visible in the kind of moral understanding people make of the choices they face and the justifications they give for how they make them. People learn how to do this and what they learn reflects the dilemmas and choices they face and the resources of moral understanding they have access to. Morality, as John Shotter (1993) has stressed, has to be approached as a matter of social practice. From this perspective, people should not simply be viewed as following principles, though many may conceive of their own action in these terms. Rather they should be viewed as struggling to see and create meaning in the choices they make. Morality from this perspective is something being constantly created and re-fashioned. The moral outlook of individuals cannot from this perspective be seen apart from the ways in which they experience their lives. And experience itself is never raw; it is always interpreted. For this reason our understanding of moral experience cannot be separated off from the frameworks of understanding and discourse publically available to people to enable them to understand their own moral choices and values.

Public discourses

Britain is at the moment in the throes of a moral panic. Bishop Chartres, quoted earlier, is reported in the same article as having said that Britain is running out of moral capital and is threatened with barbarism. A recent publication of the National Forum for Values in Education (SCAA, 1996), a body sponsored by the School Curriculum and Assessment Authority, has re-asserted the values of family life and urged the importance of teaching morality in schools. The newspapers are full of stories of crime and immorality. A few crimes have captured the sense of a general moral rot. One of the most poignant recently was that of the murder of James Bulger, the Liverpool toddler. His death focused a great deal of concern about child abuse, the break-up of inner-city communities and out of control children, living symbols of a decline in family values. A recent MORI poll of 500 people taken in Chester, an archetypal 'middle English' town, reported that 60 per cent of people thought that a lack of respect for authority was to blame for Britain's social problems (*The Observer*, 3 November 1996). In the same survey 63 per cent of respondents thought there had been a decline in children's behaviour over the past 20 to 25 years and 45 per cent believed family values worsened.

The image of a decline in family life and in the quality of parenting is a potent one. It situates the moral state of Britain in the structures of the family and the responsibility for its decline on parents, particularly lone parents, most of whom are women. The ideological alchemy of this is to be marvelled at. Some of the most disadvantaged and powerless members of society are then held responsible for what the powerful take to be its moral decline. To blame the family is not, however, a new phenomenon. Thirty years ago there were similar fears about the family focused on the growing numbers of divorces and what was taken to be growing evidence of a decline in sexual morals. The same links now being drawn between family decline and troubles at school were made over thirty years ago. The Archbishop of York, Dr Coggan, told the National Union of Teachers' Conference in April 1962 that, 'It is part of the sickness of modern society that many parents have abdicated from their share of their responsibilities . . . The schoolteacher today finds himself necessarily concerned with the total health and with the character formation of the child in his care' (quoted in Fletcher, 1962, p.15).

Fletcher (1962, p. 16) ironically summed up this particular moral panic:

> Compare us with earlier generations of parent, and we are seen to
> be a very shabby crowd. We are in a state of moral decay, lacking
> firm convictions to protect our children from evil, losing those
> permanencies which were ingrained in all earlier generations. We
> are so concerned with our selfish pursuit of wealth that we ignore
> and ill-treat our children; we have taken advantage of our new
> equality of opportunity to be irresponsible; the emancipated
> women amongst us have contributed to our moral deterioration;
> the kinder and more tolerant fathers amongst us have lost our awe
> and all our majesty; indifferently, uncaringly, without affection
> and concern, we hand our children over to the care of expert
> school masters. A black generation indeed!

There are at least two discourses at work here; the parody of the conventionally dominant view of moral decline is only possible because of the other which is liberal, tolerant, sceptical and pragmatic. In 1962, it was not as fully articulated as it was later to become and nor, perhaps, widely supported or understood.

The moral climate in which these debates took place was a very different one to that of the present day. Britain came through World War II with institutions intact and a new world to build around the values of democracy, decency, fairness and a Welfare State. Fears that the war had rocked the moral foundations of society were expressed but evaporated as people returned to the ordered lives of austerity. Kenneth Morgan (1990, p. 61) summed it all up: 'Britain presented to the post-war eye a spectacle of a somewhat drab society, but one where the workforce was docile and hard at work, sports crowds cheerful and peaceable, schools tranquil and orderly, family life secure. It was not, of course, quite like that; there were differences of income and wealth and not everyone subscribed to the values of the welfare state.

There was no overarching commitment to a particular moral code in the immediate postwar years. The sociologist, Maurice Ginsburg, characterised the mood of the time (that is, 1944) as of 'moral bewilderment' (1956). People, he felt, struggled to understand the consequences of the moral nihilism that they had seen in Nazi Germany but their bewilderment in seeking to do so was not evidence of moral decay but of something else: of a 'moral ferment' which reflected genuine moral difficulties. These included, in his view, the morality of war, the relative importance of freedom in the debates between 'capitalism' and the 'socialised economy', the role of propaganda which breeds suspicion and insincerity about all political ideals, moral fanaticism and the ethics of violence, the discrepancy between private and public morality and the right balance between the opposing ideals of the individual and the community. Because discussion of these issues involves the grading of values, he argued, it was inevitable that people will experience bewilderment and perplexity. But it does not mean they lacked moral courage or that they should accept some faith unquestioningly.

For 20 years after World War II, Britain remained a world power with colonies. Questions of morality always had, therefore, a strong international frame to them. These appeared among the intellectuals in debates about the Cold War and in the late 1950s about the ethics of nuclear weapons. They covered issues of national independence and freedom for colonial dependencies. Subtly woven into the fabric of British patriotism there was a strong line of racism which continues to be an element of British political culture and has been a powerful force shaping the moral outlook of some people.

If the social role of black people was highly circumscribed, so, too, was that of women. In postwar Britain, women who had been in the armed forces or the factories were quickly returned to the family and the home. And it did not take long for the old divisions of class inequality to re-assert themselves. The grid lines of power and control, of attitude and sentiment were quickly drawn. The lifestyles of people from different social classes could easily be distinguished, along with their differences in moral attitude. Moral panics in the 1940s occurred around attempts to defeat the rationing regulations and centred on the character of the Spiv. In a 1970s TV comedy serial the spiv returned as a figure of fun but the values he represented were real enough and resonated with much of the attitudes of many ordinary working class people. Richard Hoggart (1956) had characterised these in the 1950s as short-run hedonism and saw in the emerging materialism of modern attitudes a move away from the stoical but warm-hearted caring for one another of the traditional working class.

The 1960s is a story all of its own. In art and literature, public affairs, popular culture, international relations and in the patterns of everyday lifestyles, the world changed. The 'expressive revolution' as Bernice Martin (1981) called it, opened up a re-evaluation of all values. The public discourse about morality focused on sexuality on ground prepared in the late 1950s with important legislation on prostitution and homosexual law reform. Debates about abortion law reform heightened questions about the morality of the young and the rights of women to the control of their own bodies. It covered the behaviour of the young and their fashions in music and dress. The moral panics of the 1950s, over Teddy Boys, spiralled into those of the 1960s and 1970s over Mods and Rockers and this particular moral theme runs on.

Irreverence was a keynote of the 1960s. Satirical programmes like *That Was the Week that Was* and shows like *Beyond the Fringe* extended the voice of the Angry Young Men of the 1950s and brought into question the legitimacy of all Establishment institutions and forms of traditional authority. The Profumo scandal which conjured up images of prostitutes and spies in high places, of peculiar sexual practices among the rich and of moral rot at the heart of government, was a powerful example of a wider moral malaise. Commentators at the time, as Kenneth Morgan (1990, p. 226) pointed out 'drew inflated parallels with the moral decay that accompanied the later Roman empire, orgies and all, with extensive and inflated Gibbonian comparisons'.

It was all made worse, some believed, by the collapse of moral conviction at the centre of society. Bishop John Robinson was pilloried in 1962 for publishing his book *Honest to God* which questioned over-simplified images of God in Christianity. It all amounted to the view that traditional values were under threat and that the moral centre of society could not hold. As the means of mass communication improved through television and the press, the images of moral decline became much more obvious and the insular, always prurient worlds of conventional society broke down.

The shift in moral discourse evident in postwar Britain is from a widespread concern about the organising values of society as a whole to the morality of private lives. The cataclysmic changes of the 1960s brought the whole question of individual freedom to the heart of every public debate – about sexuality, family life, abortion, drugs, education and so on. In the bleak years of the late 1970s the terms of these debates altered and in the period of Mrs

Thatcher's premiership, the moral agenda changed profoundly. She detected in British society an eroded sense of the moral responsibility of the individual. She wished to promote self reliance, family life and values, individual responsibility, national pride and to roll back the frontiers of the state.

She stood accused, even by members of her own party, as a reactionary, someone who upheld Victorian values and someone who, in Gilmour's view, 'danced with dogma' (Gilmour, 1992). Other critics had harsher things to say, condemning the greed, hypocrisy, the lack of concern for the needs of the poor and the unjustifiable moral blindness of Tory foreign policy. Tory social policy victimised and demonised the poor, particularly single parents; they blamed the unemployed themselves for their lack of work and took a strong and illiberal line on questions about immigration and race relations. In the realm of personal morality – paradoxically, given the behaviour of many senior Tories themselves – Thatcher governments took a hostile view of homosexuality, claiming to reinforce the natural values of family life and married love.

Yet the moral project of the Tory Right failed. During the years in which it sought its hegemony, other values asserted themselves: feminism, gay rights, the environmental movement and the peace movement of the 1980s articulated different moral concerns and heightened a broader public awareness of the ways in which values and action are related. Campaigns to defend the health service, to fight off privatisation of public services, to protect the environment and to develop public services in tune with the needs of the vulnerable and dependent, all contribute to reinforce the values of decency, fairness, public service and respect for the rights of others. In this respect Britain is a much more open society than it once was and one in which people have a much greater awareness and sophisticated, undogmatic understanding of the moral issues in their lives.

Private narratives

Changes in the public discourse about morality are one thing. To understand what they imply for the ways in which adults construe the moral meaning of the own lives, another approach is needed. An effort has to be made to trace out the relationships between personal experience and moral understanding. The moral dilemmas and ambiguities of individuals are related to the logic of the social situations in which they find themselves. These are structured within the parameters of class, gender, age and ethnicity, or, in short, the structure of inequality and power in society.

Such structures shape moral sentiment in three ways. First, they define the ways in which people experience the other people in their lives. It is in this context that people are either valued or devalued, treated with respect or not. Second, they constrain the ways in which people can give an account of the moral rationale behind their thoughts and their deeds. All human groups seek to legitimate their beliefs and behaviour. These take the form of narratives which members can draw upon to confer meaning on experience and they differ from one group to another in a complex society where there is no overarching framework of beliefs. Finally, structures of inequality and power shape the ways in which people construe their personal needs and interests and the commitments towards other people which flow from these.

The link between structure and sentiment is not, however, direct; one cannot be read off from the other. The link is mediated through what people learn about the moral principles guiding them in what they do and in how they modify those principles in the light of their changing experiences in the principal domains of their lifeworld in the family, work and in the communities in which they live their lives as citizens. From this perspective, the moral fragmentation of modernity takes on a new meaning. It does not refer to some profound transformation of a formerly ordered system of morality which held society together. Rather it refers to a process of increasing differentiation of experience and understanding of moral choices. This could be a cause for celebration. In a society with open channels of communication, the understanding of the Other which is at the heart of morality, could be widened and deepened. Moral discourse could be broadened. Moral precepts could be tested in open debate. At the end of World War II, Maurice Ginsburg argued that the way to reduce moral perplexity and bewilderment was not through the unquestioning acceptance of faith, religious or otherwise. 'What is needed' he wrote, 'is greater moral courage and above all greater knowledge of social facts and a development of ethical theory equal to the task of evaluating and interpreting them' (1961, p. 9). With such conditions in place, morality could have a much firmer foundation.

The danger, on the other hand, is that with complexity and diversity in lifestyles comes prejudice, a narrowness of perspective and an atrophy of sympathy and respect for the Other. People who themselves are insecure and uncertain about their beliefs are not likely to be open to others in ways which might challenge their moral outlook. People of strong moral convictions are just as incapable of understanding the Other, but for different reasons. Moral choice is always complex. Human beings cannot always anticipate all the consequences of the choices they make. They cannot understand all the conditions of their action or perceive clearly the needs of the Other. Moral rigidity is itself immoral.

The fluidity and complexity of change which challenges all moral understanding has to be understood. This is what Ginsburg meant by knowledge of the social facts. If the full meaning of moral fragmentation is to be understood, it is important to find out both what people claim to know about the moral order of their society and how they know about and justify the moral choices they have to make. This huge task must be broken down into more manageable steps. We must explore the questions in respect of different domains of moral experience and examine them from the perspectives of different groups of people which reflect the contours of social differentiation in modern society.

The family domain

This is not the place to try and describe the full moral complexity of family relationships in modern society. It is important, though, to consider how such a description could be built up, given the kinds of information we have in our society about the private domain of the family. Two general points stand out immediately: first, the family has been for a long time the central focus of moral concern. Family failure has long been held to be at the root of many other kinds of failure in society – of crime, violence, delinquency and immorality of all kinds. The current moral panic in Britain about parenting is a telling example of this point. Second, the psychological interior of family life has become much more public. Social research and a wider public interest in family life has been stimulated by political concerns about the stability of the family as an institution, about the roles of men, women and children within it and about the moral complexity of those roles and relationships. Issues like contraception, abortion, violence, the abuse of children, the separation of parents and the effects of poverty on family life, have generated research and public commentary, not to mention political action and legislative change, which has blown away the secrecy that once surrounded them.

The social changes which debates about these issues reflect are experienced directly by individual people. The diverse textures of that experience, unique to each individual and the unpredictable features of their lives, reflect also the differences in age, gender, class and power within society and the precise forms these take at different points in time. These are the features of the organisation of society which structure private experience and moral choice. The legitimating rhetoric of family life encourages a view of the family as the site in which people should find love and security and in which children can be properly cared for.

This is not and never has been, however, how family life has always been experienced. For every account of happy family life there are others which contradict it. Love, trust, support, care, recognition, safety, personal growth, happiness, are qualities associated with family life. Violence, betrayal, indifference, exploitation, denial, danger, emotional trauma, uncertainty and fear are the features which, to varying degrees, have characterised the family life of significant numbers of people in each generation of this society. For them, the dominant rhetoric of family life describes an alien reality. The sense of the Other to grow in the minds of people who have experienced such extreme circumstances, is a severely diminished one. Their understanding of the moral choices of their lives is formed in a restricted frame in which their own needs for personal survival and their impoverished sense of what their interests are, predominate over any care or concern for the Other.

The dominant discourse about the values which govern family life bears little resemblance to the way the family functions or how it is constituted. In the past quarter century there have been profound changes in the composition of households in the developed industrial societies. Single-person households represent about 25 per cent of all households. In the past decade there has been a doubling in the number of one-parent families. Between one-third and one-half of marriages now end in divorce. More than half of all wives now work in paid employment.

Changes in structure have been accompanied by shifts in values. The old nostrums are no longer credible. When divorce increases, what does 'till death do us part' mean? Evidence of the growth of adultery which Annette Lawson (1988) interpreted as the masculinisation of sex, raises profound questions about the changed meaning and significance of values such as fidelity. Between one-quarter and one-half of all married women have affairs. Lawson did not discover moral decline in her interviews with people who were unfaithful to their partners. She did discover that people still valued such things as fidelity and did recognise their moral dilemmas. They did, however, find ways to neutralise them claiming, for example, that they were not the agents of their own infidelity. Some claimed they had affairs on impulse; others that they were seeking to realise other important values in their lives. Some justified their actions in terms of changes in the moral climate and drew liberally on literature, for example D H Lawrence or on feminist writers such as Marilyn French, to justify their actions and to renegotiate the marriage contracts they had with their partners. 'Rarely' writes Lawson, 'did people consider their own behaviour to be directly the result of early influences . . .' (1988, p. 105).

Those caught between the attractions of an illicit affair and the compelling expectations that they should be faithful, have to resolve their moral dilemmas somehow. The social and economic changes that have taken place, especially increases in employment opportunities for women, have increased the range of opportunities available to people to be unfaithful. Through infidelity, people experience a change in personal identity underlying the point that the moral personality is not a fixed element of the self but is something which alters as circumstances alter and people find new meaning in their lives.

This general point is poignantly reinforced in the experience of Muslim women in Britain trying to come to terms with complex changes in both the world of their religion and of the society they live in. The clear moral codes of Islam provide no easy solution to the dilemmas of living as a woman in a secular western society. Studies of the experience of Muslim women in West Yorkshire (Afshar, 1994) have shown how many young women who have grown up in Britain and have been educated here, now turn to their religion and wear the veil to fashion for themselves a status and identity which the host society does not offer them.

This is not just an intergenerational acceptance of values. It is a response to a complex situation. The central hypothesis of this research conducted over a decade with three-generational households in West Yorkshire proved false. The researcher had expected that the younger generation would rebel against older family and religious values. Not so; for, as Haleh Afshar puts it, 'history had intervened, as had deteriorating economic conditions and political exigencies' (1994, p. 129). Many young women adopt the veil to assert their political independence, nationality and to reject consciously western values, establishing a new sense of self and a new understanding of their place in history and society.

In both examples in the case of those who are unfaithful and in respect of the changing values of ethnic minority young women, people are struggling with the moral ambiguities which are part of their lives in their families. In neither case could their problems be seen as part of a contrast between human failing and moral absolutes. Their moral choices can only be understood in the context of their life situations and the resources of understanding available to them to find meaning in them.

This broad approach to moral conduct in the family could be focused on any number of complex issues. They include the values governing the rearing and treatment of children, the care of the elderly, decisions on family-building and sex, on the sharing of household work and on the choices to be made dealing with the vast complexity of adolescent behaviours. The choices people do make in relation to these issues describe very different patterns of family life and behaviour. They cover the spectrum of loving devotion to systematic violence.

Each point on that spectrum is a structure of learning in which people forge some understanding of the moral rules by which they try to live. Each issue they struggle with builds up their experience and understanding and their practical capacity to make moral choices and formulate the basic precepts to govern them. When those rules depart from the conventional discourse of family values, their justifications – what Matza (1969) once referred to as the 'techniques of neutralisation' – have to be learned too.

There are many situations, however, when people do not act in accord with principles or when the urgency of the moment overrides their capacity to control themselves. Family life generates stresses which can be well beyond rational control. How people make sense of such stress and the complex feelings which are part of it, is a facet of how they learn and is shaped by the resources of moral learning open to them. These include the media – particular soap operas which now cover issues like domestic violence and incest in their story lines – friends, counsellors, social workers and priests. Above all, however, they learn from the patterns of family interactions themselves. Where there is violence, it is unlikely that trust and respect will flourish.

Surveys suggest that adult people most frequently cite their parents as the source of their own moral values. A recent *Guardian*/ICM poll found that 88 per cent of respondents (a random sample of 1,202 adults) cited their parents as the ones who had set the kind of moral lead they would wish everyone to follow (*The Guardian*, 7 November 1996). Moral actuality is much more complex than this. The family of origin can provide only the broadest of ethical orientations. As with education, what is learned in the home is not sufficient to help people resolve the moral ambiguities and doubts which adults experience.

The moral framework of early family life is something people can reject or re-define. Only this is certain: the experience of one generation is necessarily different from previous ones; the settings, dilemmas, and choices people face in their lives are bound up with profound changes in society and moral discourse. That people will say they got their values from their families is not evidence that they have done so; it is evidence that in this kind of society, people lack a clear perception of the sources of and justifications for the values they imagine they live by.

The dominant discourse about the values of family life is a fractured one. Half a century ago, the family was perceived as the fundamental institution of society, the bedrock of the Welfare State. It was the institution through which people, through love and the self respect it nurtures, absorbed into themselves an understanding of and sympathy for the Other. It was the firm foundation for effective and responsible citizenship. It existed to promote the well being of its members but was seen as having a wider public role in relation to a wider community. Throughout much of the postwar period, the thrust of social policy – in housing, education, health care and income maintenance – was to support the family.

Radical criticism of the family in the 1970s challenged this discourse but did not damage it. Now the family is a site for the achievement of entirely private hopes and ambitions: love, happiness, security, being cared for. It is also the stage on which people can parade their social status and their material possessions. It is a site of private consumption and of private obligations. When it works, it works well. But high expectations of private happiness are severely tested by the normal realities of insecurity, illness and isolation. Against the additional challenges of violence, infidelity and blighted hopes, the private family has few moral defences.

The world of work

The Other is experienced also in the world of work although this domain of human experience is not normally discussed in relation to morality. Yet work is fundamental to the moral order of society. Through the division of labour people are dependent on one another. The market economy only works because of what Emile Durkheim once called the 'non-contractual elements of contract, that is, the general commitment to the moral principle that people have a duty to fulfil their legal obligations to one another (see Coser, 1971, p. 35). In contemporary management theory this has come to be discussed as the importance of trust in business.

The quality of services available to people in health, education, legal practice, and the manner of public administration in respect of all the decisions of government, depend on the existence of high levels of professional ethics among doctors, nurses, lawyers, teachers, social workers and civil servants. These ethics stress the importance of values like impartiality, confidentiality and respect for persons, accountability, truthfulness, honesty and responsibility.

The whole world of non-professional work presupposes that people understand contractual obligations and will give a fair day's work for a fair day's pay. Organised work depends on values like honesty, responsibility and respect for persons. At work people are expected to co-operate with each other and not to discriminate against colleagues on grounds of their race or gender. There is a presupposition of loyalty to the enterprise and its goals and an expectation, often embedded in negotiated contracts, that people will be dealt with fairly and legally and not, for example, be exposed to dangers which threaten their health. Some organisations see themselves, in the language of business ethics, as 'ethical organisations'. Both in the way they treat their employees and deal with suppliers and customers, they seek to be governed by clear moral principles and acknowledge that there are different 'stakeholders' in business – shareholders, managers, employees and customers – whose needs and interests need to be balanced out. They try to respect employees by involving them in decision-making or by developing training plans for them.

In the conflictual world of capitalist production, however, there is not always harmony of interest and purpose between employers and their employees. The historic roots of values like solidarity and support for the weakest members of society which are embedded in the trade union movement, are in reaction to the ways in which human beings are treated as means to the employer's ends rather than as ends in themselves. At the heart of the history of organised labour is an ethical imperative: a demand for justice and fairness. It has manifested itself as demands that the rights of workers – to be free to join trades unions, to withdraw their labour, to have a job, to be treated fairly, to be governed by procedures, not to be discriminated against – should be acknowledged by employers and protected by the state.

In the daily experience of work, people encounter others in ways that require moral decisions. People have to be reliable; they have to be loyal to one another; they have to offer each other support. Or they can choose to be governed by none of these principles. It is clear that the world of work is part of the moral order of society. It is through the processes of socialisation into work that young adults acquire some of the most important moral lessons of their lives. Wolfgang Lempert (1994) has made this point very effectively in a study of the ways in which 21 young fitters in a German firm acquired their understanding of morality. Their experience of work was very important. Their understanding of themselves as moral agents with obligations and responsibilities derived from their need to take responsibility for their work. Their understanding of values like love and empathy for others was forged in relation to questions of solidarity with and loyalty towards people with whom they worked.

Two issues arise from this: first, how are the moral imperatives of work experienced in different contexts of employment? Second, how have the moral contours of work changed? What changes have taken place in the dominant moral discourse about work?

The language of work provides clues to the answer of the first question. We talk about jobs, about work, about careers and about professions. We talk about needing a job and having a vocation. Joe Kincheloe (1995) has developed the idea of 'good work' as a way of building an ethical basis for economic institutions. Work, he claims, involves a sense of completion and fulfilment. The good workplace is one which builds on democratic principles and in which people are respected as persons with rights – to participate in decisions, to work creatively and to grow as human beings. The contrast he draws is between the idea of work and the idea of a job which describes necessary, often uncongenial tasks done only to enable someone to have a wage with which to buy things. Jobs are necessary, but they lack the moral imperatives of 'good work'.

Kincheloe's argument, rooted in a tradition of critical social theory, echoes back through time to the major challenges in politics and social theory to the ways in which the organisation of work in capitalist society dehumanises the worker. It alludes indirectly to countless studies of industries and jobs and Fordist production methods which have highlighted the boredom, monotony and destructive character of industrial work. The history of trades unionism and of the Labour Movement over this same period is one of working people fighting to regain their dignity and security against circumstances which promoted ruthless self interest; it is a history of a search for solidarity and belonging against policies which exploit people and divide workers from one another.

Much of the work millions of people are expected to do demands little of their creativity, their intelligence or their capacity to work constructively with one another. The premium is placed instead on restricting what they do to the narrow confines of the task. The settings in which many people work prevent creative communication among them and the organisations they work in elicit little loyalty or respect. The value placed upon people by the employing organisation is invariably reflected in the value people themselves put on the work they do. Work becomes a means to another set of ends which are essentially private and self interested and which people pursue with energy and, if necessary, with aggression.

Nevertheless, the absence of employment is a real threat to personal dignity and security. Unemployment is a mark of Cain which excludes people from the wider society in which they live. People have to balance the demands of their jobs with their prospects if they were to lose them. Keeping a job can often involve uncomfortable moral compromises. Employees may have to do things they regard as morally wrong, for example colluding with actions which damage the environment or which treat customers as fools or turning a blind eye to malpractice in the work place. To take a principled stand in relation to such issues is a great risk; not to do so is equally difficult.

Yet there are work places which nurture, require and reward staff who do take such a stand. Nurses in hospitals are effective to the extent that they act responsibly to patients and to other colleagues; they have to be caring, tolerant, non-judgemental, honest and truthful and able to reflect critically on their own professional practice. There is much in their daily experience of work which reinforces theses values. At the same time, of course, there is much to erode them and the same would be true of other professionals working in public sector human service organisations which are being driven to reflect the values of the market place. Job advertisements for senior staff in Social Service organisations invariably demand qualities in people normally associated with managers in the private sector – drive, negotiation skills, strategic planning, customer-focused work orientation and an ability to prepare their organisations for competition. In such a climate, many staff experience real tension between the values of the service for which they work and the pressures of the management systems governing what they do.

Human service organisations with a duty of care to people do not necessarily nurture a climate of caring and concern for the other. There are too many reported examples of children who have been abused in local authority care or in children's homes, or old people subjected to violence and intimidation in nursing homes, for anyone to feel complacent on this point. Where there are real imbalances of power between carers and their dependants and where the work of carers is outside the effective view of a wider public, the abuse of power and the denial of the rights and freedoms of individuals is a real possibility. Under such circumstances the values of a profession or of a particular service are not strong enough to prevent people acting immorally towards one another. The moral personality of employees has to be rooted in something stronger than the workplace itself. The moral understanding of people, their underlying sense of right and wrong and their ability to continue to learn to understand the differences between the two, is something bound up with their own experience of being cared for themselves and for the ways in which they have learned to value the broader community and society in which they live.

The world of community

It is for this reason that a description of the moral contours of society has to go beyond the organisation of work environments. People can, within limits, select the kinds of work they wish to do. However much work shapes the ways in which people build up their moral understanding and commitments, their values cannot be read off simply from the jobs they do. The history of organised labour validates this general point. So, too, does that of charity and philanthropy. Had the circumstances of their labour which brutalise human beings been decisive, the visions of a better world which emerged from that history would never have been articulated. But they were. If wealth and privilege necessarily meant blindness to the needs of the dispossessed, there would not have been a resilient tradition of philanthropy in Britain. What Frank Prochaska (1988) has called 'the voluntary impulse' still informs philanthropic practice and has had such a profound effect in shaping moral and democratic sentiment in Britain.

People from different social backgrounds can be inspired by ideals which are not tied to the circumstances of their class. History shows they can be inspired by wider ideals: from religion, from the tenets of political ideology and from a fundamental empathy with the plight of fellow human beings and a sense that the world could be built on different moral principles. The voluntary impulse always implied an attachment to a particular locality. 'The impulse to organise oneself and one's neighbours in a cause,' writes Prochaska (1988, p. 6) 'is one of Britain's most distinctive traditions'. And it is not confined to the actions of the rich or the great charitable institutions. There is a potent tradition of philanthropy among the poor and working class people themselves. The twentieth century has seen the development of state provision of services where once the charitable foundations worked, but the voluntary sector is still vast and still vital to the functioning of the Welfare State. Through donations, fundraising events, relentless committee work, visiting and spending time with others, volunteers express directly a generalised commitment to the welfare of their fellow human beings. In doing so they learn much about the needs they seek to address and their involvement transforms them as human beings.

The springs of such involvement lie deep in the structures and sentiments of local communities and flow through the patterns of social relationships, commitments and social identities they sustain. From this angle, morality is tied into how people experience the society around them and how that society facilitates their understanding of and respect for other people. For many people, community is a myth. Some writers have argued that civic responsibility is in deep decline and that the social capital of society has been run down to a dangerous level (Knight and Stokes, 1996). Membership of voluntary organisations is declining; church membership is falling; trades union membership has fallen by 40 per cent in fifteen years. Knight and Stokes claim that the decline is so bad in many urban areas that they can be described as war zones where people, trapped into dealing with their own personal safety from the threats of crime and violence, develop either a siege mentality or leave.

In the urban geography of modern societies, there is an affluent suburb for every inner-city wasteland. But the lifestyles they sustain are highly privatised and individuated. This is not just a matter of personal preference, but of economic necessity. The growth of home ownership presupposed the employment of women and the two income family. Households structured around conventional notions of family life have very little time to service needs other than their own.

The structure of consumer society depends on the high levels of private affluence of the majority and the social exclusion of significant minorities. The unequal society is a way of securing the social conditions of a flexible labour market: the willingness to take any work on offer to avoid the slippy slope of being at the bottom of the pile and, more importantly, to maintain the convenient fiction that the excluded have only themselves to blame. They too could work hard and save and be respectable if only they choose to do so. J K Galbraith (1992) characterised this state of affairs as the 'culture of contentment' and it does not bode well for the development of redistributive social policies and for the development of a more tolerant and open society.

From the point of view of the excluded, such a society appears uncaring, without real hope for them and beyond their ability to influence. Exclusion takes many forms: poverty, homelessness, racism, homophobia. It can be experienced in many different ways: as deprivation, violence, loss of personal dignity and hopelessness. Different groups respond to it in different ways: some organise to combat it; others retreat, finding some solace in drugs or in a lifestyle so private that they can remain immune to the wider society around them. Some turn to crime, a popular option among the young. Thousands of others spend their time in a daily struggle to retain some semblance of ordinary life and dignity on the rim of an abyss and trapped to look after themselves alone for there is no space in their lives to care realistically for others.

   Each choice brings its own moral predicaments and contradictions. Is it really wrong to steal if there is not enough money to feed the family? What is the meaning of personal responsibility if there are no jobs? How can the values of family life be nurtured when people who are homeless are driven to live in bed-sits or cramped hotel rooms? Is it wrong to deny gay and lesbian couples the possibility of adopting children just because of their sexual orientation? Why should the Protestant values of hard work and individual responsibility be taken seriously when some people are obscenely wealthy on the basis of gambling, inherited wealth, political and social connections or shifting interest rates? Is it so wrong to steal when shops can pass on the cost of shoplifting to the consumer or households can recoup the losses from burglary through insurance? Is it so irrational to live dangerously and irresponsibly in the present tense when there is no future? Is it so wrong to lie when the truth leaves everything unchanged? If someone is taught by their social position that they are not valuable people, why should they attach value to anyone else? How, if people never have contact with those who are at the edges of society, is it possible for them to empathise with and understand them?

   The point is this: moral values can never be absolute. They are always likely to conflict with one another and because the social situations of individual people are so different, it is never possible to apply rules of a universal kind to the choices people face. There is a social shape to moral choice and the ethical dilemmas people confront reflect their social position, the resources of moral understanding available to them and the prevailing moral discourse in the major domains of experience: family life, work and community.

Conclusion

The thrust of the argument developed here is this: as people grow older they experience their world in different ways. The moral capital they inherit from their families – which is in any case a very variable inheritance in a highly differentiated society – is not sufficient to guide them through the 'moral maze' of adulthood in the different domains of their lives. What people learn about morality is shaped by the circumstances of their social position and the narrative resources available to them to enable them to understand the justifications for and the contradictions and ambiguities of the moral choices they make. These narratives are not private; they are drawn from a wider range of discourses in society, some of which claim dominance over others. The public discourses about morality change through time. They change in response to political challenge, for example the Women's Movement over the past quarter century has shifted the moral discourse on family life. They change in response to new information, new technology, scientific discovery and new ways of thinking about society.

Changes in public discourses become part of the changing experience and moral understanding of adults as they struggle to make sense of their own priorities, values and choices. Some people respond to change by clinging tenaciously to older belief systems. Martin Jacques (*The Guardian*, 9 November 1996) has characterised the efforts of the 'political class' and religious leaders to re-assert traditional values as 'authoritarian nostalgia' for a moral golden age. Such an age did not exist. If anything, Jacques argues, things have got better. 'Far from living in less moral times,' he writes, 'we now live in a more demanding moral climate. When I was a boy in the fifties, child abuse, the sexual division of labour, violence against women, paedophilia and environmental awareness, to name but a few, were undiscussed and largely unrecognised. Our moral repertoire has expanded enormously. We are now far more morally aware.'

The expanded moral discourse is not, however, enough. Aristotle explained two thousand years ago that morality is inseparable from how people live in the particular circumstances of their lives. I hope to have shown in this chapter that the rapidly changing social and economic arrangements of modern society are a constant challenge to the moral understanding of adults. The moral franchise of modern society has broadened but the focus of moral concern remains surprisingly narrow. The dominant discourse about morality is largely limited to the domain of family life and sexual behaviour and when it broadens out to include the values of society as a whole, it is fixated on the bad behaviour of the young. The moral contours of work and of community are largely ignored leaving intact structures in society which erode moral sensibility.

Pleas for more moral education of the young or for a return to traditional moral values miss the main moral point: morality cannot be legislated; it has to be lived. Its character derives from two sources: from the kinds of lives people are expected to live and in the ways they experience one another and, second, from within the resources of moral understanding of the society and the ways in which these are articulated by different groups of people. Morality is learned. If we want to understand it we must enquire further how the social circumstances of people's lives govern their access to different ways of comprehending it.

10 Personal change in adulthood

The fox condemns the trap, not himself.

William Blake, *Proverbs of Hell*

Know Thyself.

Temple inscription, Delphi

Personal identities in adulthood are not fixed. People change. Each development in a human life has to be fitted into the frameworks of understanding that people have evolved to interpret their experience and this invariably involves new learning. La Rochefoucauld in his *Maxims*, saw this in the seventeenth century. 'We come quite fresh to the different stages of life, and in each of them we are usually quite inexperienced, no matter how old we are' (1986, p. 89). Sometimes changes are profound and dramatic. The wars and revolutions of the twentieth century shattered the hopes and dreams of millions profoundly altering how people could make sense of their lives and their world. Even within the contexts of the routines of ordinary everyday life, personal tragedies unfold which require fundamental changes in lifeplans, attitudes and understanding. Death, illness, accident, family breakdown all require change in how people view themselves and interpret their experience.

Some changes take place quickly. Religious conversion – Damascus Road experiences – are examples of this. Or perhaps, too, falling in love! Others unfold slowly over time and are experienced as a growing conviction that something should and will change, that a new direction will be found. Such changes involve a dialogue with the self, a re-assessment of purpose, a new attitude to the past. Once the conversation is started there is no end to it; as a new attitude towards the self emerges a new self is born. None of us ever escapes the past. The personal biographical past cannot be erased. It can be redefined, coloured, distorted, and repressed; it can be cherished, despised, regretted. It can be hidden but it cannot be ignored. All newer versions of the self, all claims to new identity have to be manageable within the persistent claims of the old.

All personal change is a form of learning or questioning. For some it is a search to discover who they are or what they might be. This kind of searching is the key existential task of the young. For others all is clear; they know who they are and what their fate is. None can escape the requirement continually to verify who they are and the truth of what they believe about themselves. Personal insight is for some almost impossible; they require the help of therapy. Others display a form of rigidity that entertains no doubt, no contradiction. They cling to a clear view of themselves for there is so much for them to lose if they were to question what they know.

In modern societies, people can choose the identities they wish to have. Giddens (1991) has captured this in the idea that modern identities are 'open'. We are not confined to the identities ascribed to us by the social positions into which we were born. In contrast, therefore, to countless past generations of human beings, there is both openness and uncertainty in how people in societies like ours will come to think of themselves and their destinies. The openness has, of course, limits. These are set by the social and political arrangements of the society which constrain human ambition into narrower channels and limit the choice of identities to a range that are credible and valued. Those who try to become what they cannot be risk being confined to the asylum. Those who pretend too much to be what they are not are invariably caught out. Failures in projecting the self images people wish others to accept is, as the sociologist Goffman (1971) pointed out, a permanent risk in all performances on the social stage.

These broad observations have many implications for the ways in which we understand the idea of lifelong learning. For the purposes of this chapter, the most important of these is this: learning throughout life embraces much more than the continuous development of skills and understanding in particular areas of human knowledge and practice. It embraces, too, self knowledge and this covers both thoughts and feelings and includes knowledge of how people can explore their own self understanding. The ancient Greeks knew full well that knowledge of the self was the starting point of all knowledge and that it was among the most difficult intellectual tasks of them all to acquire.

The development in modern societies of psychoanalysis, counselling and a vast range of other means to seek personal insight and understanding, reflects both the difficulties people have in making sense of themselves – for all of us need help in doing so – and the fact that the forms of self understanding open to us, are not personal and private, but are part of a wider cultural discourse which supplies particular ways of reflecting on personal experience and identity. The culture also supplies a range of identities to choose from, both legitimate and illegitimate. The criminal and the priest are members of the same society. From an infinity of possibilities, however, societies are so structured to value and nurture a more limited range of options. The roles and identities geared to the economic order of society are very strongly defined. So, too, are those tied to the life of families, kinship and communities. Whatever choices people feel they have made to become what they are, it is always possible to detect those felicitous patterns of correspondence between private hopes and choices and the requirements of society for particular kinds of roles to be performed. People end up, though of course not always or indeed inevitably, doing the things that society requires of them.

Since the order of society defines the life chances of different groups of people, it follows that what people can become is something related directly to their social position. The distinct and highly variable cultural nuances of different social settings, each reflecting the tangled history of class differences, regional cultures, nationality and ethnicity, provide signposts for identities that point in many directions. Some routes can be more freely chosen than others. Some are debarred to most people or require particular skills or commitments before the journey can begin.

Differences in the symbolic importance of roles and identities within and between different societies – for some roles are more highly valued than others – reflect more than any functional importance that can be attached to them. The exercise of power by those groups who possess it is decisive in determining what roles and identities will be publicly acknowledged and valued.

Contemporary culture, which some have characterised as 'postmodernist' to capture the idea that the old certainties about knowledge, culture and society itself have evaporated, provides a vast range of resources and ideas from which people can build their unique personal identities. From this perspective, modern society can be shown to be highly differentiated, essentially unstable and fast-changing, and reflecting in its fragmented diversity the complexity of the global cultural influences available to everyone through world-wide communication technologies. Under such conditions people can become whatever they like or, at least, to believe in the possibility of it. They are no longer trapped by the force of tradition. All can escape the constraints of their original families and communities or the effects of their first schooling. Not only can people redefine the meaning of the past, they can reconstruct themselves and insulate themselves from their previous identities as they build new ones.

The relationships between personal experience, personal identity and social change are fluid and complex for they are mediated through changing patterns of culture in society and shifts in structures of power and communication. The outcome is this: groups of people differ profoundly from one another in terms of the resources open to them to enable them to reach new descriptions of themselves, their experience and their hopes. Many people remain trapped within ascriptive images of themselves which have been built up for them and which are imposed by others. Lacking the means to question this they remain confined within the narrow assumptions of their lives.

But never without unease and, sometimes, dis-ease. Behind all the masks of social conformity people search for authenticity and meaning. They strive to discover the central core of meaning in their lives and to ground the mundane details of their everyday reality in a wider purpose. Religion provides the framework for this for some people. In a secular society, however, it has to have a different basis and many are available: to be happy, to be free, to be rich, to care for others. The old Protestant virtues of hard work and salvation no longer provide the rationale for what people do with their lives.

What David Reisman (1961) called 'inner-directedness' which described a highly individual approach to life stressing values like autonomy, responsibility and being true to oneself, has given way to 'other-directedness' in which people search desperately for the acknowledgement of others. They find it in fashion, in the shared icons of popular culture and in being the same as other people, consuming the same things, thinking the same thoughts. This is the paradox of postmodern individuality: people ground their sense of personal uniqueness in their embrace of the common patterns of living of their society.

This tryst with the Devil carries great risks of failure. The sustained fashionable identity requires money. The consumer role must be serviced with a continuous flow of income which can be turned into expenditure or credit. Failure in the market for consumer goods is a prerequisite for the success of those markets for they depend on unrealised hopes and ambitions, jealousies and unfulfilled desires. But failure to be the successful worker, wife, neighbour, holiday maker, becomes a mark of Cain, a symbol of personal inadequacy and failure.

Erich Fromm tried to capture these dilemmas in the form of an existential choice: we can choose either to 'have' or to 'be'. He meant by that we can choose to construct our individuality in ways which allow us to realise the material ambitions of modern society to have money, wealth, consumer goods, or we can focus on how we relate to other people and on values concerned with authenticity and love in human relationships. He comes from a tradition of writers whose central concerns are with the condition of human *alienation* from themselves and from others. It is a tradition focused on the many ways in which people fail to acknowledge or understand the real nature of their humanity and through that are unable to find the firm foundations for a coherent, purposeful and ultimately realistic sense of self.

Under such conditions people fail to find significant meaning in their lives. The danger in this, as Erich Fromm and many others have so movingly shown, is that in the absence of such meaning, there is a real danger that totalitarian forces can find fertile ground on which to impose their version of it equating meaning with the pursuit of power and the exercise of violence. The history of the twentieth century – of Fascism and genocide – is that of a world in which people were manipulated to purse deeply inhuman political ends and to fuse their own personal identities and purpose into those of the state or the party.

Václav Havel (1991), reflecting on his understanding of the world of Eastern Europe and the People's Democracies, pushed the argument further into a theory, not of alienation, but of absurdity. His concerns are with 'matters like the alienation of man from the world, the dehumanisation and the incomprehensibility of the "order of things", the emptiness and unintentional cruelty of social mechanisms and their tendency to become ends in themselves, how things get out of control, fall apart or, on the contrary, evolve to the point of absurdity, how human existence tends to get lost in the mechanised contexts of life, how easily absurdity becomes legitimate . . .' (1991, p. 288).

The world he hates is one which accepts violence, which renders people impotent to act, where there is 'centrally directed desolation and boredom'; it is a world without real mystery where 'nothingness' has been, as he puts it, 'materialised' (1991, p. 186). In such a world people are not thought of as possessing free will or reason, they are merely units in society which stands over them as if it had powers of its own.

Havel is thinking not only about Communism here; he is reflecting on the absurdity – the absence of meaning – throughout all modern societies. What worries him is apathy, the absence of spontaneity, real individuality, authenticity and rebellion. People do not live 'within the truth' and because of this fail both to comprehend the society they live in and themselves. Havel does not deny that people enjoy their pleasures or that they do not take themselves and their families seriously. Of course they do. What worries him are the relentless pressures of a machine civilisation and of forms of economic life which brook no failure and which require high levels of control and predictability in the workplace and, through that, in all other spheres of human life. People conform to these pressures and expectations and do so without a cultivated sense of the absurd; they take the organisation of society and the lives they lead within it for granted.

This is the normal state of affairs, the way in which daily lives are constructed. In the flow of its everyday concerns – working, shopping, eating, sleeping, seeing to the children, looking after the garden, the car, planning the holiday – people experience some continuity and stability. One day fades into the next, one week into another and the months and years slide by. For those on the margins of society – the poor, the rejected, the homeless, the mentally ill – daily life is not predictably under control. It is a nightmare of uncertainty, a series of threats to be avoided.

Change, though, is unavoidable; as time passes people review what they have left behind. For some this is an experience of regret; for others of relief. Whichever is the case, there is an inevitable distancing from a former self. Human beings are condemned to think of themselves through time, to look back to when they were young, or fit, or happy. Even if the backward glance is to a time of hardship they are glad to be free of, there is still the inevitable sense of a personal life slipping by and each moment of that reflection is a contemplation of the inevitability of the final demise.

For some, change opens the prospect of new hopes; for others the future is threatening. Whichever is the case, contemplation of the future involves self awareness. People have to consider whether they believe they can realise their hopes, whether they have the energies and resources to do so. They have to judge whether the society around them will sustain their ambitions. All such calculations reflect back on those making them to underline the uncertainty and risks we all face in leading our ordinary lives. When people calculate that the societies they live in will not enable them to realise themselves in the ways they desire, there is a leeching out of legitimacy, the social arrangements of society and its governing values are no longer respected. Compliance with social expectations becomes sullen. The People's Democracies of Eastern Europe before 1989 can be exactly described in these terms. Outward compliance to the demands of the state and the party concealed a private distancing from both.

When that distancing took a public form it was punished and the identity of 'dissident' was created. When it became uncontainable by the forces of the state and when the *Apparatchiks* themselves lost faith, the whole order of communist Europe collapsed. New identities became possible which reached beyond the immediate constraints of people's lives.

The secular order of international communism collapsed under the weight of its own internal contradictions. The private hopes of its citizens were unrealisable within the frameworks of power and social control on which the system depended. At the point when its mission to outdo capitalist prosperity with its socialist alternative had obviously failed, it fell apart. Some commentators see in the debris of its collapse a pent up store of stress and despair, of resentment and regret which the new order in Eastern Europe can barely cope with. Maaz (1991) an East German psychiatrist characterised this as a *Gefuhlsstau*, a log jam of repressed feeling which finds outlets in rising levels of mental illness and stress.

New identities have emerged in Eastern Europe: of the unemployed, the excluded, of entrepreneurs and, worryingly, of neo-Nazi skin heads who target immigrants as the source of their troubles. The old identities of the party faithful or the good worker have receded. Many older people look back on their lives building the anti-Fascist order of Eastern Europe after 1945 as having been pointlessly wasted.

The rise of the radical Islamic *Umma* which is one of the most potent revolutionary phenomena of our times, provides further illustration of the force of the point being made here. The Islamic revolution is a rejection of the Godless civilisation of modernity in both its capitalist and communist forms. That is the external aspect of it, a complex cultural response to imperialism, colonialism and underdevelopment. By defining themselves against what they take to be the Godlessness of the West they can affirm a new identity. It can build upon older traditions but not on positive images of the recent past, for few such exist. The Islamic world of the nineteenth and twentieth century provides too many images of failure, of defeat, compromise, corruption and loss of Islamic identity to provide positive new images for the future.

The images that can be retrieved are those of the martyr or the religious purist. Commenting both on the massive changes in the relationship between Islam and the West and on the social and demographic changes within Muslim countries themselves, Ernest Gellner (1996) put it this way: 'Puritanism and fundamentalism became tokens of urban sophistication' (p. 22). 'For the masses,' he writes, 'the High form of Islam ratified their move to urban status, it defined them against the foreigner whom they encountered in the colonial conflict . . . . and it provided them with a charter, a moral entrenched constitution, against their own newly emerging, morally often suspect, technocratic leadership' (1996, p. 22).

With this as the background it is easier to see the foreground images of Islam which haunt the West: the frenzied, breast-beating crowds of Shia Muslim demonstrators, the fundamentalists who demands Muslim schools or those, following the publication of Salman Rushdie's *The satanic verses* responded to the Iranian Fatwa and called for the book to burned and its author executed. The terrorist who is prepared to die for a God-justified cause – the struggle against American imperialism or the state of Israel – is the archetypal Muslim fanatic. The negative image embraces, too, the veiled women students in universities who simultaneously project their Islamic identity and assert their rejection of modern decadence.

The emerging identity of the one reinforces through fear and incomprehension the self-awareness of the other. Where the two identities clash – in the experience of migrant workers in Europe or in the political and military conflicts of the Middle East – they reinforce one another. Edward Said (1993) put it tellingly when he commented on the ways in which, through the world-wide media of communication and the geopolitical fractures of the modern world, distorted images are self-reinforcing. 'The fear and terror induced by the overscale images of "terrorism" and "fundamentalism" – call them figures of an international or transnational imaginary made up of foreign devils – hastens the individual's subordination to the dominant norms of the moment' (1993, p. 375–76). The senselessness of it is that conflicts escalate, identities become fixed and the critical awareness of the real complexities and causes of the problems the world itself faces, does not emerge.

The argument to this point may seem highly political and abstract but the relationships of power and identity which have been discussed can be translated into the real experience of individual people. The people who captured, beat and tortured Brian Keenan in his makeshift prison cell in Beirut, the experience of which he described in great moving detail in his book, *An evil cradling* (1992) did so often after prayer in a state of religious delirium inseparable from their understanding of the politics of the Middle East. Their torturing of Keenan was an affirmation of their Islamic identity. The thugs who attack Turkish *Gastarbeiter* (migrant workers) in German cities or those in France who commit acts of racial violence against Algerians, are affirming a distorted image of themselves as white Europeans. There is no moral justification for their action though they do believe they have right on their side. They have learned to believe that their actions are legitimate. Their view of the Other – the Arab, the Jew, the Black, the immigrant – is one which dehumanises and distorts but it is essential to their own image of themselves.

The psychology of those who cling to a rigid definition of their own cultural exclusiveness and who sharpen that sense of self by defining others as being radically different to themselves, is the psychology, ultimately, of fear. It is a frame of mind which finds security and safety in the exercise of power and which brooks no uncertainty or doubt. Our understanding of that personality in the twentieth century is inseparable from our understanding of authoritarianism and all its political forms. The unloved, authoritarian personality finds some security in the safety of social and political movements which provide order and predictability and self respect based on belonging to something which transcends the shallow misery and insecurity of their ordinary lives.

Identification with the Party or the Faith confers meaning and recognition on lives which have no other social or moral anchorage, no other authentic purpose.

The psychology, then, is well enough known. It is history and change and conflict which provide the contexts for the particular development of such personalities and the identities they can embrace. And if history has lessons for us, the most important is surely this: that there is no necessity to the ways societies change. The nineteenth-century conviction, expressed in its highest form in Marxism, though existing, too, in liberal versions of progress, that there are laws of history, is a belief which finally failed when the Berlin Wall came down. Historicism is dead.

So, too, is essentialism, the belief that people are in some way fixed in their identity – as Muslims, Europeans, Whites or Blacks, Men or Women. Dead, maybe; but certainly not yet forgotten. The political frameworks through which the affairs of the modern world are conducted rest still on personal identities defined in terms of nationality, religious faith, ethnicity, class and gender. Writers like Edward Said (1993) are surely right in pleading for a new framework, one which recognises the 'startling realities of human interdependence on a world scale' (p. 400), and which enable personal identities and forms of thought radically different to those which have catalysed the conflicts of the twentieth century. Only on that basis can we expect a better future.

Whether people can break free of the chains which bind them to particular identities and the beliefs which accompany them is a matter of their capacity to learn and to think about their own lives and to have insight into how they have become the people they are. It is not enough merely to remind them that they are flawed because they are human or that they are as they are because of destiny, or biology or class or nationality. People live their lives in time; their experience is historical. Because of that it is relative. Because they can think about it and reinterpret it, they are not trapped by it. And because of that, they can change it, but only if they understand it.

Understanding is not, however, an individual act of cognition or insight. All attempts to gain such insight into the self are shaped by the resources of understanding available to people to do so. Psychoanalysis has been such a powerful framework of self-awareness for people in the twentieth century, at least in the West. Through therapy and counselling it has provided a vocabulary and theories with which to explore the self. But it has not displaced other ways of thinking about personal experience and of interpreting how people see themselves and how they feel and how they make sense of the changes which have taken place in their lives.

This process of making sense is at the heart of what Jerome Bruner (1990) has called 'folk psychology'. And at the heart of the process itself is narrative, story telling. Bruner's key point is this; the self should not be conceived as a set of properties belonging to an individual. People do strive for a coherent sense of themselves but they do so always in social settings which provide them with the appropriate language and culturally legitimated frameworks for thinking about what they are doing. Narrative enters into the analysis at the points where there is a difference between what people are actually doing and what the culture would lead everyone to expect they should do. This is the point where stories fill the gap, where, as Bruner puts it, a link is forged 'between the exceptional and the ordinary' (1990, p. 47), and where both meaning and comprehensibility are established.

An example Bruner gives makes the point clearly. We would not expect someone in America to waive the national flag in a bank. If this occurred we would be at a loss to explain the behaviour or to know whether our surprise was a sensible response to it. If, on the other hand, we were told that it was Independence Day and the man was celebrating, both the behaviour itself and our reaction to it would be understandable. It would have meaning and the frameworks for making sense of the world through which we order our experience would remain intact and be reaffirmed. The example might seem to be a trivial one but the general point is profoundly relevant for the ways in which we can understand how people make sense of their experience. They do so by framing it into narratives which provide explanations and often justifications of what is and what has taken place in their lives. Selfhood from this perspective cannot be set apart from the shifting circumstances of and changes within people's lives.

Bruner's perspective invites questions about how the resources of narrative that are available to people are distributed among them. And it invites more questions about how different groups of people resolve the differences between the exceptional and the ordinary in their lives. Studies of human behaviour *in extremis* provide some clues. In his powerful account of his concentration camp experience in Dachau and Buchenwald, the psychologist Bruno Bettleheim (1960) observed that those who survived the camp experience best were those with a clear understanding of the nature of Nazism. The communists, some religious prisoners and some of the other political prisoners knew Nazism for what it was and understood well why they themselves would be persecuted by the Nazis. For them the extraordinary was not in the least inexplicable.

On the other hand, conventional middle class Jews had no way of comprehending what was taking place. The extraordinary in their lives was beyond any understanding they could supply. Some dealt with this by dissolving into madness. Bettleheim's account of those who lived in a trance-like non-communicating state of total and oblivious conformity to the camp – they were known as 'Muselmänner' [Muslims] is a moving one. It is of people reduced by violence and fear to a total inability to make sense of anything. They did not survive long.

The concentration camp, it might be claimed, is such an exceptional case on which to hang a general argument that it is not really relevant to the generic question of how human beings search for and provide meaning to their lives. This is not, however, the case; the extremism of the camps has its counterpart in the ways in which some people are forced to live their lives today. Not only have we seen in Europe – in Bosnia – the return of the concentration camp and of genocide, there are many settings where people experience violence and the arbitrary exercise of power or where people are oppressed because of their racial identity or simply, as in families where women and children are abused, because of their powerlessness.

The extraordinariness of insecurity, unemployment, low incomes, poor housing, ill-health, family break-up, crime and mental breakdown is not so far beyond the ordinary experience of millions of people struggling to lead their lives in the freed-up, flexible labour markets of contemporary capitalism. What narrative resources are available to them to bridge the gap between the ordinary and extraordinary? And how do those resources differ between different social classes, different generations and between men and women? How do they relate to the differences between individual people with their different attitudes, values and degrees of self awareness?

Public discourse, private narratives

The answer lies in the subtle interplay between the accounts of personal experience that people can draw upon which are made routinely available through the conventional patterns of thinking within a culture and those forms of self-awareness and insight that individuals have built up for themselves. The two are connected; selfhood and self-awareness and the language available to people to describe them, are bound to the interpersonal contexts of people's lives. What is more, they are inseparable from the moral contexts and valuations of those lives. In our society some social identities are valued more than others. The identity of people whose prime working obligations are in the home is typically judged to be a socially inferior one. Compare the terms 'housewife' with 'business executive', 'manager' and 'secretary', 'young man' and 'black youth'. In each case one description carries a higher social evaluation than the other and nurtures a more positive self image.

The public forms of self-awareness include the standard narratives in terms of which people can give an account of themselves. Some of these are very positive. The businessman who celebrates his achievement with some version of the 'rags to riches through hard work' story is a case in point. The working man who looks back over his life through the interpretive frame of the 'we didn't have the opportunities' story is another. Both accounts – which can be thought of as a kind of learned script with individual embellishments – are often offered to justify and explain why people's lives have taken the tack that they have taken. They provide a convenient summary of a host of diverse facts and individual experience into a coherent, publicly recognisable account. Some people can look back through their lives and see images of themselves which they are proud of and which strengthen a positive self image. Others experience themselves as failures. The first image cannot be fully articulated publicly because of prevailing norms of modesty, the second is often suppressed because it is too painful to confront.

Some people look back over their experience and see a record of continuity; their lives may not have changed very much. Others, an increasing group in an highly mobile, fast-changing society, see only discontinuities. Previous selves slip by into oblivion. Former selves seem to be those of strangers. Those who 'come out' as adults to announce that they are gay or lesbian are examples of people who experience a dramatic change in identity. Those pitched from employment into unemployment, or from health into chronic illness, or from being with a partner to be being without, those who lose faith in their religion or are ostracised by their group, all experience a radical discontinuity of the self.

The self is for some unexplored territory, for others a source of constant interest and fascination. There are people who actively throw up barriers to prevent themselves from peering too deeply into their lives, their thoughts and their feelings. They are afraid to confront what they may find. Others, as we now have been taught by Freud, repress their awareness of particular experience to render them beyond conscious recall. Some reinterpret their experience and identity to adjust the past to what they would prefer for the present. We all know people who insulate aspects of themselves to such a degree that they never come into public view, who keep only the surface of themselves on view. The deeper layers are never revealed, perhaps not even to themselves.

There are people who actively search for themselves and explore how they feel; they are people who try to 'get in touch with themselves'. It can be done, though the means to do so may be diverse and are sometimes drug-induced. Others, as we shall see, cannot do it because they lack an appropriate vocabulary or the support to do so. George Eliot commented in *Adam Bede*, that 'we can't say half what we feel, with all our words' (Penguin edition, p. 163).

Individual difficulties in realising higher levels of self-awareness and understanding are not just a consequence of personal inadequacies of one kind or another. They reflect, too the contexts of people's lives and the choices people have made in deciding how to live them. People select the social contexts which confirm their sense of themselves and avoid those contexts which do not. Identity and some of the personal memories of which it is constituted – the biographical self – can be seen from this perspective as something inseparable from the social contexts of people's lives.

An extreme example of this concerns the memories and experiences of those who survived the Holocaust. Lawrence Langer (1991) in his book *Holocaust Testimonies*, noted that the camp experience of people was so brutal, so shocking, so traumatising, that they have been unable to find a language to communicate it to others. They fear they will not be believed. They fear the recall of the person that they themselves were in the camp. Their memories of it all, as well as their capacity to comprehend it, has been deeply contained and insulated from their present sense of self. They remain, however, hostages to it. Speaking of her Auschwitz experience, one survivor told Langer, 'I don't live with it. It lives with me' (1991, p. 23). Another is quoted as saying that the camp experience sets its survivors apart. 'You don't sort of feel at home in this world anymore' (p. 35).

Since our understanding of ourselves is set in a social (and moral) frame and the language and narrative forms available to us to describe ourselves and our experience are publicly legitimated, the precise things that people say about themselves, or struggle to say, cannot be set apart from the contexts in which they are talking. The point can be illustrated with a dramatic historical example and a simpler everyday one.

The dramatic one comes from some of the surprising findings of life history research. Oral history research in Italy has had to confront a profound silence in the way older people account for their lives. The work of the Italian historian, Luisa Passerini (1982) on the Fascist period is telling. Many of her interviews remain strangely silent about their experience during the Mussolini years. It is not that they have forgotten what they did; it is more that there are few contexts which would occasion them to provide an account of those years and none that would allow them to give a positive description of them. How different it would have been if the Fascists had won the war! In Germany there remains a profound difficulty in recovering from people their experiences of the Nazi period related to the genocide of the Jews. Apart from the problem of silence itself which insulates the past from the present, there is the problem of what Saul Friedlander (1992) has called 'the limits of representation'. Modern Germans have a problem: how to understand the Holocaust, how to account for it and how to construct their personal identities as Germans with the knowledge of the Nazi destruction of the Jews. The terms available to us all to describe the Holocaust and the historical narratives which seek to render it all comprehensible, to explain it, are quite inadequate for the task. For the Holocaust goes far beyond moral understanding, far beyond any account that can be given of man's inhumanity to man, far beyond all the representations we have of political repression, or nationalism and therefore beyond our capacity to describe it fully. How then can individuals give an account of their own experience in relation to it?

People can only make sense of themselves in terms of the prevailing ways of doing so made available to them in the societies and communities in which they live. Private experiences and the ways people order it into a meaningful account are from this perspective never merely private or unique. They are held in public frames and these, together with the language in which they are embedded, change through time, enabling people to re-write their own biographies and interpret their experiences in fresh ways as they continue the search to know themselves.

A telling example of this, it has been suggested (by Eric Santner, 1992), is the example of the German film *Heimat*, Edgar Reitz's drama documentary of the fortunes of a family in the rural area of the Hunsruck. The effect of this popular eleven-episode film, has been, according to Santer, to enable Germans to use the word *heimat* (which means home) in a new way. It is now no longer a place uniquely theirs because it has been cleansed of Jews – the Nazi version of the term – but something which they have lost and can now feel nostalgic about. Edgar Reitz saw his film as a way of giving back to Germans a way of talking about their own past and their own individual memories in ways which were not distorted by the heavy overlay of deeply critical historical narratives of twentieth-century German history centred on the Holocaust. To that extent the film was successful, for the millions of German people who saw it will have been enabled to think of their own past, their own personal experience in a different light.

The simpler example concerns men. It is commonplace to note that men do not cry, that men can hide themselves successfully behind their masks of masculinity. Men who act violently towards women or children have an atrophied sense of themselves and of their relationships with others. Their actions centre on their own power and they lack a capacity to empathise with those they attack. They lack insight into their own behaviour. They cannot acknowledge weakness or doubt; they resolve conflict through the exercise of power.

The extreme case of the violent man does not prove the general rule that all men are capable of such violence. Men's lives are, however, touched with violence. Generally they are the ones who fight the wars; they are much more likely than women to be involved in violent crime and many of the images available to young men to model themselves on are built around themes of violence and power. Peter Middleton (1992) has tried to characterise the emotional insight of men using the phrase 'blocked reflexivity'. His point is that men have been denied a chance to develop an emotional language which gives themselves access to their innermost feelings, doubts and uncertainties. The outcome is that men are often 'silent' about their emotions. It also explains why they are suspicious about revealing weakness and uncertainty and why in their friendships men can still remain guarded and relate to one another in ways which do not expose their vulnerabilities but which emphasise their strengths. Male banter, joking, mutual teasing and conversations centred on issues external to their personal relationships – sport, business, politics – all serve to preserve both the public identity of the successful male and the private inability to have any kind of personal emotional insight.

Breaking through the barriers

The case so far presented perhaps overstresses the degree to which identities are held in social frames from which people can only break free with great difficulty. People do, however change; they do cast off the constraints of the identities offered them. They do redefine themselves and develop a new understanding of themselves. Some achieve this in the context of therapy or in conscious inward reflection on biographical experience. For some it is a matter of finding new personal challenges – a new job, new relationships, climbing mountains, painting pictures, learning a foreign language, running a youth group. Others achieve an inward personal transformation through communion with others in religious revelation or practice or in social and political movements seeking to change the world. In each case, personal change is a consequence of new learning and of the emergence of a new sense of self rooted in a new narrative, a new account of personal experience.

The work on depression by the psychologist Dorothy Rowe (1987) is instructive in this regard. It is built on the view that 'Depression is a prison which we build for ourselves. Just as we build it, so we can unlock the door and let ourselves out' (1987, p. viii). The key to the door is knowledge 'of learning to live wisely and harmoniously' (p. 164). Good health, relaxation, self-awareness and reflection, risking being more open to and trusting of others are key elements of the process of becoming mentally healthy again. For the therapist it is a question of helping the patient rewrite the narratives of their lives to develop a new understanding of their experience.

Some people cannot break free of the prison; they remain trapped in their own self loathing and their fear. Rowe is convinced that after years of clinical work, it is through deeper self-awareness people can overcome depression. They learn their way out of it. But not by themselves alone; all of us need help to gain personal insight upon which new personal development can take place. All the help in the world would be insufficient, however, if the context of our lives, the historical and social setting in which we live them, did not in some ways facilitate and justify the changes we struggle to make.

It took Janina Bauman 40 years to have the courage to write about her experiences surviving the Warsaw Ghetto and the Nazi occupation of Poland (1986). Until then she had preferred to forget. When, in late middle age, she started to write about those terrible years, she was amazed at how much, through active recall, she could remember. In her case, though, it took 40 years, exile from her homeland and a totally new life in Britain – she now possesses a very strong sense of belonging nowhere – to create the mental space to be able to feel it was the right thing for her to do.

Having written two volumes of stunning autobiography she none the less commented that her life story is still to her, as it is to strangers, confused and ambiguous. She writes that that part of her self which enabled her to tell her own story remains to her a puzzle. 'She is a puzzle, that woman, to me. She has brought me here. Let her account for that' (1986). This feeling is wholly bound up with her sense of her Jewishness, but that, too, has altered its meaning. In Poland, after the war, and, perhaps too, now, in Britain, she is not sure what her Jewishness means to her. But she comments darkly, that for a Jew 'it was easier to know where you were under the German occupation' (1986, p. 14). Jews had a clear identity imposed upon them by the violence of Nazism. Janina Bauman was part of that; she cannot escape that, but the context of her self-awareness now is different.

Janina Bauman's life is marked by profound discontinuities. For other people it is the continuity of belonging which is problematic. For some, intense belonging – to a peer group, to a party, to a faith, a class – is a rigid frame of self-awareness which prevents new growth, development and understanding. That same belonging can become a terrible frame of regret, nostalgia or bitterness as the social contexts which once supported it changes or disappears.

History is no iron cage. Hope can be transformed. People can escape the prisons of their lives. It is not always, however, in ways which keep alive liberal hopes of tolerance, personal growth and freedom. New identities can be forged in promoting the opposite of these things. History – of the Holocaust, of colonial oppression, Stalin's gulags, of East European secret services, of Bosnia and ethnic cleansing, of terrorism and of the everyday horrors of racial violence and the routine oppression of the weak – is an ever-expanding archive of evidence of the ways in which individual identities can be forged on the anvils of hate. People learn to do this, too; they learn to suppress their sympathy for the Other and to close off from themselves the full moral horror of their actions. At the core of the history of genocide in the twentieth century is a story of how ordinary, decent people can become killers.

Zygmunt Bauman (1989) in his work on the Holocaust, has explained how it can happen. It is a facet of modernity itself and of the capacity which exists in all modern, bureaucratic societies, to harness the means of rational administration to the task of genocidal destruction. All it takes is for a group of people to be defined as an outgroup and to be stripped of their ordinary claims to be treated morally as human beings. It is not difficult for tyrants to feed on weakness, moral gullibility and ignorance and to create opportunities in which people can be valued as killers. Prevented from human contact with the 'Other', it is easy for people to come to feel that the strangeness of the 'Other' – the Jew, the Black, the Muslim, the foreigner, the 'do-gooder', the junkie, the unemployed, 'youth', gays and lesbians or whoever else is 'not us' – justifies treating them as a danger and a threat and a legitimate target for violence and abuse.

In the worst circumstances, however, in civil wars – as in Yugoslavia, or in long-running conflicts, for example between Arabs and Jews over Palestine, or in South Africa where the Commission on Truth and Reconciliation is at work following the collapse of Apartheid – there is always another way. In his moving reflections on his attempts – in Nigeria, Israel, South Africa and, more recently in Bosnia to promote peace and non-violence – Adam Curle (1995) has drawn the lesson from his work, particularly in Osijek, that to combat violence, people need help to realise their potential as human beings. It is not just a question of politics and diplomacy and mediation – though each is vital. It is about how people perceive one another, understand themselves and make sense of their experience of one another. To put it into the language of narrative, it is a question of what stories people can tell about one another.

The 'fullest possible development of our humanity, our potential as human beings' means:

> becoming able to escape from the mindless automatism that
> governs so much of our lives, from senseless worries and fears,
> from prejudice, from ego cherishing and irritability, from vanity,

from illusions of guilt or badness, from a belief in a separate existence. These and all other negative emotions are like a fist tightly closed around the heart. They imprison our consciousness within the narrow confines of the self. But to be fully human our consciousness must expand, gradually embracing others, including all non-human others with whom we share the planet. It means losing the lonely sense of separation. It means to be rather than to do (1995, Curle, p. 119).

To achieve this, Curle believes, new learning is required. His peace workshops are means to promote this learning in ways which promote listening, self reflection and joint analyses of complex problems of history, politics and identity. It is a slow way to solve problems, but there is no other way for all questions of politics are ultimately bound up with history and with issues of personal identity. To know oneself, therefore, is the first step to knowing about the world.

11 Dialogue and learning: towards a new model of citizenship

> Always be ready to speak your mind, and a base man will avoid you.
> William Blake, *Proverbs of Hell*

The central idea developed in this chapter is this: people learn through dialogue with one another and in the process of doing so they transform their understanding both of themselves and their world. It is not a new idea but it does have major implications for the practices of education and learning and for the organisation of the social institutions in which both take place. Above all, this chapter seeks to show that dialogue is not merely a technique to facilitate learning; it is, as Wallis and Allman (1996) have stressed, both a powerful model for and a process of change in society and for a renewed vision of democracy itself.

Dialogue is a special form of communication. It is more than conversation and the simple exchange of information. It is communication undertaken within a commitment to arrive at an agreed understanding of something. For it to occur, a number of prior conditions must be met: those engaged in it must respect one another's right to their opinions. They must share the same language. They must be aware of the logical principles of argument. They must have knowledge about the problem being discussed and they must be prepared to change their views if the argument and the evidence being examined justifies them doing so. Dialogue requires, then, the main elements of what Habermas (see Bernstein, 1995) has described as the ideal speech situation. In the absence of these conditions human communication is 'distorted'. In Habermas's social theory, the conditions of non-distorted communication can only be secured in a society in which truth, freedom and justice prevail; the conditions of non-distorted communication are therefore not simply linguistic; they are social and material.

The theory of dialogue is a powerful tool with which to develop a critical understanding of social institutions for it points to the conditions which prevent people from searching for the truth of things together. It explains, therefore, why people fail to learn to the levels they are capable of and why social institutions and work organisations do not change as rapidly or as successfully as they might. It explains the mechanisms of deceit, manipulation and ideological control through which the powerful can maintain their dominance. It carries also the promise that people can find better ways of working together to solve old problems in new and creative ways. In so doing they can contribute to the resources of collective knowledge of people in society and, indeed, throughout the world. Dialogue is at the heart of successful learning and of the successful, open society. It is the key concept of lifelong learning.

The argument of this chapter is built up as follows. First, the centrality of the concept of dialogue to a range of moral and political problems is set out. Then the idea of knowledge itself is discussed. Knowledge is shown to be a facet of collective human experience, a social product rather than an individual possession. Since all claims to knowledge can and must be contested, the point is strongly made that knowledge grows most successfully under the conditions of an open society in which the rights and freedoms of individuals are fully protected by law and respected in practice. The society which can nurture dialogue has to create the institutions and opportunities in which it can take place.

The theories of learning which inform the theory of dialogue are then set out. These theories stress the situated, intersubjective nature of human learning and relate structures of cognition to the organisation of social institutions and the patterns of power and culture which define them. The processes of learning are discussed to reveal their dialogical character. Next, the practices and structures in modern society which hinder dialogue are discussed to reveal, simultaneously, how they must be changed if the open society is to nurture an effective model of citizenship and the democratic means to bring about social change. The chapter closes with observations about how the dialogical approach to learning transforms the practice of education and training at work, in the community and in formal educational institutions. More than that, it transforms the functioning of society itself and the forms of knowledge and understanding on which it is based.

Dialogue: evolving perspectives

The view of dialogue as a distinctive process of human communication has its roots in several traditions of enquiry and of educational practice. In what follows, the aim is to clarify the nature of the social and psychological processes at the heart of dialogue and through that to try to specify more precisely what its distinctive features are and the ways in which they differ from those of other forms of human communication.

A great deal that is relevant to the theme of this chapter has developed in areas which are beyond the fields of conventional educational practice. There is, for example, a great deal of highly relevant work on interfaith communication among the major religious denominations where the special problems of understanding and communication across different belief systems have been confronted (Dupre, 1994). Our understanding of what dialogue is has emerged also from work done in the field of international relations and is focused on the themes of peace and reconciliation. The work of Adam Curle (1995) in the field of peace-making has shown how distorted, non-dialogical thinking – which for him is a form of ignorance – can result in violence but also that there is a way out of it based on new forms of discussions and debate.

The area of practice known as community development which some writers see as a form of community education and learning or social education (see Smith, 1994; Kirkwood and Kirkwood, 1989) has been informed directly by theories of dialogue drawn from the work of Paulo Freire. A central tenet of the field of development studies is the fundamental requirement to engage people in the development process itself so that through direct participation in all the decisions which affect their lives, people will learn new skills and be better placed to shape their own destinies and resist the continuing colonisation of their societies (Apffel-Marglin and Marglin, 1996).

On a more narrowly focused theme, Frankie Todd (1994) has developed a view of dialogue as central to professional education. Taking a view of dialogue rooted in the work of the literary critic, Bakhtin (1994) and reflecting on the attempts of the Toronto Police Department to counter racism within the force, she develops the view that dialogue is a powerful tool of cultural and organisational change. Only when members of the force were confronted with representatives of ethnic minority groups who could make their complaints about routine police practice vivid, were police officers able to think about their work in a new way.

The physicist David Bohm (1996) developed a practice of dialogue rooted in a particular view of the nature of knowledge as something which is essentially collective in nature and not the possession of individuals. His view of dialogue is that it is not to persuade others of something they do not hold to; it is to help people suspend their normal assumptions about a problem, to become critical of those assumptions and to engage in uninhibited collective discussion in full awareness of the elements within the group which render that discussion difficult.

Social scientists who write in the social constructivist tradition and who conceive of the selfhood, understanding and identity of individuals as being a feature of the ways in which they are members of society and use language, have stressed the importance of dialogue as a mode of social learning (Crossley, 1996; Shotter, 1993; Billig, 1992; Burkitt, 1991). In the course of their conversations people stimulate one another into having thoughts and ideas which they did not have prior to the conversation itself. It is the intersubjectivity of dialogue that binds people together into a group, according to each a place and an identity in a wider social world.

Linguists are now considering the distinctive properties of dialogue as a form of communication in which the patterns of thought and belief within a culture and society are both revealed and reconstituted (Weigend, 1994; Windisch, 1990; Myerson, 1994). The already-mentioned work of Jürgen Habermas (see Bernstein, 1995) – in particular his notion of communicative rationality – is centrally concerned with structure of communication in modern societies and his notion of the 'ideal speech situation' is a powerful tool to help us analyse the ways in which communication can be distorted.

Once it is acknowledged that language itself is not a neutral means of communication but encodes in its own structures – its metaphors, allusions and symbols – the ideas, values and modes of perception of a society or culture, it follows that its distortions can be overcome. The more open and democratic the society, the more likely this can be achieved. The language of the totalitarian states in the twentieth century was closely policed so that words like 'Jew' or 'Comrade' never lost the meanings the Party intended them to have. The most frightening and pernicious feature of George Orwell's *Nineteen Eighty-Four* was that the new language of 'Newspeak' was so laundered that no one could think an oppositional thought. No dialogue was possible under Big Brother. It is therefore easy to see why movements of social and political liberation and oppressed peoples generally, have to find their own voice, their own language, in order to reclaim and express their own thoughts and identities.

What the theologians, social theorists, philosophers and linguists are telling us is that dialogue is concerned with the most fundamental problems of knowledge and of being a person and has direct and profound implications for the practice of education and learning. It concerns the ways in which people communicate with one another, the forms their disagreements take, the conditions which must be met if they are to understand one another better and to be able to articulate their own views of the world without fear and with confidence. Differences in the power and authority of social groups limit the ability of their members to communicate effectively and creatively with each other and limit what they can together discover and learn about the problems they discuss.

Science and reason are not the ways out of the kinds of impasse which exists between different views of the world or disagreements about how something – a scientific puzzle, an issue of social policy, a problem at work – can be resolved. For as George Myerson (1994) has show in his account of 'dialogic rationalism', reason itself is embedded in particular forms of argument and discourse which shape the forms its practice takes. Educators must understand these issues because what takes place in the encounter between a learner and a teacher – in whatever setting they meet – is a process of communication in which dialogue is either facilitated or inhibited and in which, therefore, learning and creative problem-solving, either flourishes or is stifled.

In what follows, an attempt is made to build upon this work and clarify for educationists the essentials of a theory of dialogue and to relate it to educational practice with adults. My concern, however, is not only with the ways in which dialogue is part of learning; it is also to relate it to social practice and in particular to the processes involved in building up an open, democratic society. The thrust of the argument here is that adults can be helped through dialogical practice to learn and to effect change in the major domains of their lives: in their families, in work, in the community and in their roles as citizens.

Dialogue and the learning society

In a global society, the citizen role is without precise boundaries. The horrendous problems faced by all modern societies require for their solution new kinds of learning and practice which transcend those of any one society or community. The problems of the environment are not containable within the legal boundaries of nation states. International action is required to save the global environment. The security of communities within any nation state is related to a greater encompassing security which must be achieved through negotiations in transnational institutions. Underdevelopment and world poverty are great catalysts of conflict and war and the full range of problems they generate – genocide, disease, crime, terrorism and environmental degradation – are threats to the security of everyone.

All these problems demand solutions. New solutions will have to be found repeatedly for the problems themselves change with each intervention. The old solutions, models and practices no longer suffice. Neither the environmental conditions in which people live, or the current patterns of social and economic organisation of modern societies, are sustainable without serious damage to the global quality of life. It is only on the basis of new learning that new solutions can be found to old problems. To do so, however, we require new forms of learning and wider opportunities to act on the basis of new knowledge. We need, in short, a learning society.

Dialogue has to be at the heart of any credible version of the learning society. It is the necessary catalyst of lifelong learning. The outlines of the learning society of the future cannot be precisely drawn. Only this is clear: it will measure up to the ideal to the extent that it is an open society in which informed citizens, searching for new knowledge, are in active dialogue with one another to explore ways to overcome their problems and define the future of their society and its institutions. It is a society in which people will be prepared to change their minds, to think afresh about what they once previously believed. Jack Mezirow (1987) has discussed this as a process of 'perspective transformation'. Stephen Brookfield (1987) has tried to capture it as the process of helping people think critically.

The learning society will certainly be a talkative society in which people are open both to other people and to new ideas. In the context of world-wide communication networks, the learning society of the future will also be a global one. Communication across cultures will require more than the development of the technical skills of information technology; it will demand new forms of understanding between people together with new kinds of communicative competence.

Work done on interfaith dialogue is directly relevant here. When people from different faiths come to be aware of the structures of thought and forms of communication of their own faith and through that have acquired a deeper understanding of it, they can appreciate more fully the logic of other systems of belief and the ways in which interfaith communication can be distorted (Dupre,

1994). The outcome – despite a long history of religious repression – is not that one faith would supersede another, but that all faiths would be enriched through the realisation that they deal with common human predicaments. In peaceful, open-ended dialogue with others, members of different religious traditions will come to appreciate more the universal significance of the particularities of their own faith.

The principles of dialogue rest on a moral foundation: if people are to solve the problems they face in their ordinary lives and those that beset modern societies as a whole, they have to learn to think and learn in new ways. Their own integrity as human beings, their right to have the respect of others has to be protected. Peter Jarvis (1992) has explained very clearly that all learning embraces the whole person and that the full and authentic personal development of human beings can only be realised through their relationships with others. It requires freedom and autonomy and self-determination. To live and to learn otherwise, as millions of people are forced to, is not only to deny the basic moral integrity of human beings, it is to create conditions in which people cannot develop their personhood through authentic and effective learning.

Authentic learning on the other hand, engages with the ideas of other people; it is a process in which people learn from one another. It requires a minimum of respect for the needs and interests of the Other and a sympathetic disposition to listen to his or her point of view. It presupposes a competency, a confidence and an opportunity to engage in dialogue which many people do not possess but which they must be helped to acquire. From this perspective, learning must be seen as a social process that cannot be separated from the contexts in which people live their lives. It follows that education has a central moral purpose: to help people acquire the understanding, confidence and capability to engage critically in all discussions which concern the organisation of society and its institutions. The purpose of dialogue is not to win arguments; it is to establish understanding, even if this only means that people come to understand why others hold such different views.

From the perspective on learning outlined here, much of what passes for education (and, as was seen in Chapters 5 and 6, has passed for education) in modern society, as well as what takes place in the more restricted domain of professional and vocational training, hardly passes muster. Measured against what human beings are capable of and what society itself requires if its long term survival is to be assured, much conventional education has to be judged a failure. The evidence is clear: it turns people off from learning to such a degree that most of them never return to it. The loss to individuals of not having an opportunity to develop their potential to the full is only matched by the loss to society of people whose creativity and ideas could have enriched it.

Much of the learning that takes place in the workplace can be judged by the same criteria to be narrow, uninspiring and narrowly functional. This is not a new observation; it has been forcibly and more effectively stated elsewhere – in respect of higher education by Barnett (1993) and in relation to vocational training by, among many others, Hyland (1994) and Kincheloe (1995). A great deal of vocational training is narrow in the range of skills it nurtures and is limited, too, in the conception of the future career needs of employees it embodies. It hardly begins to acknowledge the real potentiality of the work place as a site for learning and personal development.

What is emerging from these debates are new insights into the practice of teaching and learning which, were they to be adopted, would transform the educational institutions of modern society and through doing so, the nature of the learning experiences they offer. Educational institutions do not, however, change easily. In Chapter 7 it was shown that the forms of learning and of communication in educational institutions reflect those of earlier times and can be profoundly didactic and hierarchical and quite unsuited to the more open forms of dialogue being discussed here. Learning at work is constrained too tightly by the short-term requirements of commercial profitability to be a really effective way of transforming the creativity of people in employment. In both cases, what is missing is a real vision of possibility for a new kind of society which is really open and in which everyone can find a secure place and in which it is not assumed the answers to all important questions are somehow already known by those with power and authority to impose their decisions on others.

Knowledge and dialogue

The model of dialogue developed here presupposes a particular theory of knowledge. In essence it is the view that knowledge is an aspect of the collective experience of a society and a culture and is not the property of individuals. Knowledge can, of course, only exist in the minds of individuals but the frameworks of cognition within which people build up their knowledge are intrinsically social. This is true not only of the everyday knowledge in terms of which people manage the ordinary business of their daily lives; it applies, too, to what we think of as scientific or objective knowledge.

The objective knowledge of science is embedded in the work of scientific communities. Scientific training is a process of being inducted into the ways of thinking of a scientific community. Scientific knowledge does not exist apart from the ways in which the scientific community validates particular ways of thinking and of judging the claims of its members to have made discoveries or to have demonstrated the veracity of particular propositions. What passes for knowledge and is accepted as valid, is something made legitimate by particular communities of learning at particular moments of time. In universities, these communities crystallise into particular subject areas and academic disciplines each with their own preoccupations and perspectives, identities and professional commitments.

Modern science and technology are themselves part of a broader discourse of rationality and reasoned argument which is connected historically to the distinctive forms of thought that are part of western culture and civilisation. The empirical, reductionist, objective character of scientific knowledge and the value distinctions central to it – those for example between the subjective and the objective, the factual and the normative – has left (see Chapter 2) a particular stamp on the patterns of thinking of the culture as a whole and of the ways in which people within it make sense of themselves and their world. One element of this is a widespread view that scientific and technological knowledge – indeed expert knowledge of all kinds – is in some way objective and known and valid and completely neutral in its implications.

More powerful still in the prevailing cultural model of scientific knowledge, is the belief that through it mankind will be able to solve its most pressing problems – what Aron (discussed in Chapter 2) referred to as the 'Promethean Ambition' (1968, p. 216). The cultural force of such claims cannot be underestimated. As Agnes Heller noted, we live in a science-saturated culture (1984). Our world views are 'encapsulated'; science percolates into all aspects of experience and that people feel dependent on the solutions science is believed to offer to all the problems faced by people in modern societies. Scientists, or, at least, the more thoughtful among them, do not think in this way. Sir Peter Medawar (1986) pointed out forcibly that science is the 'art of the soluble' and scientific method is very productive in solving the problems that science can solve. But there is a vast range of questions about human experience which cannot be understood using the methods of science but which nevertheless need discussion and analysis so that people can make decisions about how to act.

One of the features of scientific thought which would carry over into other areas of enquiry is its essential contestability. Karl Popper (1963) explored this is the principle of falsifiability. Scientific statements are always formulated in ways which would allow their truth claims to be falsified. There has been a great deal of debate about whether this is the defining feature of scientific thought. What is not contested is that scientific understanding grows out of rigorous questioning, debate; it is a process of conjecture and refutation among scientists and presupposes a framework of community and communicative competence among them. To assess the veracity of a proposition, scientists have to be able to understand it and debate it. They have to have the freedom to think that something is wrong and to have the courage and conviction to say so.

These conditions have to be met in the social arrangements which support scientific work. Jürgen Habermas has tried to specify them in his account of the ideal speech situation (see Bernstein, 1995). This idea can be simply expressed: discourse of a kind likely to lead to an agreed understanding of the truth of a proposition, requires a number of conditions. People have to acknowledge that the consensus they arrive at has been achieved on the basis of argument; that people are free to step outside conventional ways of thinking about the problem being discussed and that they are motivated only by a commitment to the truth so that claims to truth based on other kinds of claims, for example status or power, are ruled out of the discussion. The conditions which must be met are therefore social in character. They concern the values of truthfulness and freedom as well as those of justice, so that all can join in the debate free of any coercive pressure to think one way rather than another.

These conditions are ideal in the sense that they are difficult to achieve in practice. In all societies there are social arrangements which prevent such conditions being realised. The fate of the powerless – whoever they may be – is not to be heard and to be required to accept the views of the powerful and the articulate. Those who cannot join in the argument, because they lack either the communicative competence or the opportunity to do so, cannot be taken into account. They are forced to remain silent. The understanding they have is then lost to the discussion. Their needs remain unarticulated. Dialogue among specialists then remains exclusive. Knowledge gained under those circumstances is necessarily incomplete and untested.

The conditions under which modern science actually develops do meet some of the criteria of the ideal speech situation. Scientific research has to be justified to the science community; its results are evaluated in debate among scientists. Once the scope of debate widens to include the social sciences, however, and concerns the existing arrangements of society itself, the prevailing patterns of discourse reveal all the characteristic features of 'distorted communication'. The problem of knowledge that arises then is that decisions are taken based on forms of understanding about how society itself is working that have not been fully tested in open debate.

This is a problem both for the validity of dominant forms of understanding and for the practice of democracy itself. The preconditions of scientific thinking are those of the open society. Of course, the history of the past two centuries, particularly of the twentieth, provides many examples of science deployed to serve the needs of a dominant ideology or to have developed under conditions of almost absolute secrecy. The danger then is that science is detached from both its moral context and the open communicative conditions which are essential to its growth and validity.

There are many examples of such closed science in the domain of military research and development, the development of atomic weapons being a major example. The science which spawned the technology was unconnected with the political morality which governed the rationale behind the development of those weapons. The moral emptiness of science during the Third Reich is a key element in the historical configuration which made the Holocaust possible (Bauman, 1989). There is closure, too, in the more mundane contexts of commercial Research and Development. And in all areas of professional practice there is a risk that knowledge will be kept exclusive to preserve the power of those who use it.

The specialised knowledge of managers in industry and commerce is often deployed in exclusive ways to justify managerial decisions and authority. It is invariably more effective, however, to broaden out the base of decision-making to incorporate a wider range of points of view and to work towards innovative solutions to old problems by broadening out the frameworks through which problems are approached. Knowledge, however, (as was shown in Chapter 2) is inseparable from power and indeed is a form of power; people who wield it are unlikely to want to share it lest they lose their control of the organisations they manage.

From this angle, dialogue can pose a real threat to some groups of people and to the prevailing modes of thinking within a group. Yet, if the full creative potentiality of people is to develop and new knowledge is to be discovered, there must be dialogue and people must learn to live with the contradictions and the doubts it opens up. It is through discussion with others in which the thoughts of the others are grasped and evaluated, that individuals become critically conscious of their own thoughts and aware of the relative nature of their own understanding and experience. Conversations with others broadens out both.

Conversation which takes the form of dialogue, in which there is acute sensitivity to the perspectives of others participating is something which generates new understanding and changed awareness. Knowledge is not a fixed system of propositions. Whatever the domain of human experience and enquiry, knowledge changes. Individuals think the thoughts that make this possible but the structure of their thinking is bound up with the collective experience of their culture. This view of knowledge has profound implications for teaching and learning and, as we shall see, for our understanding of the organisation of society and its institutions. In particular it implies a radical change in the ways in which change itself should be understood, achieved and managed. The open society in which dialogue flourishes is profoundly different in its working arrangements to those which currently obtain in modern societies where, too often, and for a variety of different reasons, though with one generic rationale – the exercise of power – dialogue is suppressed.

Theory of learning

The theory of dialogue requires a theory of learning. People need to learn new ideas, acquire new information and understanding before they can engage in dialogue. Dialogue is itself, however, a process of learning, of hearing the other's point of view and of having the opportunity to enlarge on one's own arguments and in so doing reflect on them and refine them. Dialogue itself nurtures insight and awareness; people become clearer about the strengths and weaknesses of their own views.

Learning is a psychological process which takes place in particular settings of social interaction. Lave and Wenger (1991) have made this point in their notion of 'situated learning'. Learning cannot be separated off from the social and ideological conditions in which it takes place. Some contexts facilitate it, others inhibit it. Some contexts of learning are formal; others informal. All contexts of learning involve the interpersonal transmission of ideas, skills and understanding. Sometimes, as in formal education, this is done in an explicit way; in other contexts it is achieved implicitly or tacitly. In both cases the learners come to be aware of the ways of thinking, values, tacit understandings, forms of expression and practice of the group or culture or profession into which they are becoming members. Lave and Wenger have argued that some settings of learning actively inhibit it because they deny the autonomy of the learner and their freedom to ask questions. Other contexts impose very artificial constraints on the opportunities open to people to learn new things. Too often people are simply expected to do as they are told or are helped to learn only the minimum of what is needed to complete a routine task.

The theory of learning that can be derived from a dialogical model of knowledge predicts that the most successful learning that individuals engage in occurs in situations when the following conditions apply:

- People can participate in the learning process by setting its goals and its methods. Learning must have relevance to the needs and interests of people. It must be meaningful to them. It must be purposeful and people learn most effectively when it is fun.
- People feel secure that they are valued and are being taken seriously; trust between facilitator and learner is crucial. Without trust, learners can never be sure of the motives of the facilitator or the veracity of what they are being helped to understand.
- People are confident that they can ask questions and challenge the views of others without fear of humiliation or reprisal; if the needs for safety and security are at the forefront of learner's concerns, their ability to learn is undermined.
- People are given support to articulate their questions and their points of view, when their interests and enthusiasm are reciprocated by those who facilitate their learning.
- People are helped by the circumstances of their learning to be open to others. It is important to be able to listen and to communicate effectively in a group.
- People are helped to understand their failures in learning so that their 'meta-cognitive' awareness improves. Another facet of this is that people learn more effectively when they have a heightened awareness of the deeper structures of their own understanding and a greater appreciation of their own styles of learning.
- People are helped to become aware of the ways in which others build up their understanding of the world and communicate their thoughts and try to justify their claims to knowledge. This is the corollary of a heightened individual meta-cognitive awareness; it is a strengthened critical awareness of the forms of debate used by others.
- People can see the immediate consequences of their learning in their ability to do new things and to act in new ways and apply what they have come to know. When this takes place, the motivation to learn improves dramatically and people experience a deep sense of personal growth and satisfaction. It is an experience of self-actualisation and is arguably a profound human need.

- People experience the joy of personal growth and a deeper understanding of what interests them. Under these conditions people extend themselves in fresh ways; they gain new insights into their past and the possibilities before them in the future.
- People experience themselves as agents, as being able to determine their own fate and to be able to act to influence the decisions that shape their lives. This condition, in conjunction with the others set out above, is a facet of self-actualisation and authentic selfhood which can flourish only in creative collaboration with others.

The importance of these ten propositions can be easily underlined for they all highlight a key point: all learning (as was discussed in Chapter 10) engages the self and results in changes to the ways in which people make sense of themselves and their world. Unless they feel it is safe to do so, or that they themselves have made the choice to make the changes, they will not be open to new ideas. It is an existential requirement that people reach a view of themselves which is credible, authentic and sustainable. New knowledge and ways of thinking can threaten this process profoundly. New experiences can be negative; they can result in new forms of self-awareness in which people come to see themselves as inadequate or unworthy.

Learning situations do exist which reflect principles opposite to those set out above. Too many people have experienced dull, didactic teaching. Many have had their intellectual confidence undermined by educational failure and have been poorly supported in their efforts to learn. In defensive mode, too many people have responded to new ideas by clinging on to their older beliefs thus closing off possibilities for personal growth and development. Too few people have been privileged enough to encounter teachers who helped them understand their own learning styles and failures in a supportive way. Millions of people have experienced their education as something which took away all the pleasures and possibilities of growth and development through learning. People have too often been socialised into an ordered world in which it was not their place to ask critical questions, where they were expected to trust those with authority and power. And it is a matter of great concern that the majority of adults do not engage in opportunities for adult education so they never compensate for the weaknesses of the education they received at school.

When people learn new things their world alters and there is a real sense in which people are learning all the time. Lifelong learning from this perspective is a necessary and inevitable existential requirement of survival. Simply by living through the experiences of an ordinary life, people adapt to and come to terms with its complexities. They experience its important transitions from youth to adulthood and old age. They suffer its traumas of birth and death and of broken relationships. They engage with the changes taking place around them – in technology, styles of life and fashion – and cope with the consequences of wider patterns of social and political change.

All of this involves personal gain and loss. People experience joy, grief and suffering. They have occasions to be hopeful and others to be sad. In the course of the twentieth century, people have experienced wars and revolutions and have lived in fear of their lives. We all have to come to terms with the past, including our personal past (see Chapter 4 for a fuller discussion of this) and this is also a process of learning and personal change. And for all of us there is a need to anticipate the future. Modern identities, as modern social theorists stress, are peculiarly open and people can define for themselves the kinds of people they would like to be. Such hopeful openness, however, is not a luxury available to everyone. Many people experience their lives as a series of traps or dead ends and see no way out of them. Their sense of who they are is part of the powerlessness of their position and is something shaped by others. Powerless inauthenticity is, none the less, a mode of experience and learning but not of a life-enhancing critical kind.

Experiential learning is not, therefore, enough. Experience without the ideas through which it can be interpreted is no guide to action. Understanding requires the development of concepts, ideas, information and skills which enable people to reorganise the perspectives through which they view the world (see Chapter 3 for a fuller discussion of this point). There can be no learning without experience but learning must go beyond experience to reframe it and interpret it from new points of view. Such re-framing is not and cannot be an entirely private or individual process; it occurs in and through engagement with others so that the experience of one individual is extended beyond their immediate world by the experience of the others. More than that; the capacity of individuals to interpret their experience is based upon the resources of understanding available to them through the categories of their culture which they come to know only through communication with others.

This observation leads to two major points: the first is that those who seek to facilitate the learning of others must begin with an understanding of what learners already believe they know. Put differently, they must appreciate the perspectives and frameworks of understanding – some writers have referred to them as paradigms, others, taking their cue from the work of Piaget, talk about cognitive structures – through which the learners approaches both the process of learning and the materials to be learned. It is only on this basis, as the Russian psychologist Vygotsky (see Moll, 1990) noted, that the facilitator can know what the problems are the learner most overcome to be able to develop to the next stage of learning. What Vygotsky called the 'zone of proximal development' needs to be clearly in view in the mind of the facilitator and this presupposes a sound understanding of what the learner currently understands.

Second, facilitators must understand and acknowledge that learners have different attitudes towards and views about knowledge and develop what Belenky et al (1986) have described as different 'ways of knowing'. These 'ways of knowing' are different, it has been claimed, between men and women. Women are said to judge claims to truth by subjective rather than objective criteria and therefore have different relationships to knowledge itself. They do this, it is claimed, because they occupy different roles to those of men and communicate with one another in qualitatively different ways as well.

The same general point can be related to patterns of class and ethnic differentiation in society and to a range of other social differences which sustain different conceptions of the nature of knowledge and of understanding. Black people and working class people encounter formal education as an alien world built on patterns of thinking and on claims to knowledge which are very different to those of the society from which they come. To the extent that their concerns are not reflected in what schools and colleges offer them, their experience of learning is one of alienation and anonymity; it is of a world in which their role is to remain silent and without power.

But it is not just in schools and colleges where people learn. The experience of paid employment or of community can be for many people one in which they feel ignored or undervalued, even rejected. But people always strive to live in hope. The history of protest at the conditions of work in modern societies – through trades unionism and all other battles at 'the frontiers of control' in the workplace – and all the struggles over basic rights and freedoms that punctuate the development of democratic ideas in the modern world – testify to a deep-rooted potentiality within people to reject oppression and to demand a better world.

The rights and freedoms enjoyed by people in modern western societies were won at great cost. The social movements through which the demands for a better society have been and continue to be articulated – the labour movement, the movement for women's liberation, the movement against racism or for a better environment or for peace – each of which find particular expression and local commitment in the myriads of groups through which people press their political interests, all involve learning and the development of new ways of thinking, feeling and acting. The larger moments of change of the twentieth century – the wars and the revolutions which have carried forward radical visions for a new future – all involved forms of conflict and experience which transformed those caught up in them.

Human beings (as argued in Chapter 8) simply cannot live in the world as it is; they search constantly for new futures. They redefine their understanding of both themselves and their world and struggle to act on the basis of that. Sometimes they do so as individuals and strive creatively to achieve their personal ambitions. At other times, out of conviction or necessity they act together in groups to achieve their ends. Collective action provides myriads of opportunities for individuals to redefine themselves and to acquire new knowledge and understanding. It also clarifies what more needs to be understood. Through political action people come to a deeper understanding of political processes and of the society they seek to change. Through co-operative effort to change their circumstances, people come to understand those circumstances in new ways.

Dialogue and democracy

Dialogue is a special kind of human communication. It does not develop in a natural way; the social and political conditions for it to be possible have to be created. This is why a theory of dialogue requires also a theory of democracy and a revitalised model of democratic citizenship.

These are testing times for democracy. Representative, liberal democracy is a framework of government which manages to elect representatives to governing bodies whose decisions, by and large, are regarded as legitimate. But it is neither the only model of democracy available or one guaranteed to prevent the emergence of non-democratic forms of government. It is a system of government to which millions of people throughout the world aspire, but it is not necessarily the kind of society which delivers what they also want: ever-increasing personal wealth and economic growth. Its underlying assumptions about human nature – that people are capable of articulating their needs and interests rationally and are willing, in the essentially secular contexts of modern government, to resolve their differences through the ballot box – are assumptions which disqualify most of the societies of the modern world from ever becoming democratic.

So, too, with citizenship. The rights people claim to be treated equally before the law, to be allowed to vote their politicians in and out of office and to be treated fairly and decently by the state, are the inalienable rights of modern citizenship. They do not necessarily imply an obligation on the part of citizens to participate fully in the decisions which affect their lives or to abide by those with which they disagree. In practice, however, modern democracies have developed a very narrow model of democratic citizenship. Some writers (eg Etzioni, 1997) believe that model lays too much emphasis on the rights of citizens and not enough on their responsibilities and obligations.

A far more serious criticism, however, is that the modern citizen has been depoliticised; that the public realm of society – the realm of the political – has become so complex and remote that people neither feel involved with or are able to influence the decisions taken on their behalf. Mass electorates are expected to show loyalty to the parties that solicit their support, but are not expected to be fully engaged in the political debates about the future of their societies. The result is that people are alienated from politics and cynical about politicians. Politicians must become popular but do so at the expense of serious political debate. Richard Hoggart (1995) has noted that in modern societies there is a growing relativism which discourages serious discussion about society. There is, he feels, 'neither language nor tone for proper demotic discourse . . . the cheapjacks, the flatterers, the glib thrive; but "The best lack all conviction . . ." ' (p. 285). What is missing, he believes, is the 'critical literacy' of genuine democracy which enables people to disagree, quarrel, question, resist and ensure that democratic debate itself is protected from everything that currently threatens to erode it.

The problem is how to secure the social and political conditions of democratic dialogue in the face of developments in the modern state and in the modern economy and in the culture of modern societies themselves, which currently threaten them. The centralisation of big government, the globalisation of economic life, the loosening of all the bonds of mutuality which hold civil society together and, finally, the loss of conviction among many intellectuals about the future viability of liberal principles, are the conditions which both exclude people from political life and leave politics prey to the powerful or the irrational.

Under these conditions, which some writers (see, for example, Gray, 1995) see as the final end of the Enlightenment project to root human affairs in a rational discourse in which human rights and freedoms are respected, a number of responses are possible. Among them we would have to include apathetic resignation and fatalism. Millions of people throughout the modern world feel detached from the political processes of their societies. The world is for them out of control and they are not the agents of their own fate. Another is the abandonment of democratic ideals and the development of a passionate commitment to a faith or an ideology which contains within its own assumptions all the solutions to all possible problems, so can be supported wholeheartedly and imposed on others who doubt it. Religious fundamentalism and totalitarian politics are both versions of this response. Those who disagree can be removed.

None of these responses contain the promise of an open critical dialogue about the prospects for change in modern societies. None envisages change based on new knowledge and understanding. From each of these positions people expect change to occur. In one it happens unpredictably and uncontrollably; in another it is imposed in an effort to realise some future end state when the good society will be attained.

Is there another way? The answer is a resounding yes. But it cannot be pre-programmed or read off from some grand political design. The Enlightenment project of reason and progress is dead and no one believes any longer that there is a message in history. Were there to be one it would be: the future is intrinsically open-ended and unknowable. What it becomes is the result of human agency, of hopes and conflicts which political institutions sometimes hold in check and sometimes promote. The direction of change in society is decided by those with the most powerful voices. Alternative voices can be heard, however. History is a story of power and resistance, of change and struggle, negotiation and compromise. It is a continuing story of how people imagine different futures for themselves and seek to achieve them in practice.

Each change in the story, each movement in the plot is possible because the people involved nurture new hopes and learn new ways to realise them. Each step involves new learning and a reinterpretation of the past, new kinds of communicative competence so that formerly silent people can be heard. The new thoughts and feelings – new 'structures of feeling' as Raymond Williams (1973) described them – involve new ways of perceiving and of comprehending the world which open up new lines of action and further enquiry. The history of organised labour exemplifies this precisely. So, too, do other social movements – the Women's Movement, the Peace Movement, the Dissident Movements of Eastern Europe and all the tentative, searching, demanding actions to combat racism and other forms of oppression and social exclusion.

The evidence is also clear from several generations of adult education and practice, especially in the last two decades, that adult people can be helped to think in critical ways, to build on what they know and, through co-operative work with others, generate new knowledge and understanding. What often prevents them from doing so is not their intelligence, but the opportunities open to them in the different settings in which they live their lives. Neither the world of work nor that of communities (as discussed in Chapters 6 and 8) is particularly conducive to the development of open, democratic and critical forms of discussion and learning. People do not have the chance to experience themselves as citizens with a voice. They are valued as producers of, or as consumers of goods but not as active citizens at work with a responsibility for the ways in which their companies are organised, or should develop and change. There is much discussion in the literature of modern management theory and community work practice, of how best to 'empower' people to take more control of their lives and participate in making decisions and solving problems. The weakness of it is that all the empowerment in the world would be pointless without real opportunities to change the conditions under which people work and live.

Even on the narrow, ballot-box versions of citizenship which prevail in modern democracies, people are not expected or enabled to participate continuously in the policy-making processes which shape their destiny. Insofar as democratic citizenship has to be learned through the experience of participating in political life, there are too few opportunities for people to do so.

The problem is that no one can simply provide such opportunities. They are not something to given but to be insisted upon or seized, for they are facets of the structure and distribution of power in society. Opportunities to make a difference to how such power is exercised have to be opened up and created. This requires understanding, confidence, commitment which can only grow through debate, disagreement and dialogue, each demanding the free flow of ideas, the right to express them and the freedom to do so without fear of threat or reprisal.

This process has not been and is not easy. In repressive regimes, such as Apartheid South Africa or in the darker days of Stalin in the People's Democracies of Eastern Europe, it has required political struggle and much sacrifice. In the developed democracies of the West, the rights of minority groups – of black people, women, religious minorities, homosexuals, migrants, the disabled, the wrongly imprisoned – and of socially excluded members of society, still fall far short of what a strict democratic standard requires. Lacking power, their voices are not heard. What the history of each of these groups has shown, however – and what the rich and powerful have always known and never taken for granted – is that power is something to be acquired and maintained through learning, co-operation, organisation and action.

In the global economy and in the inter-governmental world of trade, political alliances and multinational institutions like the United Nations, UNESCO, the World Bank, OECD, the European Union, the GATT trade conference and other institutions of this kind, including temporary organisations and alliances to deal with specific problems – in the Gulf, Bosnia – power is exercised on a global scale. The nation state is no longer the tight frame of democratic citizenship. In an interdependent world, the boundaries of the citizen role are global and the values that nurture democracy have to be defended and defined in a wide international framework.

The need is for a model of citizenship which is active rather than passive and one which is general rather than specific. The active principle is clear enough: people either learn democratic practice through practice – at home, in school, at work, in the community and in the ways they play their roles as citizens – or they do not. If we wish seriously to strengthen the foundations of a democratic societies, education for democracy has to become part of how all social institutions function. A general model of democratic citizenship envisages the participation of people in shaping all of the decisions which affect their lives – at work, in the community and in the formal public realm of government.

This is not a new idea. John Dewey, as Philip Selznick (1992) has noted, captured it in his idea of 'democracy-in-depth'. Selznick himself has taken it further to emphasise that democracy cannot be restricted simply to the majority rule of mass politics. It has to have a much stronger moral frame than that and be connected directly to the ways in which people experience their lives in the communities in which they live. For Selznick (1992, p. 523), the modern need is for active citizenship:

> Active, purposive, reflective citizenship is an alternative to undisciplined participation. Citizenship binds participation to public ends, creates obligations of duty and service, and presumes a framework within which dialogue and compromise may proceed. Thus civic participation is far more than the exercise of options by registered voters. It requires a public formed and regulated by the machinery of deliberation and by the experience of exercising responsible choice.

Democracy from this perspective rests on a willingness and an ability of people to engage in shared discovery and to possess what Selznick calls a 'shared resolve' to prefer and perfect dialogue and deliberation. The whole edifice rests on a 'covenant of reason' and on the view that the existence of a plurality of ways of thinking and feeling is not an obstacle to democratic discourse but something to celebrate. It provides, to adapt a term from Ernest Gellner, the cognitive pluralism upon which the search for new knowledge, new solutions to problems, depends.

That public realm of shared resolve cannot, however, have narrow geographical boundaries. For many purposes e.g. the development of ethical foreign policies or the management of the global environment or the development of aid and trade policies directed at the poor societies of the world, and certainly in relation to all decisions bearing on peace and war, the public realm of discourse and debate has to be conceived of in global terms. The development of such democratic discourse does not imply some historical end state to be reached when the world is finally democratic. What democracy means in practice is something which necessarily evolves and changes as existing social and political arrangements are judged against a well-debated vision of what they might be if the rights and freedoms of everyone were properly respected. So, too, with democratic citizenship. What it means to be free, to have rights and responsibilities, is not something to predefine. As circumstances change, so do the responsibilities, the understanding, the rights and democratic identities of citizens themselves.

The thrust of the argument of this chapter has been this: the development of new knowledge is a process intimately connected with the conditions of open communication which are the hallmark of democratic, open societies. Democracy is a broad and learned ideal which is realised as it is practised and lived. At its core, there is a special form of communication and debate which is dialogue. This form of human communication requires freedom, an awareness of the needs and perspective of others and a capacity to reason and debate with confidence. People enter into dialogue with open minds and are prepared to change their views and opinions if the evidence and the logic of the arguments they hear justify it.

Of course, these conditions are never fully met. Self interest, mistrust of others, prejudice, the ruthless pursuit and use of power over others, political or religious fanaticism and pervasive ignorance, continue to corrode democratic sentiments and capabilities. As modern societies change in pursuit of economic growth, they generate social exclusions which deny people any opportunity to shape their own lives. Nevertheless, the conditions of the open, democratic society are understood; many of them are met in the ways modern societies function. Much more is yet to be done in schools, communities, the world of work and in the institutions of government to develop the moral commitment, the shared resolve and the communicative competence which a healthy democracy requires. It can be done. We must all act continuously as if we really did live in a democratic, open society and commit ourselves to finding new solutions to the complex problems of global modernity.

References

Afshar, H (1994) 'Muslim women in West Yorkshire', in H Afshar and M Maynard (eds), *The dynamics of 'race' and gender: some feminist interventions*, Taylor and Francis, London.

Allman, P and Wallis, J (1996) 'Challenging the postmodern condition: radical adult education for critical intelligence', in M Mayo and J Thompson (eds), *Adult learning, critical intelligence and social change*, NIACE, Leicester.

Anderson, B (1983) *Imagined communities: reflections on the origins and spread of nationalism*, Verso, London.

Aron, R (1968) *Progress and disillusion: the dialectics of modern society*, Pall Mall, London.

Altbach, P G (1982) 'Servitude of the mind? Education, dependency and neo-colonialism', in P G Altbach, R F Arnove and G P Kelly (eds), *Comparative education*, Macmillan, London.

Altbach, P G (1987) 'What do you know? How the West dominates the worldwide distribution of knowledge', *The Times Higher Education Supplement*, 20 February, p. 16.

Apffel-Marglin, F and Marglin, S (1996) *Decolonizing knowledge: from development to dialogue*, Clarendon Press, Oxford.

Bakhtin, M (1994) *Dialogism: Bakhtin and His World* (by M Holquist), Routledge, London.

Barke, M and Turnbull, G (1992) *Meadowell: the biography of an 'estate with problems'*, Avebury, Aldershot.

Barnett, R (1990) *The idea of higher education*, The Open University Press, Buckingham.

Barnett, R (ed.) (1995) *Academic community: discourse or discord?*, Jessica Kingsley, London.

Bauman, J (1986) *Winter in the morning*, Virago, London.

Bauman, Z (1989) *Modernity and the holocaust*, Polity, Oxford.

Bauman, Z (1993) *Postmodern ethics*, Blackwell, Oxford.

Becher, T (1989) *Academic tribes and territories: intellectual enquiry and the cultures of disciplines*, Open University Press, Buckingham.

Beck, U (1992) *Risk society: towards a new modernity*, Sage, London.

Belenky, M F *et al* (1986) *Women's ways of knowing: the development of self, voice and mind*, Basic Books, New York.

Bell, D (1976) *The cultural contradictions of capitalism*, Heinemann, London.

Berger, P, Berger, B and Kellner, H (1973) *The homeless mind: modernization and consiousness*, Penguin, Harmondsworth.

Bernstein, B (1971a) *Class, codes and control vol 1*, Routledge and Kegan Paul, London.

Bernstein, B (1971b) 'On the classification and framing of educational knowledge', in M F D Young (ed.) *Knowledge and Control: New Directions* for the Sociology of Education, Collier-Macmillan, London.

Bernstein, J M (1995) *Recovering ethical life: Jürgen Habermas and the future of critical theory*, Routledge, London.

Bettleheim, B (1960) *The informed heart*, The Free Press, New York.

Bianchini, F and Parkinson, M (eds) (1993) *Cultural policy and urban regeneration, the west European experience*, Manchester University Press, Manchester.

Billig, M (1992) *Talking to the Royal Family*, Routledge, London.

Boguslaw, R (1965) *The new Utopians: a study of systems design and social change*, Prentice Hall, New York.

Bohm, D (1996) *On dialogue*, Routledge, London.

Bourdieu, P (1974) 'The school as a conservative force: scholastic and cultural inequalities', in J Eggleston (ed.), *Contemporary research in the sociology of education*, Methuen, London, pp. 32–47.

Brookfield, S (1987) *Developing critical thinkers: challenging adults to explore alternative ways of thinking and action*, Open University Press, Milton Keynes.

Brown, P and Scase, R (1994) *Higher education and corporate realities: class, culture and the decline of graduate careers*, University College London Press, London.

Bruner, J (1986) *Actual minds, possible worlds*, Harvard University Press, Cambridge, MA.

Bruner, J (1990) *Acts of meaning*, Harvard University Press, Cambridge, MA.

Burkitt, I (1991) *Social selves: theories of the social formation of personality*, Sage, London.

Castells, M (1990) *The informational city: information technology, economic restructuring and the urban – regional process*, Blackwell, Oxford.

Castells, M (1996) *The rise of network society*, Blackwell, Oxford.

Chaplin, S (1969a) 'The Iron North', *Newcastle Journal*, Supplement, 29 September, Newcastle Upon Tyne.

Chaplin, S (1969b) *A tree with rosy apples*, Frank Graham, Newcastle Upon Tyne.

Chaplin, S (1987) 'A Credo', in *In blackberry time*, Bloodaxe Books, Newcastle Upon Tyne.

Chomsky, N (1992) *Deterring democracy*, Vintage, London.

Clignet, R (1971) 'Damned if you do, damned if you don't: the dilemmas of the colonizer – colonized relations', *Comparative Education Review*, October, pp. 296–312.

Coffield, F and Williamson, B (eds) (1997) *Repositioning higher education*, Open Univesity Press, Buckingham.

Collins, R (1979) *The credential society: an historical sociology of education and stratification*, Academic Press, New York.

Colls, R (1995) 'What is 'Community' and how do we get it? A message for the member for Sedgefield', *Northern Review*, Vol. 1, Spring, pp. 9–27.

Coser, L (1971) *Masters of sociological thought: ideas in historical and social context*, Harcourt, Brace and Jovanovich, New York.

Crossley, N (1996) *Intersubjectivity: the fabric of social becoming*, Sage, London.

Curle, A (1995) *Another way: positive response to contemporary violence*, Jon Carpenter, Oxford.

Delors, J. *et al* (1996) *Learning: the treasure within*, UNESCO, Paris.

Derber, C, Schwartz, W A and Magrass, Y (1990) *Power in the highest degree: professionals and the rise of a new mandarin power*, Oxford University Press, Oxford.

Dupre, W (1994) *Patterns of meaning: reflection on meaning and truth in cultural reality, religious tradition and dialogical encounters*, Kok Pharos, Kampen.

Edelman, G (1992) *Bright air, brilliant fire: on the matter of the mind*, Penguin, Harmondsworth.

Etzioni, A (1995) *The spirit of community: rights, responsibilities and the communitarian agenda*, Fontana, London.

Etzioni, A (1997) *The new golden rule: community and morality in a democratic society*, Profile Books, London.

European Communities (EU) (1995) *Teaching and learning towards the learning society*.

European Communities (EU) (1996) *European Year of Lifelong Learning*.

Fanon, F (1973) *Black skins, white masks*, MacGibbon and Kee, London.

Finger, M (1995) 'Adult education and society today', *International Journal of Lifelong Education*, Vol. 14, No. 2, March – April, pp. 110–19.

Fletcher, R (1962) *The family and marriage in modern Britain*, Penguin, Harmondsworth.

Fieldhouse, R (ed.) (1996) *A history of modern British adult education*, NIACE, Leicester.

Friedlander, S (ed.) (1992) *Probing the limits of representation: Nazism and the 'Final Solution'*, Harvard University Press, Cambridge, MA.

Fukuyama, F (1995) *Trust: The new foundation of global prosperity*, Hamish Hamilton, London.

Fussell, P (1991) 'The american spirit of pure BADness', *The Guardian*, is 15 August, p. 32.

Galbraith, J K (1992) *The culture of contentment*, Sinclair and Stevenson, London.

Gardiner, H (1993) *Creating minds: an anatomy of creativity*, Basic Books, New York.

Gellner, E (1996) *Conditions of liberty: civil society and its rivals*, Penguin, Harmondsworth.

Gibbons, M *et al.* (1994) *The new production of knowledge*, Sage, London.

Giddens, A (1990) *The consequences of modernity*, Polity, Cambridge.

Giddens, A (1991) *Modernity and self identity: self and society in the late modern age*, Polity Press, Oxford.

Gilmour, I (1992) *Dancing with dogma: Britain under Thatchersim*, Simon and Schuster, London.

Ginsburg, M (1961) *On the diversity of morals: essays in sociology and philosophy*, Heinemann, London.

Goffman, E (1971) *The presentation of the self in everyday life*, Penguin, Harmondsworth.

Gray, J (1995) *Enlightenment's wake: politics and culture at the close of the modern age*, Routledge, London.

Habermas, J (1976) *Legitimation crisis*, Heinemann, London.

Harre, R (1986) (ed.) *The social construction of emotions*, Blackwell, Oxford.

Havel, V (1987) *Living in truth*, Faber and Faber, London.

Havel, V (1991) *Letters to Olga*, Faber and Faber, London.

Heller, A (1984) *Everyday life*, Routledge and Kegan Paul, London.

HMSO (1996) *Family expenditure survey*, CSO, London.

HMSO (1997) *Social trends*, CSO, London.

Hobsbawm, E (1994) *Age of extremes: the short twentieth century 1914–1991*, Michael Joseph, London.

Hockey, J and James, A (1993) *Growing up and growing old*, Sage, London.

Hoggart, R (1956) *The uses of literacy*, Penguin, Harmondsworth.

Hoggart, R (1991) 'The Abuse of Literacy', *The Guardian*, 27 June, p. 21.

Hoggart, R (1995) *The way we live now*, Pimlico, London.

Horton, R (1971) 'African traditional thought and western science', in M F D Young (ed), *Knowledge and control: new directions for the sociology of education*, Collier-Macmillan, London.

Hudson, M (1995) *Coming back brockens: a year in a mining village*, Vintage, London.

Hyland, T (1994) *Competence, education and NVQs: dissenting perspectives*, Cassell, London.

Jarausch, K H (1982) *Students, society and politcs in imperial Germany*, Princeston University Press, NJ.

Jarvis, P (1992) *Paradoxes of learning: on becoming an individual in society*, Jossey Bass, San Francisco.

Jarvis, P (1997) *Ethics and education for adults in a late modern society*, NIACE, Leicester.

Josselson, R and Lieblich, A (eds) (1993) *The narrative study of lives*, Sage, London.

Keats, J (1988) *Collected poems*, Penguin, Harmondsworth.

Keenan, B (1993) *An evil cradling*, Viking, New York.

Kiernan, V G (1989) *Poets, politics and the people*, Verso, London.

Kincheloe, J (1995) *Toil and trouble: good work, smart workers and the integration of academic and vocational education*, P Lang, New York.

Kirkwood, G and Kirkwood, C (1989) *Living adult education: Freire in Scotland*, Open University Press, Milton Keynes.

Knight, B and Stokes, P (1996) 'Self help citizenship', *The Guardian*, 30 October, p. 2.

Kuhn, T (1962) *The structure of scientific revolutions*, Chicago University Press, Chicago.

Kumar, K (1995) *From post-industrial society to post-modern society: new theories of the contemporary world*, Blackwell, Oxford.

Langer, L (1991) *Holocaust testimonies: the ruins of memory*, Yale University Press, New Haven.

Lave, J and Wenger, E (1991) *Situated learning: legitimate peripheral participation*, Cambridge University Press, Cambridge.

Lawson, A (1988) *Adultery: an analysis of love and betrayal*, Oxford University Press, Oxford.

Lempert, W (1994) 'Moral development in the biographies of skilled industrial workers', *Journal of Moral Education*, Vol. 23, No. 4, pp. 451–68.

Maaz, H-J (1990) *Der Gefuhlsstau: Ein Pyschogram der DDR*, Argon Verlag, Berlin.

MacIntyre, A (1981) *After virtue: a study in moral theory*, Duckworth, London.

Mannheim, K (1950) *Diagnosis of our time: essays of a wartime sociologist*, Routledge and Kegan Paul, London.

Marglin, S (1990) *Dominating knowledge*, Clarendon Press, Oxford.

Martin, B (1981) *A sociology of contemporary cultural change*, Blackwell, Oxford.

Matza, D (1969) *Becoming deviant*, Prentice-Hall, Englewood Cliffs, N J.

McLellan, D (1971) *The thought of Karl Marx*, Macmillan, Basingstoke.

Medawar, P (1986) *The limits of science*, Oxford University Press, Oxford.

Mezirow, J (1987) 'A critical theory of adult learning and education', in M Tight (ed), *Education for adults vol 1, Adult learning and education*, Croom Helm/Open University Press, Beckenham.

Middlehurst, R (1993) *Leading academics*, Open University Press, Buckingham.

Middleton, P (1992) *The inward gaze: masculinity and subjectivity in modern culture*, Routledge, London.

Mills, C Wright (1959) *The causes of World War Three*, Secker and Warburg, London.

Moll, L C (ed) (1990) *Vygotsky and education: instructional implications of socio-historical psychology*, Cambridge University Press, Cambridge.

Morgan, G (1986) *Images of organization*, Sage, London.

Morgan, K O (1990) *The people's peace: British history 1945–1989*, Oxford University Press, Oxford.

Morley, L (1997) 'Change and equity in higher education', *British Journal of Sociology of Education*, Vol. 18, No. 2, pp. 231–42.

Myerson, G (1994) *Rhetoric, reason and society: rationality as dialogue*, Sage, London.

National Institute of Adult Continuing Education (NIACE) (1996) *Learning cities*, NIACE, Leicester.

Oppenheim, C and Harker, L (1996) *Poverty, the facts*, Child Poverty Action Group, London.

Organisation for European Economic Co-operation and Development (OECD) (1992) *City strategies for lifelong learning*, CERI, Paris.

Orwell, G (1954) *Nineteen Eighty-Four*, Penguin, Harmondsworth.

Passerini, L (1982) 'Work, ideology and working class attitudes to Fascism', in P Thompson (ed.), *Our common history; the transformation of Europe*, Pluto Press, London.

Peat, F D (1995) *Blackfoot physics: a journey into the native American universe*, Fourth Estate, London.

Popper, K R (1963) *Conjectures and refutations: the growth of scientific knowledge*, Routledge and Kegan Paul, London.

Popper, K R (1992) *Unended quest: an intellectual autobiography*, Routledge, London.

Prichard, C and Willmott, H (1997) 'Just how managed is the McUniversity?', *Organization Studies*, Vol. 18, No. 2, pp. 287–316.

Prochaska, F (1988) *The voluntary impulse*, Faber and Faber, London.

Ranson, S (1994) *Towards the learning society*, Cassell, London.

Ranson, S, Martin, J and Dixon, J (1997) 'A learning democracy for co-operative action', *Oxford Review of Education*, Vol. 23, No. 1, pp. 117–33.

Reisman, D (1961) *The lonely crowd: a study of the changing American character*, Yale University Press, New Haven.

Rochefoucauld La (1986) *Maxims*, Penguin, Harmondsworth.

Rowe, D (1987) *Depression: the way out of your prison*, Routledge, London.

Rundell, J (1994) 'Creativity and judgement: Kant on reason and imagination', in G Robinson and J Rundell (eds), *Rethinking imagination*, Routledge, London.

Rushdie, S (1989) *The satanic verses*, Viking, New York.

Said, E W (1993) *Culture and imperialism*, Chatto and Windus, London.

Santner, E (1992) 'History beyond the pleasure principle: some thoughts on the representation of trauma', in S Friedlander (ed.), *Probing the limits of representation: Nazism and the Final Solution*, Harvard University Press, MA.

SCAA (School Curriculum and Assessment Authority) (1996) *Education for adult life: the spiritual and moral developmet of young people*, PO Box 590, London.

Seabrook, J (1997) 'Story of a slum', *New Internationalist*, No. 290, May.

Selznick, P (1992) *The moral commonwealth: social theory and the promise of community*, University of California Press, Berkeley.

Sennett, R (1978) *The fall of public man: on the social psychology of capitalism*, Vintage Books, New York.

Sennett, R and Cobb, J (1972) *The hidden injuries of class*, Cambridge University Press, Cambridge.

Shotter, J (1993) *Cultural politics of everyday life*, Open Univesity Press, Buckingham.

Sloboda, J *et al.* (1994) 'Is everyone musical?', *The Psychologist*, August, pp. 349–60.

Smith, M K (1994) *Local education: community, conversation, praxis*, Open University Press, Buckingham.

Stehr, N (1994) *Knowledge societies*, Sage, London.

Tardif, T Z and Sternberg, R J (1988) 'What do we know about creativity?' in R J Sternberg (ed.), *The nature of creativity: contemporary psychological perspectives*, Cambridge University Press, Cambridge, pp. 429–41.

Tawney, R H (1964) *Equality*, Unwin Books, London.

Taylor, C (1992) *Sources of the self: the making of the modern identity*, Cambridge University Press, Cambridge.

Taylor, R (1996) 'Preserving the Liberal Tradition in "New Times" ', in J Wallis (ed.), *Liberal adult education: the end of an era?*, Continuing Education Press, Nottingham.

Todd, F (1994) 'Professional learning for ethno-cultural diversity' Part 1 and 2, in *International Journal for Lifelong Education*, Vol. 13, No. 2, March – April, pp. 81–125.

Tuckett, A (1996) 'A mature higher education system?', in F Coffield (ed.), *Higher*

Education and Lifelong Learning, University of Newcastle Upon Tyne, Department of Education, Newcastle Upon Tyne, pp. 41–54.

Usher, R, Bryant, I and Johnston, R (1997) *Adult education and the postmodern challenge: learning, beyond the limits*, Routledge, London.

Wakeford, F and J (1974) 'Universities and the study of elites', in P Stanworth and A Giddens (eds), *Elites and power in British society*, Cambridge University Press, Cambridge.

Ward, K (1997) 'British university adult education and working class communities', *Community Development Journal*, Vol. 32, No. 1, January, pp. 65–77.

Ward, K and Taylor, R (eds) (1986) *Adult education and the working class: education for the missing millions*, Croom Helm, London.

Weber, M (1970) 'Science as a vocation', in H H Gerth and C Wright Mills (eds), *From Max Weber: essays in sociology*, Routledge and Kegan Paul, London.

Weigend, E (ed) (1994) *Concepts of dialogue considered from the perspective of different disciplines*, Niemeyer, Tübingen.

West, L (1996) *Beyond fragments: adult motivation and higher education – a biographical analysis*, Taylor and Francis, London.

Westwood, S and Thomas, J E (1991) *Radical agenda? the politics of adult eduation*, NIACE, Leicester.

Williams, R (1973) *Marxism and literature*, Lawrence and Wishart, London.

Williams, R (1983) *Towards 2000*, Penguin, Harmondsworth.

Williamson, B (1982) *Class, culture and community: a sociological study of community through biography*, Routledge, London.

Williamson, B (1992) 'Lifeworlds and learning' in *Studies in the Education of Adults*, Vol. 24, No. 2, October, pp. 176–91.

Windisch, U (1990) *Speech and reasoning in everyday life*, Cambridge University Press, Cambridge.

Index